Selected Upanishads

A Collection of 14 Upanishads with Devanagari Script, Translation and Notes

Jayaram V

Editor & Translator

Published by
Pure Life Vision LLC
New Albany, Ohio

Selected Upanishads

Copyright © 2013 by Jayaram V. All rights reserved.
Published and Distributed Worldwide by Pure Life Vision LLC., USA.
First edition 2013

This book is copyrighted under International and Pan American conventions. Printed in the USA. All rights reserved. No part of this publication may be reproduced stored in a retrieval system, or transmitted in any form or by any means, electronic, mechanical, photocopying, recording, scanning or otherwise, without the prior written permission of the publisher or the author. Requests to the publisher for permission or for bulk purchase of the book should be made online at http://www.PureLifeVision.com.

Limit of Liability/Disclaimer of Warranty: While the publisher and the author have used their best efforts in preparing this book, they make no representation or warranties with respect to the accuracy or completeness of the contents of this book and specifically disclaim any implied warranties of merchantability or fitness for particular purpose. No warranty may be created or extended by sales representatives or written sales materials. The advice and strategies contained herein may not be suitable for your situation. You should consult with a professional where appropriate. Neither the publisher nor author shall be liable for any loss of profit or any other commercial damages, including but not limited to special, incidental, consequential or other damages.

Pure Life Vision books and products are available through bookstores and online websites. For Enquiries, please visit http://www.PureLifeVision.com.

Cover illustration the Vedic Universe © Jayaram V

Publisher Cataloging-in-Publication Data

V, Jayaram, (Vemulapalli)
Selected Upanishads
    p. cm
    Includes bibliographical references
    ISBN- 13: 978-1-935760-06-1
    ISBN -10: 1-935760-068
    1. Upanishads. 2. Upanishads. English. 3. Upanishads.-- Commentaries. I. Title.

BL1124.52.V152013
294.5/9218 — dc22   2013904776

Printed in the United States of America
10 9 8 7 6 5 4 3 2 1
First Edition

To my parents, grandparents and ancestors

About the Author

Jayaram V is an author of 12 books on Hinduism, Spirituality and Self-help. He is the founder president of Hinduwebsite.com. He has been writing regularly for the last several years on Indian religions, spiritual subjects, yoga, self-help, current affairs and information technology. He holds a Masters degree in Botany, a Diploma in Journalism, and a Bachelor of Science in Information Technology.

His recent works include The Bhagavadgita Complete Translation, Brahman, Introduction to Hinduism, The Awakened Life, Chandogya Upanishad, and Brihadaranyaka Upanishad. He is currently working on a book on the philosophy and teachings of the Upanishads and a translation and commentary on the Yogasutras.

Jayaram is an Indian American born and raised in India. He worked in India, Nigeria and USA in both public and private sectors in various positions before he turned to writing fulltime. He writes regularly for Hinduwebsite.com and other websites, apart from managing a hectic schedule to publish several books on Hinduism, Buddhism, Yoga and related subjects.

ALSO BY JAYARAM V

1. Think Success: A Collection of Writings on Success and Achievement through Positive Thinking, Volume I
2. Think Success: A Collection of Writings on Success and Achievement through Positive Thinking, Volume II
3. Think Success: A Collection of Writings on Success and Achievement through Positive Thinking, Combined Volume
4. The Awakened Life: A Collection of Writings on Spiritual Life
5. Brahman
6. The Bhagavadgita Complete Translation
7. The Bhagavadgita Simple Translation
8. Essays on the Bhagavadgita
9. Introduction to Hinduism.
10. Brihadaranyaka Upanishad
11. Chandogya Upanishad

FORTHCOMING

1. The Secret Knowledge - Essays on the Upanishads
2. The Yogasutras – Translation and Commentary
3. Perspectives on Hinduism
4. Selected Thoughts and Quotations

Selected Upanishads

A Collection of 14 Upanishads with Devanagari Script, Translation and Notes

Jayaram V

Editor & Translator

Contents

Author's Note	19
Introduction	21
The Upanishads	29
Aitareya Upanishad	**37**
Editor's Note	37
Invocation	39
Chapter 1	39
Creation Of The Worlds And Beings	39
Placing The Organs In The Human Body	41
Creation of Food and the Embodiment of the Self	43
Chapter 2	47
The Triple Births of the Embodied Self	47
Chapter 3	48
Different Types of Intelligence	48
Kausitaki Upanishad	**51**
Editor's Note	51
Chapter 1	53
The Worlds Where the Souls Go After Death	53
Chapter 2	59
The Greatness of Breath	59
Chapter 3	72
The Superiority of Breath	72
Chapter 4	81
Partial Definitions of Brahman	81
Kena Upanishad	**89**
Editor's Note	89
Invocation	91
Translation	91
Who is the True Lord of the Body?	91
The Difficulty of Knowing Brahman	93

  A Brief Encounter Between Brahman and Gods........................ 95
  Brahman, the Highest and the Supreme 97

Tattiriya Upanishad..101
Editor's Note...101
Chapter 1 - Siksa Valli..103
Invocation..103
  The Study of Pronunciation 103
  The Great Combinations 104
  A Teacher's Prayer for Knowledge and Prosperity 105
  The Four Mystic Utterances... 106
  Meditating Upon Brahman 107
  The Fivefold Aggregates 108
  The Significance of Aum... 109
  The Order and Regularity of Life.. 109
  Trisanku on Knowledge and Wisdom 110
  Farewell Advise to Students 110
  A Joint Invocation for Divine Help 112

Chapter 2 - Brahmananda Valli 113
  Brahman and Creation... 113
  The Importance of Food 113
  Breath and Mind.. 114
  Mind and Intelligence.. 115
  Intelligence and Bliss 115
  Brahman, the Self in the Body 116
  The Blissful Nature of Brahman 117
  Progressive States of Bliss... 118
  Offering Actions to the Self Within 120

Chapter 3 – Bhrigu Valli 121
  Varuna's Teachings to Bhrigu 121
  Food is Brahman.. 121
  Breath is Brahman 122
  Mind is Brahman.. 122
  Intelligence is Brahman 122
  Bliss is Brahman 123

- Food and Breath 123
- Food and Water 124
- Food and Earth 124
- The Importance of Offering Food 124

Isavasya Upanishad 127
Editor's Note 127
Invocation 129
Translation 129
- All This Belongs to Brahman 129
- The Transcendental Self 132
- knowledge and Ignorance 135
- The Prayers of a Dying Person 138

Katha Upanishad 141
Editor's Note 141
Invocation 143
Chapter 1 143
- Naciketas' Death and Journey to Yama's World 143
- The Two Paths 150
- What Leads to Rebirth and Salvation 155

Chapter 2 159
- Knowing the Self, the Eternal Lord 159
- What Happens to the Self Upon Death 162
- Asvattha Tree - The Tree of Creation 165

Mundaka Upanishad 171
Chapter (Mundaka) 1 173
- Two Types of Knowledge 173
- The Inferior Nature of Sacrifices 175

Chapter (Mundaka) 2 179
- Brahman as the Source of All 179
- Knowing the Self 181

Chapter (Mundaka) 3 183
- Truth Alone Triumphs 183
- The Self is Known By the Self 186

Mandukya Upanishad **191**
   Editor's Note **191**
   Invocation 193
   Translation 193
      The Four States of Consciousness 193
   Free Translation 197
Prasna Upanishad **199**
   Editor's Note **199**
   Invocation 201
   Question 1 201
      Manifestations of Prajapati 201
   Question 2 206
      Deities in the Body and Breath 206
   Question 3 208
      The Origin and Manifestations of Breath 208
   Question 4 211
      Who Remains Awake in Sleep 211
   Question 5 214
      Significance of Aum Meditation 214
   Question 6 216
      The Being with Sixteen Parts 216
Svetasvatara Upanishad **219**
   Editor's Note **219**
   Invocation 221
   Chapter 1 221
      Brahman Perceived as a Wheel with Parts 221
   Chapter 2 226
      An Ancient Prayer to Savitr 226
   Chapter 3 229
      Rudra, the Lord of the Universe 229
   Chapter 4 233

    Two Birds on the Tree of Life 233
  Chapter 5 238
    The Supreme Self and the Individual Self 238
  Chapter 6 241
    The One God Who Liberates 241

Paingala Upanishad 249
  Editor's Note 249
  Invocation 251
  Chapter 1 251
    The Process of Creation 251
  Chapter 2 255
    Creation of the Body and Beingness 255
  Chapter 3 262
    Mahavakyas, the Great Sayings 262
  Chapter 4 266
    The Life of a Jivanmukta 266

Kaivalya Upanishad 273
  Editor's Note 273
  Invocation 275
  Translation 275
    The Knowledge of Brahman and Liberation 275

Vajrasucika Upanishad 283
  Editor's Note 283
  Translation 285
    The Knowledge of Vajrasuci 285

Jabala Upanishad 289
  Editor's Note 289
  Invocation 291
  Chapter 1 291
    Avimutka - The Bound Self 291
  Chapter 2 292

The location of the Self	292

Chapter 3 293
The Importance of Satarudriyam 293

Chapter 4 293
The Practice of Renuciartion 293

Chapter 5 295
The True Sacred Thread 295

Chapter 6 296
Description of Great Souls - Paramahansas 296

Bibliography 299
Symbolism Of The Cover Design 307

Author's Note

No translation is better than the original. It is difficult to avoid dilution of the meaning or of the aesthetic appeal of the original text when you translate a well known manuscript from one language to another. You are bound to face difficulties in your choice of words and construction of sentences and in conveying the intended meaning. It is also difficult to avoid in a work of translation unintended errors and distortions that may arise due to the differences in the use of the languages, and the changes that time and tradition hews upon them and upon our very knowledge and understanding of them. It is more so, if the original text was composed thousands of years ago and you do not know the exact conditions in which people lived and the hidden motivation behind their actions and beliefs.

I therefore consider writing a book on a spiritual subject or translating an ancient scripture such as an Upanishad is more like an austerity rather than a mere intellectual exercise. In accomplishing the goal, you experience certain pain and discomfort as you apply your mind and body to the task. In the end, you emerge more purified, knowledgeable, vigorous and transformed, having completed it with concentration, dedication and discipline. The austerity of translating a sacred text, such as an Upanishad or the Bhagavadgita, is perhaps the best austerity you can think of in the modern world. It is more purifying and satisfying than indulging in rituals and contemplative practices. It gives you an opportunity to spend quality time in the company of great souls; and experience certain admiration as you try to formulate a mental picture of their vision and wisdom. I hope these translations will fill certain gaps in our understanding of the ancient wisdom. I hope they will open the minds of aspiring souls to an eternal wisdom and help them to make progress on their spiritual path. The Upanishads have the potential to ignite the flame of knowledge in the minds of seekers of knowledge. If you are interested in becoming a spiritual person and develop higher knowledge, wisdom and sensitivity towards the world and yourself, then the Upanishads are the best choice for you.

Jayaram V

Introduction

Upanishad (up+ni+shad) means sitting down near. They are so called because the knowledge of the Upanishads was considered secret in the Vedic world and was meant to be taught in person by the teachers to their students, after choosing them carefully through a rigorous testing process. There were many reasons why they did it and one of them was to preserve the sanctity and purity of the knowledge, which they considered very sacred.

The teachers taught this knowledge to those who were either related to them or whose moral purity and spiritual readiness were beyond doubt. Even this was done in the end, when the students spent nearly two decades serving their teachers and learning the ritual portions of the Vedas from them. When they became proficient in other branches of the Vedic curriculum, they were allowed to approach the teacher and learn from them this secret knowledge. Not all teachers were equally proficient in the Upanishads and hence, not all students were able to learn this knowledge. We find ample illustrations in the Upanishads where even learned scholars were ignorant about certain aspects of the Upanishads. Therefore, sometimes people approached men of wisdom even at a ripe age to overcome their ignorance and perfect their knowledge.

It is also believed that the word Upanishad has multiple meanings. Shankara suggested that Upanishads were so called because they destroyed ignorance and led one to the knowledge of Brahman. The knowledge was considered a secret within the secret (atiguhya) because the Upanishads were the hidden secret within the Vedas, which were in themselves secretive. If the knowledge of the ritual portions of the Vedas was restricted to a few selected Brahmana lineages, the Upanishads were even more secretive parts hidden within them which were imparted to even lesser number of people.

Philosopher kings

Originally, the knowledge of the Upanishads was not under the exclusive ownership of the Brahmanas. In the early Vedic period, the Kshatriya clans worshipped Brahma and considered him the highest god of creation. They possessed the knowledge of several Upanishads. The Brahmanas specialized in ritual worship of the Vedas, while the Kshatriyas in the spiritual knowledge of Brahman. In the earliest Upanishads such as the Brihadaranyaka and Chandogya Upanishads, we find this dichotomy. We find several Brahmana scholars approaching kings such as Ajatasatru for knowledge.

The kings certainly played a key role in the development of the Vedanta, until scholars such as Yajnavalkya and Uddalaka Aruni arrived on the scene. They commanded respect for their knowledge from the Brahmanas who visited their courts and participated in sacrificial ceremonies and religious discussions. Occasionally, they exposed the ignorance of vain scholars like Balaki who boasted of their limited knowledge, but were generous enough to impart the sacred knowledge to willing Brahmanas, such as Uddalaka Aruni, who approached them with humility.

Eventually the original Kshatriya clans of the ancient Vedic kingdoms disappeared, leaving the high moral ground entirely to the Brahmanas. With that development, the Brahmanas became the sole guardians of the Upanishads. As new kings emerged in the power struggle, who worshipped different gods and belonged to different social backgrounds, it became imperative for the Brahmana families that were migrating from arid regions in the west to the Gangetic valley to secure their patronage. In exchange for that they accommodated new beliefs and practices into their religion, and began making offerings to several new deities, who now became part of their pantheon.

As a result, by the time the westward migration was complete, the highest god of the Upanishads and gods such as Indra, Varuna, Soma, Mitra, Brahma, Yama, Aditya and others whom the Kshatriyas worshipped as the gods of Kshatra power yielded place to the deities such as Vishnu, Siva, Rama, Krishna and Kartikeya. The legend of Parasurama alludes to the conflicts and tensions within the Vedic society and the emergence of a new social order dictated overwhelmingly by the Brahmanas. In their new role, they became the primary guardians of the Vedic knowledge, supported by the ruling class who had now the obligation to follow the code of conduct laid out for them in the law books as part of their duties. A king certainly enjoyed a higher status in the early stages of a horse sacrifice, but in the end he had sit down on a lower ground before the Brahmana priests and accept their blessings.

The Vedas

The Upanishads form the end part of the Vedas. To those who are not familiar with the Vedic literature, here is a brief exposition of the subject. The Vedas constitute the heart and soul of the Vedic religion, major elements of which found their way into the present day Hinduism.

The Vedas are not the only important scriptures of Hinduism and not every Hindu considers them inviolable. However, they do occupy a significant place in the sacred literature of Hinduism, as the highest and the most reliable knowledge. The Vedic scholars regarded the knowledge of the Vedas as inviolable and their statements as the measure of truth (sabda pramana).

In other words if there were disputes among the scholars as to the veracity of a statement, doctrine, or philosophy, they would look to the Vedas for its validity. If the Vedas contained some reference to it even vaguely, they would accept it as a valid argument and allow the debate to continue.

The Vedas were also called revelations or not manmade (apaurseya). The Vedic seers held that the Vedas were eternal, that is they were not created by humans, but existed eternally in the realm of Brahman, who transmitted them in the beginning of each time cycle to the worlds through Brahma, the First Born and the creator of the worlds and beings. Since they were eternal, none had the authority to change them or distort them. None had the permission to mix them up with manmade ideas and religious knowledge. Since they were eternal and received only through the inner ears of the earliest seers, who are now recognized as the originators of different lineages of priestly classes, the Vedas were considered srutis, that which were heard. Rest of the knowledge, which came out of our memory, knowledge, experience, perceptions and intellect was grouped under the heading smriti, meaning memorial texts. The Dharamasastras, the epics, the Puranas, the Vedangas and the sutra literature for example, form part of this branch of knowledge.

The Vedas are four in number. Originally, there were only three and they were called in the earliest Upanishads as the triple knowledge. The fourth Veda was added subsequently as part of the changing sociopolitical conditions of ancient India. These assimilations might not have happened smoothly and without resistance. There might have been conflicts and internal differences among different lineages of Brahmanas, until the new knowledge and practices were integrated into the fourth Veda.

The four Vedas are the Rigveda, the Yajurveda, the Samaveda and the Atharvaveda. They are not simple, ordinary texts. They are very large, containing hundreds and thousands of hymns and verses of varying lengths and metrical forms. A lifetime may not be sufficient to study them completely or translate them with a detailed exposition. Their imagery is very complex. Their meaning is hidden. While they may look deceptively simple, they can be interpreted variously.

The fourteen Upanishads, which are included here constitute just a fraction of the Vedas. With all the modern facilities and references available and with limited explanatory notes, it took me over six months to translated them. Imagine how long it would take to translate the entire corpus of the Vedas and then dwell deep into their ritual imagery and hidden symbolism.

Learning the Vedas

In the ancient world, the students spent over two decades to study the Vedas. Most of their study time went into recitation and memorization, rather than the actual study and understanding of the knowledge they contained. Their primary aim was to remember the hymns by heart because upon that depended largely their livelihood, family name and professional reputation. Such a system had obvious drawbacks, since human memory was fallible and subject to decay.

Therefore, even after completing their formal education, the priests practiced regular recitation and study of the Vedas as part of their self-learning (svadhyaya), and to consolidate their knowledge they participated in religious debates and discussions, while practicing their profession, as apprentices, novice priests or experienced masters. The male members of the family or other close relations also helped one another to keep their knowledge and memory intact

The study continued during the entire course of their lives as they discharged their duties as householders and skilled professionals. They did it while pursuing the aims prescribed by the Vedas and honoring their family obligations. Most of them specialized in particular aspects of ritual worship and specific branches of Vedas, as Hotris, Udgatris, Prastoris, Adharvayus and so on.

Their study continued even after they retired from active duty and went to forests to fulfill their age specific obligations (ashrama-dharma), where they would contemplate upon the deeper aspects of the ritual knowledge and the advanced knowledge of the rituals and their symbolism. During this stage in their lives, they would internalize the ritual symbolism and begin a contemplative life, bringing the model of sacrifice into their very being and making it a part of their spiritual practice.

We notice from the Upanishads that not all scholars in the Vedic world possessed correct knowledge or a perfect understanding of the Vedas and their hidden significance. I have no doubt that, despite their personal drawbacks, some of them were also teachers of great reputation in their times. While they might have lacked correct understanding of certain aspects of Brahman and Self-knowledge, they possessed perfect knowledge of the sacrifices (*yajnas*) and their relevance to human life. From time to time great seers and philosopher kings appeared on the religious scene to expound the knowledge of the Upanishad and correct the errors and distortions that crept into their understanding due to the very impurities of the human mind and its vulnerability to self-interest and temptations of life.

Parts of the Vedas

Each Vedas was divided into four parts, the Samhitas, the Brahmanas, the Aranyakas and the Upanishads. The Samhita portion contained hymns called Ricks (chants), Samans (songs) and Yajus (formulas), which were chanted, sung or uttered with specific pronunciation and metrical rhythms during sacrificial ceremonies to create powerful vibrations and attract the attention of the gods in heaven from whom blessings were sought.

The hymns of the Rigveda are called Riks, those of the Samaveda Samans and those of the Yajurveda, Yajus. Each of these had a different purpose and each were sung or chanted by a particular class of priests. These different forms of hymns contained invocations to various divinities and they were supposed to be sung on specific occasions for specific purposes and accompanied by certain specific ritual observances and practices.

In others words, you cannot just wake up one morning and chant whatever hymn that comes to your mind to secure the favors of a divinity. You have to know clearly the purpose of the ritual, the deities for whom it is meant, the occasion for which it is to be used and the procedure prescribed for its practice. You also need to know for which main deity and for which associated deities the ritual and the hymns need to be addressed, what materials should be used as offerings, how they need to be gathered, purified, mixed or arranged, what vessels and tools should be used, how to prepare and purify the sacrificial fire, what austerities and initiatory ceremonies need to be performed and who should be invited to attend the ceremony or participate in them.

The Brahmanas

There is little freedom for the Vedic worshippers to take liberties with the rituals. They have to observe a strict code of conduct and comply with the procedural aspects of the sacrifices, hymn by hymn, and step by step. Such details of the procedural knowledge of the rituals are available in the second part of the Vedas, known as the Brahmanas. The Brahmanas tell you how to perform rituals, the duties of different types of priests, the various types of sacrifices, the classes of priests and their respective duties, the deities, duties and sacrifices meant for different classes of people, the knowledge of the sacraments, purification and expiation ceremonies, sacrifices to attract prosperity, sacrifices to overpower, delude or destroy an enemy and so on.

Some of the sacrifices are meant to be performed every day, using the domestic fires kept in the household, some seasonally and periodically and some occasionally. Some sacrifices are simple offerings, with little complexity; while some are very elaborate, which have to be performed in stages over a long time, with prior preparation, such as the horse sacrifice (asvamedha yajna) or mantha rites mentioned in the Brihadaranyaka and Chandogya Upanishads. Some sacrifices like the Agnicayana sacrifices require elaborate preparation, including preparation of specific types and number of bricks to be used in the construction of the sacrificial altar and need to be performed in stages stretching over several years. Most of these sacrifices are no more practiced, except perhaps occasionally or symbolically. Many sacrificial ceremonies have fallen into disuse due to the changes in the socioeconomic order and the absence of patrons and religious minded people interested in nourishing the ancient gods.

The Aranyakas

The third part of the Vedas are known as the Aranyakas or forest books. They contain advanced knowledge of the rituals, knowledge of certain sacrifices that are not in public knowledge and their significance. The knowledge of the Aranyakas was originally kept secret from the public. In the Vedic world, even the most experienced priests were not privy to the full knowledge of the Aranyakas until they reached certain age. The Aranyakas themselves are rather cryptic. Their knowledge is neither continuous nor straightforward. It is difficult to make sense out of them, even with a good knowledge of the sacrifices, unless you are guided by an experienced teacher. This knowledge was kept secret for other reasons also. Some of the rituals are meant to cast spells, repulse astral attacks, overpower resisting women or harm one's enemies. The Brihadaranyaka Upanishad, for example, contains spells to harm the secret lover of a man's wife. There is another ritual mentioned in both the Upanishads regarding attaining greatness. These are just a few illustrations of what the Vedas contain for an advanced knower of rituals.

Antiquity of the Vedas

It is believed that the Brahmanas, Aranyakas and even the Samhitas we have today are just fragments of a vast body of knowledge that had became extinct overtime from the earliest days of Vedic civilization until recent times. The tradition is at least 6000-7000 years old and in parts may be even older. It is difficult to determine the dates of early Indian history. There is nothing much we can do other than speculate about the antiquity of the Vedas and the Vedic civilization. The ancient scholars of India, rarely maintained any historical data. Secondly, there is not enough archeological data to establish the chronology through carbon dating. Thirdly, not many monuments of that period are left because the ancient Indians built their cities mostly in wood. For example, Pataliputra was a huge city that spread over several miles, but none of that remains now. Fourthly, the people in ancient India mixed up factual history with legends and myths. As a result, the Puranas and such other works we have today may present a grand picture of the ancient world, yet it is difficult to rely upon them exclusively to draw meaningful conclusions. Fifthly, the European historians of colonial India postdated most of the events of India's past because of their ignorance and their racial and religious bias. Therefore, they dated the earliest compositions of the Vedic literature to around 2000 BCE-1500 BCE. They also suggested that the Vedic civilization was the result of an Aryan invasion .

They created the premise that a warrior tribe of Aryans wandered off into the Indian subcontinent on horsebacks and conquered the native people. Having formulated the hypothesis, they looked for evidence in the scriptures and interpreted the imagery found in them in support of it. Now, there is no evidence that the so called Vedic Aryans ever invaded India or defeated the natives. There is no evidence that prior to their so called invasion, they lived anywhere, spoke Sanskrit, performed rituals or worshipped similar gods. The Vedic people, described in the Vedas, were predominantly pastoral people who lived in villages and spent their time in the service of their families, ancestors and gods, performing sacrifices and exploring the nature of existence. There is also no evidence that they ever displaced any native communities by waging wars. Whatever evidence they suggested in support of their speculation was inconclusive and ambiguous. They also ignored the fact that the Vedic religion was unique to India and had no parallel outside. Yet, the historians of the British period in India, went ahead with their theories led by the belief that since the beginning of creation God entrusted the responsibility of civilizing the world and ruling over it to a few select tribes of particular color and creed. Therefore, that part of the Indian history, centered around the notion of racial distinctions cannot be relied upon to determine the antiquity and significance of Hinduism and its literature.

The Upanishads

The Upanishads constitute the fourth or the end part of the Vedas. Since they form the end part of the Vedas, they are also collectively known as the Vedanta. Anta means, the end and Veda means knowledge. Vedanta thus not only means the end of the Vedas but also the end of all knowing and seeking. When you study the Upanishads and realize the knowledge contained in them, you reach the end of all knowing and enter into the eternal world of Brahman that has no beginning and no end.

The Upanishads, as you can verify from the 14 Upanishads included in this collection, contain a vast amount of information on the aspects of creation and human personality, the manifestation of beingness and duality, the origin and dissolution of the worlds, the divine nature of existence, the eternal nature of our hidden souls and our eternal and inseparable connection with the Supreme Universal Self.

They contain profound philosophy, which is unparalleled in the history of any religion. They allude to the flowering of human consciousness in the ancient world. They have the potential to uplift you and stretch your mind and vision far into the universe on a scale you may not imagine until you read them and assimilate them.

There are many Upanishads, composed over a long period of time, some very ancient and some very recent, numbering over 300. Some Upanishads form part of the Tantras and Puranas. Even the Bhagavadgita is considered by some as an Upanishad only. It is believed that we might have lost many Upanishads and what we have now are collections gleaned from various sources and preserved by teacher traditions.

Based upon their content, the Upanishads are classified into Vedanta Upanishads, Yoga Upanishads, and Sanyasa Upanishads. In addition, there are some Vaishnava and Saiiva Upanishads also. Based upon their composition they are classified into prose Upanishads and verse Upanishads. For example Brihadaranyaka, Chandogya, Taittiriya and Kena are prose

Upanishads. while Isavasya. Katha, Mundaka and Svetasvatara are verse Upanishads.

The Upanishads, the Brahmasutras and the Bhagavadgita occupy a very important place in Hindu religious philosophy. Together they are considered the three that lead to the Place of Brahman (prastana traya). Of all the Upanishads, Brihadaranyaka, Aitareya, Chandogya, Kausitaki, Kena, Taittiriya, Isa and Katha Upanishads are considered the most ancient, composed long before the emergence of Buddhism.

Most historians presently believe that the major Upanishads are not the work of one person or tradition, but collections or compilations gleaned from various sources by teacher traditions and arranged in a certain manner for the purpose of instruction. Therefore, you may find them in no continuity of thought but loosely arranged ideas and doctrines. However, each idea in itself is complete and has the potential to open your mind to the truths of the eternal wisdom or right knowledge (jnana).

Some of the knowledge in the Upanishads is repetitive. Some of it is symbolic. Some of it is composed to influence your thinking in a certain way, such as the Upanishads that project either Siva or Vishnu as the Supreme Brahman. Of the 300 or so Upanishads, 108 are considered sacred; and of the 108 Upanishads, 12 to 16 are considered principal Upanishads for which commentaries (bashyas) and expositions (karikas) have been written by the ancient commentators. Vidyaranya (13th Century AD) in his Sarvopanishad Arthanubhuti Prakasa mentioned the following 12 Upanishads: Aitareya, Taittiriya, Chandogya, Mundaka, Prasna, Kausitaki, Maitrayaniya, Kathavalli, Svetasvatara, Brihadaranyaka, Talvakara (Kena), and Nrisimhottara-tapaniya Upanishads.

As for the classical commentators of the Upanishads, Gaudapada, Shakaracharya, Shanakarananda, Sayana are prominent. Shankaracharya's understanding of the Upanishads is unparalleled. His commentaries of the principal Upanishads are works of excellence and no study of the Upanishads is complete without their study.

Of these principal Upanishads, we may consider the Chandogya and the Brihadaranyaka as the heart and soul. They not only contain the earliest of the Vedic philosophy, but also form over two thirds of the entire collection. As you can see in the table below, out of the 16 Upanishads included in it, these two contain over 1000 verses of varying lengths.

Not all the Upanishads form the end part of the Vedas. Some Upanishads are part of the Brahmanas and Aranyakas also. Some are associated with the Tantras and Puranas. While we do not exactly know how this happened, one reason could be because the texts we have today came to us from different traditions and each tradition possessed its own knowledge and teaching methods to impart it to their committed followers.

Whatever may be the truth, the Upanishads do not present a coherent philosophy of ideas. The knowledge is at the most disorganized and loose. If you expect them to have a linear or sequential thought process, with a beginning, a middle and conclusive end, you will be disappointed. In the Upanishads, you will find no methodical or systematic arrangement of thoughts and ideas. The same Upanishad may deal with a hundred subjects, with no overall coherence. The verses or the sections do not proceed in a methodical fashion. They may sometimes, but not always. One section of the Upanishad may have little in common with the next. It may be because, the knowledge was secretive and each teacher tradition tried to preserve what it knew, by ensuring that the succession of teacher maintained the integrity and purity of knowledge they received under an oath.

Higher and lower knowledge

The knowledge contained in the Upanishads is considered higher knowledge (jnana) in contrast to the ritual knowledge of the Samhitas and the Brahmanas which is considered lower knowledge (vijnana). They are also identified in some verses as Vidya (knowledge) and Avidya (ignorance).

The Vedas contain both ritual and spiritual knowledge. Ritual knowledge is necessary for practicing karma yoga, or performing one's duties and obligations. as part of God's Eternal Duty (dharma) to maintain the order and regularity (rta) of the worlds. But it is not an end in itself. This knowledge is useful up to a certain extent. But one should not remain confined to it, because it is not a liberating knowledge. The Upanishads state that if you focus your effort entirely upon satisfying your desires and leading a comfortable life, chances are you will eventually suffer from moral and spiritual depravity and enter the darkest hells.

Therefore, after reaching a certain stage in your life, having done your part in the service of God, family and society, not necessarily in the same order, you have to return to your higher purpose, which is liberation from this world of duality, deception and delusion and from the cycle of births and deaths. For that you have to pursue higher knowledge, which is considered the knowledge of knowledge, which is also the knowledge of the source of all sources rather than the effects, and which leads to the knowledge of the Self that is hidden within oneself.

Upanishad	Veda	Chapters	Sections	*Verses
Brihadaranyaka	White Yajurveda	6	47	427
Chandogya	Samaveda	8	154	629
Aitareya	Rigveda	3	5	33
Kausitaki	Rigveda	4	4	50
Kena	Samaveda	4	1	35
Taittariya	Black Yajurveda	3	31	55
Isavasya	White Yajurveda	1	1	19
Katha	Black Yajurveda	2	6	120
Mundaka	Atharvaveda	3	6	65
Mandukya	Atharvaveda	1	1	13
Prasna	Atharvaveda	1	6	67
Svetasvatara	Black Yajurveda	6	6	115
Paingala	White Yajurveda	4	4	55
Kaivalya	Atharvaveda	1	1	26
Vajrasucika	Samaveda	1	1	9

| Jabala | Atharvaveda | 6 | 6 | 7 |
| Total | 16 | 54 | 280 | 1725 |

* Note: The number of verses is inclusive of invocations also

This is the liberating knowledge sought by the ascetics who live in the caves and forests and practice austerities or those who have reached the end of their worldly lives and found no meaningful and sustaining purpose in it. This is where the knowledge of the Upanishads become relevant and important. They teach you how to internalize the rituals and use austere methods and contemplative practices of yoga to elevate your consciousness and become stabilized in the experience of the Self and Brahman.

In the Upanishads presented in this collection you will find an expansive vision of the human mind stretched into infinity, an advancement over somewhat primitive and ritualistic theology of the Samhitas and Brahmanas, with the focus firmly fixed upon the world within and the universe outside. You will notice in the verses an unflinching yearning for freedom and a mystic vision that descends into the arteries of the human heart, but at the same time attempts to ascend into the realms of the highest heaven, to envision a single and unitary reality that is indefinable and indescribable, yet can be experienced, with austere effort, in the recesses of the human mind.

This book contains 14 translations, with a total of 669 verses (including invocations). Of these Aitareya Upanishad belongs to the Rigveda; Brihadaranyaka, Isavasya Upanishads belong to White Yajurveda; Katha, Svetasvatara and Taittiriya Upanishads belong to Black Yajurveda; Chandogya, Kena and Vajrasucika Upanishads belong to Samaveda; and Mandukya, Mundaka, Kaivalya and Jabala Upanishads belong to Atharvaveda Upanishads. An overview of the Upanishads and their content is provided in the table.

I started the translation of the Upanishads, since last year. It took me several months to complete them. I originally intended to include all the free translations I did before and add a few more. But I was not particularly happy with the free translations I did, in which I took many liberties with the meaning as well as expression. Therefore, I decided to redo all the translations and also translate the Brihadaranyaka and Chandogya Upanishads, which are indeed very large texts. These two translations are not included in this collection. They are published separately as two books because of their sheer volume.

Perhaps, with some liberties, as in case of free translations, I would have made the texts more readable. But this time, I decided to focus upon the meaning and substance rather than the style. About 95% of this work is new. A few verses from the previous translations I chose to leave intact as I did not find them objectionable. I am sure readers will make out the meaning of the verses, even if they are not translated exactly the way we speak English in our daily lives. Even with some redundant words and twisted expressions, I believe the translations are easy to understand and you may find them useful for study, contemplation, reflection and understanding.

There is no one interpretation for the Upanishads. There is no one single authority on the Upanishads. Even the interpretation of Shankara is debatable, just as mine or anyone else's is. Scriptures such as the Upanishads challenge your learning and wisdom. When you study them and interpret them you always run into the risk of superimposing your thoughts and worldviews upon it. While that may provide unique perspective on what the scriptures teach, it may also expose the limitations of the human mind in assimilating abstract ideas and transcendental truths.

Translations

Aitareya Upanishad

Editor's Note

The Aitareya Upanishad is one of the oldest among the principal Upanishads. It belongs to the Aitareya Aranyaka of the Rigveda, which has five chapters. Out of the five chapters, fourth, fifth and the sixth, containing 33 verses, constitute the Upanishad. The earlier two chapters deal with meditation on karma, breath and material manifestation, whereas these three deal with the eternal Self. According to scholars, this arrangement is somewhat artificial, since there is no clarity why only the last three chapters form part of the Upanishad, while the first two, which deal with Karma and Prana are ignored. Shankara suggested that the first two chapters were meant for the householders, while the last three were meant for those who completed their obligations and set their minds upon liberation. The first chapter of the Upanishad deals with creation of the four worlds, creation of bodily parts, bodily parts experiencing hunger and thirst, bodily parts finding an abode in the human body, creation of food, the entry of eternal Self into the body, and the nature of true Self. The second chapter deals with the three births of a human being. The first birth is in the father. The second one is from the womb as the son. And the third one is through rebirth. The third chapter explains the correlation between Brahman and intelligence and contains the famous saying (mahavakya) that Brahman Himself is intelligence (prajnanam brahma). Intelligence is also distinguished into different types which form part of our consciousness. The knowledge of the Upanishad is meant for those who have renounced worldly life with an aim to attain self-realization, having performed their duties.

Presented here is the translation of the Aitareya Upanishad by Jayaram V with explanatory notes.

38

Invocation

aum, van me manasi pratishita mano me vaci pratisthitam; avir avir ma edhi vedasya ma anisthah. srutam me ma prahasih anenadhitenahoratran samdadhamy rtam vadisyami. satyam vaidisyami: tan mama avatu, tad vaktaram avatu, avatu mam, avatu vaktaram, avatu vaktaram. Aum, santih, santih, santih, santih.

Aum, may my speech be established in my mind; may my mind be established in my speech. He who is manifested, may He reveal Himself for my sake. Let Him be as a nail for my knowledge (Veda). May He not let go of what I have learned. By what I have studied day and night, I will speak that which is harmonious; I will speak Truth. May that protect me; may that protect the speaker. Aum, peace, peace, peace.

Notes: This is an invocation containing an assurance by the teacher that he will be true to his speech and he will speak only that which has been revealed to him. Since his speech is based upon memory, he is seeking the help of God to remember everything truthfully. The source of all knowledge is God, the Manifested One. He is also the source of speech (*vac*). Therefore, he alone can stabilize our minds in knowledge and knowledge in our in speech to ensure that we speak the truth as we know. In our tradition, a spiritual teacher has an obligation to speak truth, nothing but truth and only that he knows for sure is truth. He has to honor the wisdom he has learned from his teacher and abide by the truths contained in the scripture as the standard testimony. This verse conveys that pledge and the commitment.

Chapter 1

Section 1

Creation Of The Worlds And Beings

1. aum, atma va idam eka evagra asit; nanyat kin cana misat; sa aiksata lokan nu srja iti.

1. In the beginning this Self was but alone. There was nothing else whatsoever that batted an eyelid. He (the Self) thought, "Let me now create the worlds."

Notes: The Self is eternal and indestructible. It is prior to all and will remain immutable even after the dissolution of the worlds. According to this verse, creation did not emerge from nothing but from the Self, or Brahman. At the time of creation, other than the Self, there was nothing whatsoever. Even Nature was non-existent. It manifested subsequently when the Self desired to create the worlds. Thus, the Upanishad differs fundamentally from the Samkhya philosophy, which holds that Nature is an independent and eternal entity like the Self.

2. sa imaaml lokan asrjata; ambho maicir maram apo'do'mbhah parena divam dyauh partistha, antarisksam maricayah, prthvi maro ya adhastat ta apah.

2. *That created all these worlds, ambhas (the world in the clouds), marici (rays), mara (death)and apa (water). That which is beyond the heaven is ambhas. Its support is heaven. The light rays are the mid-region. The earth is death; and that which is below is the waters (apa).*

Notes: Sa means that. It refers to the Self or Brahman. He created four worlds or planes of existence, each supporting or supported by an entity or aspect. The highest is the *ambhas*, the cloud region, which holds the waters of life and where appear to the naked eye the sun, the moon, the Milky Way and the constellations. Physically, it is the region where the water holding clouds float, seemingly above the sky. It is supported by gods in the heaven, represented by the sky. Hence heaven or the sky is its support. The region between the earth and the heaven is called antariksham or the mid-region and by some the atmospheric region. It is the world of light rays (marici) inhabited by celestial beings such as the Yakshas and Gandharvas. The earth is the world of death inhabited by mortal beings. The subterranean world is the world of water because water is found usually in the depressions of the earth or below the earth surface such as the oceans, lakes, rivers, wells and subterranean streams. More or less this is the cosmology found in the Vedic scriptures, a four-tier universe, serving the order of creation in their respective ways.

3. sa iksata ime nu loka loka-palan nu srja iti; so'dbhya eva purusam samuddhrtyamurchayat.

3. *He pondered, "Here are then these worlds. Let me create guardians of these worlds."From the water itself, He gathered a person and gave him a form.*

Notes: Creation of the four worlds or spheres of existence was the first step. The next step was to populate them. You cannot have worlds and beings without order and regularity. Therefore, He proceeded with the creation of guardians for each world. He did it by gathering the waters of the heaven, from which He created a cosmic person with form. This Being was the first guardian, the Lord of creation.

4. tam abhyatapat, tasyabhitaptasya mukham nirbhidyata yathandam; mukhad vag vaco'gnir nasike nirbhidyetam, naskiabhyam pranah, pranad vayuh aksini nirbhidyetam aksibhyam caksuh caksusa adityah karnau nirbhidyetam, karnabhyam srotram, srotrad disah, tvan nirbhidyata, tvaco lomani lomabhya osadhi-vanaspatayah, hrdayam nirbhidyata hrdayan manah, manasas candramah nabhir nirbhidvata nabhya apanah apanan mrtyuh sisnam nirbhidyata sisnad retah retasa apah.

4. *With regard to Him, He performed austerity (tapas). From Him about whom the austerity was performed the mouth was separated, as*

in case of an egg. From the mouth came speech, from speech fire. The nostrils were separated. From the nostrils, breathe, from breathe air. The two eyes were separated. From the eyes sight, from sight the Sun. The ears were separated. From the ears hearing, from hearing the (eight) directions of space. The skin was separated. From the skin, the hairs, from the hair plants and trees. The heart was separated. From the heart the mind, from the mind the Moon. The navel was separated. From the navel, the rectum, from the rectum death. The reproductive organs were separated. From them semen, from semen water.

Notes: *Tapah* means austerity. Some scholars translate it as meditation. Meditation is a form of austerity, but *tapah* is a more elaborate practice than meditation in which the mind and body are disciplined through various practices to generate bodily heat and transform the spiritual energy into creative energy. In this verse, creation is described as an act of *tapah* or spiritual activity. Austerities, as in yoga, endow us with supernatural powers (siddhis) and the ability to manifest things. The same powers have been used by God to manifest creation. The first organ to differentiate was the mouth. It formed just as a hole would appear when a chick broke out of an egg shell. Then sense organs and internal organs (the mind and heart) of the body became separated from the indistinct form of that Person. There is a clear succession of events and separation of organs and their functions. In the cosmic person, these organs represent various divinities and powers. The Person described here is a replica of the human form. All the aspects and parts of that Person are also found in the human personality. The whole material universe is the body of the cosmic Person. His subtle body is made up of the subtle aspects of creation. So are our subtle bodies, whereby we are able to think, feel, and reason. The organs that are described here are the deities in the body. They are the sense organs and organs of action. They seek things. They grasp things. They do it because they are subject to hunger or thirst, or more precisely to desires. This is stated in the next verse.

Section 2

Placing The Organs In The Human Body

1. tad eta devatah srsta asmin mahaty arnave prapatan; tam asandya-pipasabhyam anvavarjat ta enam abruvann ayatanam nah prajanaihi yasmin pratisthita annam adam eti.

1. *These divinities so created fell into this great ocean (of life). He subjected them to hunger and thirst. They said to Him, "Find out an abode for us established in which we may eat food."*

Notes: The deities were the organs of that Cosmic Person. Neither the humans nor the divinities can survive without desires. So hunger and thirst were created. They are the most basic desires from which arise all other forms of desires. Desire, which is an obstacle on the path of liberation, is a facilitator of life in creation. Therefore, we may pursue them to perform our obligatory duties as well as to ensure order regularity in our lives. They are god's creation and have their own importance in ensuring the continuity of the worlds and the world order. A householder is allowed to pursue goals and desires, but only with detachment and as part of his duty. The ocean into which the organs fell is a reference to the waters from which Brahman gathered up the Cosmic Person. The organs cannot exist by themselves. They can exist only as parts of a body. In the body, they have to work in unison to satisfy their hunger and thirst. Therefore, they requested the Creator to find them a body where they could carry out their regular functions.

2. tabhyo gam anayat ta abruvan, na vai no'yam alam iti; tabhyo svam anayat ta abruvan, na vai no yam alam iti.

2. He brought for them a cow. They said, "No, this one is not sufficient for us" He brought them a horse. They said, "No this one is not sufficient for us."

Notes: The organs, which were subjected to hunger and thirst, needed a perfect body where they could satisfy their desires and find peace and balance. Now, the senses are also present in other life forms such as cows and sheep, but there they have lesser opportunities to satisfy their hunger and thirst. Therefore, when the bodies of the cow and horse were presented to them, they expressed their displeasure and requested for a more suitable abode where they would be able to satisfy their hunger and thirst adequately.

3. tabhyah purusam anayatta abruvan, sukrtam bateti puruso vava sukrtam; ta abravid yathayatanam pravishateti.

3. He brought for them a person. They said, "This one is well created." A person, indeed, is an excellent creation. He said to them, "Enter into your respective abodes"

Notes: The organs finally chose the human body because it was a perfect fit for them to pursue their desires and keep themselves happy. In the body of a human being, they had better chances of enjoying life and satisfying their desires. The human body is an excellent creation of God. It is the source of intelligent actions (sukrtam) as well as the result of intelligent deeds. Only through intelligent actions, man is able to nourish the divinities present in the body and sustain them. And only through intelligent actions do humans achieve liberation. Human birth, therefore, is very precious and a human body is a perfectly suitable vehicle for the sacrifice of life that eventually culminates in liberation. It is important to remember that we should not starve our bodies because the organs of the body (deities) depend upon us for their nourishment. The body is a sacred creation of God and we must honor it and respect it, with good thoughts, good actions and sacrificial offerings.

4. agnirvagbhutva mukham pravisadvayuh prano bhutva nasike pravisad, adityas chaksurbhutvaksini pravisad, disah srotram bhutva karnau pravisann, osadhivanaspatayo lomani bhutva tvacham pravisams chandrama mano bhutva hridayam pravisan mrityur apano bhutva nabhim pravisad apo reto bhutva sisnam pravisan.

4. Fire became speech and entered into the mouth. Air entered into the nostrils becoming life breath. The sun entered into the eyes becoming sight. The directions entered into the ears becoming hearing. Plants and trees entered into the skin becoming hair. The moon entered into the heart becoming the mind. Death entered into the navel becoming the outgoing breath. Water entered into the reproductive organs becoming semen.

Notes: This verse explains how, having found a suitable body, the various organs and their functions entered it and became part of it. The parts that are mentioned here are not just parts of a specific body. They are aspects of Nature (tattvas) which manifest in the bodies as the organs and in the worlds above as the deities. They body is subject to decay. We are not supposed to develop attachment with it. Nor we are expected to pursue our carnal desires. Many scriptures declare the body as impure and mortal and the cause of our pains and suffering. Yet, underlying this message is also the theme that life is sacred and divine and the human body is a city or an abode of God. The body is also sacred because it is created in the exact image of the Cosmic Person (Purusha). For one reason or another, we may not appreciate our exceptional status in creation as individuals or our dutiful roles in upholding creation. But a time will come in the lives of people when they begin to realize this fundamental truth about their existence and know that their prime duty upon earth is to serve others who depend upon them for nourishment. We have a right to enjoy our lives only while doing our obligatory duties to serve others, especially the gods. This is the selfless approach advocated by the seers in our scriptures. We should not live for ourselves, but for the sake of upholding creation. As human beings, we have an unique opportunity to serve God and his numerous aspects through our own bodies. Thus, we actually enjoy a better status in the cosmic hierarchy than even gods, because we not only nourish them through our sacrificial actions but also host them in our bodies and carry their burden. When we live our lives in their service, we become qualified for liberation; but if we misuse our organs for selfish purposes, we incur sin and remain bound to the mortal world.

5. tam asanaya-pipase abrutam avabhyam abhiprajanihiti te abravit etasve va vam devatasvabhajamy etasu bhaginnyau karomiti; tasmad yasyai kasyai ca devatayai haviri grhyate bhaginya vevasyam asanaya-pipase bhavatah.

5. To Him hunger and thirst said, "Consider providing us also with an abode." To them He replied, "For you I arrange your livelihood among these divinities and make you both sharers of their portions." Therefore, even now whichever deity receives an offering hunger and thirst becomes its sharers.

Notes: Hunger and thirst are pervasive and universal. All organs in the body are subject to them and so also all beings that have bodies with parts. The organs are also interdependent. They have to work in unison and they have to share the same food consumed by each individual. Hunger and thirst have their share in everything that we consume and whatever food is eaten by us is shared by all the organs in the body according to their share.

Section 3

Creation of Food and the Embodiment of the Self

1. sa iksataime nu lokas ca lokapalas cannam ebhyah srja iti.

1. He thought, "Now, here are the worlds and the controllers of the worlds. Let me create food for them."

Notes: First a form was created. Then parts of the form. Then the parts were accommodated inside the human body. The parts were subjected to hunger and thirst. Then food was created to satisfy hunger. As far as thirst was concerned, water was already available in the earth. Hence there was no need to create it further.

2. so'po'bhyatapat tabhyo'bhitaptabhyo murtir ajayata ya vai sa murtir ajayatannam vai tat

2. He meditated upon the waters and from the waters so meditated upon, came forth a form which was verily food.

Notes: Food is the sustaining and nourishing aspect of creation. In a general sense, food means not just what we eat. Food means all that fulfills our desires and facilitate our enjoyment and happiness upon earth. All the sense objects in the material world which we pursue for our enjoyment constitute food only. It includes our thoughts and actions, and even the air we breathe. Just as milk and honey are food for us, we are food for gods. They feed upon our offerings and eventually consume our casual bodies in the final sacrifice of our lives. However, as we will see, in the context of these verses, food means simply the food we eat.

3. tad enad abhisristam parantyajighamsat tad vacajighriksat tan nasaknod vaca grahitum sa yad hainad vacagrahaisyad abhivyahrtya haivannam atrapsyat.

3. This form so created tried to run away. He tried to seize it with speech. But speech could not take hold of it. Indeed if he could have seized it with speech, with speech alone he would have had the satisfaction of eating food.

Notes: The essence of this verse is that the primal being, who was created out of the waters of life, tried to grasp food with his speech and realized that it was futile to satisfy his hunger in that manner. Now, you cannot grasp food with your speech. Speaking about food is not going to satisfy your hunger. If that is so, none would be hungry in this world. Our words may get us food, but they cannot satisfy our hunger. To satisfy your hunger, you have to eat food actually rather than speaking about it.

4. tat pranenajighriksat tan nasaknot pranena grahitum sa; yad hainat pranena grahaisyad abhipranya;haivannam atrapsyat.

4. He tried to seize it with breath. But breath could not take hold of it. Indeed if he could have seized it with breath, with breathing alone he would have had the satisfaction of eating food.

Notes: The same goes for breath also. You cannot satisfy your hunger by breathing. Breath control (pranayama) may help you to bear the pains of hunger but not satisfy the hunger itself.

5. tac caksusajighriksat tannasaknoc caksusa grahitum sa; yadd hainac caksusa grahaisyad dristva haivanam atrapsyat.

5. *He tried to seize it with sight. But sight could not take hold of it. Indeed if he could have seized it with sight, with seeing alone he would have had the satisfaction of eating food.*

Notes: Mere seeing the food is not going to satisfy your hunger. In fact, it may even aggravate your hunger.

6. tac chrotrenajighriksat tan nasaknoc chrotrena grahitum sa; yad hainac chrotena grahaisya chrutva haivannam atrapsyat.

6. *He tried to seize it with hearing. But hearing could not take hold of it. Indeed if he could have seized it with hearing, with hearing alone he would have had the satisfaction of eating food.*

7. tat tvacajighriksat tan nasaknot tvaca grahitum sa; yad hainat tvacagrahaisyat spristva haivannam atrapsyat.

7. *He tried to seize it with skin. But skin could not take hold of it. Indeed if he could have seized it with skin, with the sensation of touch alone he would have had the satisfaction of eating food.*

8. tan manasa jighriksat tan nasaknon manasa grahitum sa; yad hainan manasa grahaisyad dhyatva haivannam atrapsyat.

8. *He tried to seize it with mind. But mind could not take hold of it. Indeed if he could have seized it with mind, with thought alone he would have had the satisfaction of eating food.*

9. tac chisnenajighriksat tan nasaknoc chisnena grahitum sa; yad hainac chisnenagrahaisyad vitsrijya haivannam atrapsyat.

9. *He tried to seize it with reproductive organs. But reproductive organs could not take hold of it. Indeed, if he could have seized it with reproductive organs, with emission alone he would have had the satisfaction of eating food.*

10. tad apanenajighriksat tad avayat saiso'nnasya graho; yad vayur anayuvar esa yad vayuh.

10. *Then he tried to seize it with apana breath. And he seized it. He who has grasped food thus is what air is. This one who lives on food is verily of the nature of air.*

Notes: The being tried to grasp food in various ways using the various organs of his body and their activities, but he was unable to grasp food by any of them. Only when he put the food in his mouth, and pushed it down with his downward breath, meaning when he actually ate it, he was able to satisfy his hunger. As we have discussed before, grasping the food with our senses, mind, breath or speech does not satisfy our hunger or thirst. In fact, they enhance it and make us desirous of food. The desire to eat or drink comes to an end, only when we actually consume food or drink water. The being that lives in the body is described to be of the nature of air. The soul is compared to air because air like the Self is subtle, invisible and formless. Besides, upon death, the Self gathers the breaths and move out of the body into air only.

11. sa iksata katham nvidam madrite syad iti sa iksata katarena prapadya iti sa iksata yadi vacabhivyahritam yadi pranenabhipranitam yadi caksusa dristam yadi srotrena srutam yadi tvaca spristamm yadi manasa dhyatam yadyapanenabhyapanitam yadi sisnena visristamatha ko'ham iti.

11. He thought, "How can this food exist without me?" He thought, "By what path should I enter into it?" He thought, "If speaking is through the organ of speech, if breathing is through the organ of breath, if seeing is through the eyes, if hearing is through the ears, if touching is through the skin, if thinking is through the mind, if breathing out is through the out breath, if ejaculation is through the reproductive organs, then who am I?"

Notes: The body is the vehicle or support for the Self. It is embodies the organs and the Self. The organs perform various functions to keep the body alive. Now, the Self, who is the lord of the body, having observed that the organs were carrying out their respective functions and breath was assisting them in satisfying their hunger and thirst, wondered what was then its own specific role and what it was supposed to do to enter into the body. This is the meaning implied in this verse.

12. sa etameva simanam vidaryaitaya dvara prapadyata saisa vidritirnama dvah tad etann andanam tasya traya avasathastrayah svapna ayamavasatho'yamavasatho'yam avasatha iti.

12. Opening the very end of the head, He entered through it. This is the opening, which is known by its name vidrti. It is (the source of) delight. For that, three abodes and three kinds of dreams exist. This is the abode, this is the abode, and this is the abode.

Notes: To know its exact role and status in the body, the Self then entered it through an aperture in the head. As per Vedas, each soul enters a body at the time of the birth through the same aperture through which it departs at the time of death. This aperture exists in the tip of the head. It goes by different names, but the name mentioned here is vidrti. The sahasrara chakra or the seventh chakra, also said to exist in this region. It is the passage to the transcendental world of divinities and celestial beings. According to Shankara, the three abodes are the places in the body where the Self resides. They are the eyes, the mind and the heart. Alternatively, we may regard the three bodies as the body of the father, the womb of the mother and one's own body where the eternal Self resides in the course of its embodiment. He also states that the three kinds of dreams are the waking state, the dream state and the deep sleep state. The waking state is also considered a dream because the world is an illusion and very much dreamlike.

13. sa jato bhutany abhivyaikhyat kimihanyam vavadisad iti sa etam eva purusam brahma tatamam apasyat idam adarsamiti.

13. *Having born, He perceived the created beings. He perceived this very Person, the all-pervading Brahman. "I have seen this," he said. What else would one desire to speak here?*

Notes: Having born, that is having entered the body during birth as the inner Lord, the Self perceives the duality and diversity of the world. This is ignorance. Then, upon Self-realization he realizes that all that is seen and enjoyed is a manifestation of Supreme Brahman, the one reality. This is the universal vision arising from the higher knowledge. When you enter into that state, there is nothing else for you to know.

14. tasmad idandro namedandro ha vai nama tam idandram santam indra ity acaksate paroksena paroksapriya iva hi devah paroksapriya iva hi devah.

14. *Therefore, his name is Idandra. Indeed Idandra is the name. Of him, who is Idandra, they speak of him indirectly as Indra. Indeed God seems to be fond of being indirect.*

Notes: Idandra is the Witness, the perceiver of this (body). He is the inner Self. However, since He is hidden, no one wants to refer to Him directly. They speak of Him indirectly as Indra, the Lord of the heavens. God Himself loves to be indirect. Therefore, he remains hidden beyond the senses.

Chapter 2
The Triple Births of the Embodied Self

1. aum puruse ha va ayamadito garbho bhavati yad etad retah tad etat sarvebhyo'ngebhyas tejah sambhutam atmany evaatmanam vibharti tad yatha striyam sincaty athainaj janayati tad asya prathamam janma.

1. *Indeed, in a person this one first becomes an embryo. That which is called semen is a culmination of the vigor coming from the limbs of the body. In the self only one bears the self. By shedding it into a female, he gives birth to it. This is the first birth.*

Notes: In the Self only one bears the Self means in the body only one gives birth to another. It also affirms the Vedic belief that a father is born again as his own son. The semen in the body is the source of that. This is the first birth. as the father.

2. tat striya atmabhuyam gaccati yatha svamamgam tatha tasmad enam na hinasti sasyaitam atmanam atra gatam bhavayati

2. *It enters into the self of the female, as if it is a limb of her. Therefore it does not cause her any harm. She nourishes this self of his that has come into her.*

3. sa bhavayitri bhavayitavya bhavati tam stri garbham vibharti so'gra eva kumaram janmano'gredhibhavayat sa yat

kumaram janmano'gre'dhibhavayaty atmanam eva tad bhavayaty esam lokanam samtatya evam santata hime lokah tad asya dvitiyam janma.

3. She is the one who nourishes, so should she be nourished. She bears him in her womb as an embryo. Before the birth he nourishes the child, so does he after his birth. He thus nourishes his own self, for the continuation of the worlds. The worlds are sustained in this manner only. This is the second birth.

Notes: This is the second birth. The birth from the womb as the son, a new person.

4. so'syayamatma punyebhyah karmabhyah pratidhiyate athasyayam itara atma kritakrityo vayogatah praiti sa itah prayann eva punar jayate tad asya tritiyam janma.

4. He who is thus born of his own self, becomes the substitute for performing the deeds. After completing his works, he departs. Departing thus he is born again. This is his third birth.

Notes: Rebirth is the third birth. From there the cycle continues.

5. tad uktam risinam. garbhe nu sann anvesam avedam aham devanam janimani visva satam ma pura ayasir araksann aghah syeno javasa niradiyamiti garbha evaitac cayano vamadeva evam uvaca.

5. This is what the seer said."While I was in the womb, I knew all the births of the gods. A hundred walls made of steel, protected me. I burst out of them with the speed of a hawk, "Vamadeva spoke this verse even when he was lying in the womb.

6. sa evam vidvan asmac charirabhedad urdhva utkramyamusmin svarge loke sarvan kamanan aptvamritah samabhavat samabhavat.

6. He knowing thus, when the body was dissolved, travelled upward and enjoyed al the desires in the heaven. He became immortal, yes He became immortal.

Chapter 3
Different Types of Intelligence

1. aum, ko'yamatmeti vayam upasmahe katarah sa atma yena va pasyati yena va srinoti yena va gandhan ajighrati yena va vacam vyakaroti yena va svadu casvadu ca vijanati.

1. *Aum, who is he whom we all worship as the Self? Which one is the Self? Is it that by which one verily sees, one verily hears, one verily smells the odors, one verily is able to speak, and one verily is able to distinguish the tasty ones from the tasteless?*

2. Yad etadd hridayam manas caitat samjnanama ajnanam vijnanam prajnanam medha dristir dhritir matir manisa jutih smritih samkalpah kratur asuh kamo vasa iti sarvany evaitani prajnanasya namadheyani bhavati.

2. (It is) that which is the heart and the mind. That is consciousness, perception, discrimination, intelligence, mental brilliance, vision, resolve, cognition, mental discipline, impulse, memory, intention, goal, life, desire, and control. All these are the names of intelligence only.

3. esa brahmaisa indra esa prajapatir ete sarve deva imani ca panca mahabhutani prithivi vayur akasa apo jyotimsity etan imani ca ksudramisraniva bijanitarani cetarani candajani ca jarujani ca svedajani codbhijjani casva gavah purusa hastino yat kin cedam prani jangamam ca patatri ca yacca sthavaram sarvam tat prajnanetram prajnane pratisthitam prajnanetro lokah prajna pratistha prajnanam brahma.

3. He is Brahma, he is Indra, he is Prajapati. He is all these gods. He is the five elements, namely the earth, air, ether, water and light, a combination of which forms into seeds of different kinds, those born out of eggs, those born out of wombs, those born from sweat, those born from sprouts, horses, cows, people, and elephants, all creatures that breath here, moving, flying or stationary. All this is moved by intelligence, is established in intelligence. The world is moved by intelligence. The support is intelligence. Brahman is intelligence.

Notes: This verse contains the great saying (mahavakya), "Prajnanam Brahma," meaning Brahman is intelligence

4. sa etena prajnenatmanasmal lokad utkramyamusmin svarge loke sarvan kaman aptvamritah samabhavat samabhavat.

4. He with this intelligent self soared upward from this world and having enjoyed all the desires in that heavenly world became immortal. Yes he became immortal.

Notes: The one who became immortal was Vamadeva.

Kausitaki Upanishad

Editor's Note

Kausitaki Upanishad, also spelled as Kaushitaki Upanishad and also known as Kausitaki-brahmana-upanishad, forms part of the Kausitaki Aranyaka of the Rigveda from chapters 3-6, which is again part of the 30 chapters of the Kausitaki Brahmana included in the Veda. The Upanishad contains the names of some of the most prominent seers of the early Vedic period, namely, Uddalaka Aruni, Svetaketu, Ajatasatru and Balaki. Although in its current form only four chapters are available, Max Mueller stated that Professor Cowell discovered another five chapters appended to the Upanishad explaining some aspects of the Aitereya Aranyaka. He also stated that various other recensions of the Upanishad were available. Here, we have followed the same version followed by Max Mueller, S.Radhakrishnan and others. The text that has been presented here is probably not the original, in the sense that it underwent many changes, and rerenditions overtime and even corrupted. However, in my opinion it is the most current and up to date.

Being one of the earliest Upanishads, forming part of the Rigveda, the Kausitaki Upanishad is also important from a historical perspective, because in this it is Brahma, neither Vishnu nor Siva, who is depicted as the supreme deity, whose world is water, who rules the immortal heaven and who receives the liberated souls into the highest heaven. He also decides before birth and after the death whether an individual should go to the ancestral world or the immortal heaven.

Following is a translation of the Kausitaki Upanishad by Jayaram V

Chapter 1
The Worlds Where the Souls Go After Death

1. citro ha vai gangyayanir yaksyamana arunim vavre sa ha putram svetaketum prajighaya yajayeti tam habhyagatam papraccha gautamasya putraste samvritam loke yasmin ma dhasyasy anyamaho baddhva tasya loke dhasyasiti sa hovaca naham etad veda hantacaryam pracchaniti: sa ha pitaram asadya papraccha ititi ma praksit katham pratibravaniti; sa hovaca, aham apy etanna veda sadasy eva vayam svadhyayam adhitya haramahe yan nah pare dadaty ehy ubhau gamishyava iti, sa ha samitpanis citram gangyayanim praticakrama upayaniti tam hovaca brahmarhosi gautama, yo na manam upagah ehi vyeva tva jnapayishyamiti.

1. Citra Gargyayani, verily, possessed of a desire to perform a sacrifice, chose (Uddalaka) Aruni. But he sent (instead) his son Svetaketu saying, "You perform the sacrifice." When he arrived, he asked, "O son of Gautama, is there a hidden place in the world where you can place me, or is there another way and will you place me in that world to which it leads?" He said, "I do not know. I will go and ask my teacher." He approached his father and said, "He asked me thus, how may I answer it?" He said, " I do not know it. Only after practicing the self-study of the Vedas at his residence (under his guidance), we should (perform sacrifices and) accept (fee) from others. Come, together we will both go there." Then, with fuel in his hands, he approached Citra Gangyayani, saying , "May I approach you." He said to him, "You are qualified to know Brahman, O Gautama, because you are not swayed by pride. Come I will help you to know it by heart. "

Notes: Citra Ganyayani (translated in some versions as Gargyayani) was well versed in the Vedas. Since he was a Kshatriya and as per the prescribed duties, he was not allowed to perform sacrifices on his own, he sought the help of Uddalaka Aruni. Uddalaka Aruni, instead, sent his son Svetaketu. It may be recalled that both these seers figure prominently in the Chandogya Upanishad also. While Uddalaka Aruni was well versed in the knowledge of Brahman, Svetaketu was not. When he went to the house of Citra Gangyayani, the latter asked him a question about the merits accruing out of the sacrifice. He wanted to know whether by virtue of the sacrifice, Svetaketu would be able to help him gain an entry into the world of ancestors by the path of ancestors or by the other path to the world of immortals. Svetaketu had no idea and even his father was not aware of the two paths, which we have discussed in the other Upanishads. A priest was required to know the results of a sacrifice. Hence, he told his son honestly that since they both lacked that knowledge, they would not perform sacrifices or accept fee from others until they knew the answer correctly. Hence, they both went to Citra Gangyayani, wishing to know from him. By saying, "May I approach," as per tradition, Aruni, a Brahmana, indicated his willingness to learn the secret knowledge from Gangyayani, who was a Kshatriya, and the latter readily accepted to teach them both.

2. sa hovaca ye vai ke casmal lokat prayanti candramasam eva te sarve gacchanti tesham pranaih puurvapaksa apyayate tan aparapakse na prajanayaty etad vai svargasya lokasya dvaram yac candramas tam yat praty aha tam atisrijate: ya enam pratyaha tamiha vrishtir bhuutva varshati sa iha kito va patango va matsyo va sakunir va simho va varaho va parasvan va sardulo va purusho va anyo va tesh tesu sthanesu pratyajayate yathakarmam yathavidyam tam agatam pricchati ko'asiti tam pratibruyat: vicaksanad ritavo reta abhritam pancadasat prasuutat pitryavatah tan ma pumsi kartaryerayadhvam pumsa kartra matari ma nisinca. sa jayamana upajayamano dvadasa trayodasa upamaso dvadasa trayodasena pitrasam tad videham pratitad videham tan ma ritavo martya va arabhadhvam tena satyena tapasa rtur asmy artavo'asmi ko'asi tvam asmiti tam atisrijate.

2. He said, "Those who depart from this world, they all do verily go to the moon. In the first (bright) half, it (the moon) deals with them with affection. In the second (dark) half, it sends them back to be born (again). The moon, verily, is the door to the heaven. Whoever responds to it rightly (with correct answer), it sets him free (to reach the immortal world). But for him who does not respond to it rightly, becoming rain it rains him down. He is born again as worm, or as an insect, or as a fish, or as a bird, or as a lion, or as a boar, or as a snake, or as a tiger, or as a person or as someone else in different, different places, according to his deeds, and according to his knowledge. When he arrives (he), asks him, "Who are you?"

He should answer, "From the yonder shining (moon), who ordains the seasons. The semen, that is me, is gathered from the moon, the home of our ancestors, during the course of the fifteen days (of the dark half). They sent me here and put me in a man as an agent to be placed in a mother with the man as the active agent. Then, growing up (in the womb) I would be born in the twelfth or thirteenth month so that I may reach the father of twelve or thirteen parts. That (father) I may know or may not know. Therefore, O Father of Seasons, help me to attain immortality. By this truth, by this austerity, I am like a season. I am of the season.

"Who are you?," (he asks).

"I am you," he replies. Then he sets him free.

Notes: Some of the wording in this verse is cryptic and it has been interpreted differently by different commentators in the past. I did took some liberties with the translation to make the symbolism obvious, and I believe it may be the true meaning. The seasons are recurring phenomena. The mortal life, like the seasons, also happens recurrently. The verse refers to the return journey of a soul that has fallen from the moon to the earth through the rain. It is about to become part of a man's semen and enter into the womb of a woman, when he is being tested by Brahma, the creator or the father of the seasons, who is also extolled in many verses as the year itself. The year consisting of 12 or 13 months is a symbol of immortality embodied by Brahma. Therefore, most likely it is Brahma who stops the souls and asks them this question. He asks the liberated soul also a similar question, which is mentioned in a subsequent verse (6). The immortal souls who travel by the path of gods reach the full year (immortality) after crossing the first six months during which the sun travels northwards, where as those who are on their way to the world of ancestors remain stuck in the six months and never reach the full year.

3. sa etam devayanam panthanam asadyagni lokam agacchati sa vayulokam sa varunalokam sa adityalokam sa indralokam sa prajapatilokam sa brahmalokam tasya ha va etasya brahmalokasyaro hrido muhurta yeshtiha viraja nadilyo vriksah salajyam samsthanam aparajitam ayatanam indraprajapati dvaragopau vibhum pramitam vicaksanasandhy amitaujah prayankah priya ca manasi pratirupa ca caksushi pushpany adayavayato vai ca jagany ambas' cambayavis' capsaraso' ambaya nadyah tam ittham vid agacchati tam brahma habhidhavata mama yasasa virajam va yam nadim prapan na va ayam jigishyatiti.

3. *He going by the path by which the immortal gods travel reaches the world of Agni (fire), then to the world of Vayu (air), then to the world of Varuna, then to the world of Aditya (sun), then to the world of Indra, then to the world of Prajapati, then to the world of Brahma. In this world of Brahma, verily, is the lake Ara, points of time called Yestiha, the river Viraja, the tree Ilya, the city Salajya, the court of Aparajita, the door keepers Indra and Prajapati, the hall Vibhu, the throne Vicaksana, the couch Amitaujas, the beloved Manasi and her twin Caksusi weaving the worlds with flowers, Ambas (mothers), Ambavayis (nurses), Apsaras (celestial beauties), and the rivers called Ambayas. To this world comes the knower of this. To him Brahma says, "Welcome, you have my glory and you have reached the ageless river Viraja and you will never age."*

Notes: This verse contains many names that require explanation. Lake Ara is described as an obstacle river containing enemies such as fear, anger etc. Yesitha means the time spent in subduing desires. Viraja means ageless. Ilya may be another name for Asvattha tree. Salajya is a city that abounds in water with bowstrings on its banks as large as the Sal trees. It has many rivers, lakes, wells, water tanks and warriors. Aparajita means unconquerable, Vibhu means mighty or powerful. Vicaksana means discernment or common sense. Amitaujah means limitless splendor.

4. tam pancasatany apsarasam pratidhavanti satam phalahastah satam anjanahastah satam malyahastah satam vasohastah satam curnahastah tam brahmalankarenalankurvanti sa brahmalankarenalankrito brahma vidvan brahmaivabhipraiti; sa agacchaty aram hridam tan manasatyeti tam ritva sampratvido majjanti sa agacchati muhurtan yeshtihan te'smad apadravanti sa agacchati virajam nadim tam manasaivatyeti tat sukritadushkrite dhunute va, tasya priya jnatayah sukritam upayanty apriya dushkritam tad yatha rathena dhavayan rathacakre paryaveksata evam ahoratre paryaveksata evam sukritadushkrite sarvani ca dvandvani, sa esa visukrito vidushkrito brahma vidvan brahmaivabhipraiti.

4. Five hundred Apsaras (heavenly beauties) come to him from the other side, one hundred holding fruits in their hands, a hundred with ointments in their hands, a hundred bearing perfumes in their hands, one hundred with garments in their hands, and one hundred with powder in their hands. Then they adorn him just like the way Brahma is adorned. Then, with the adornments of Brahma, goes the knower of Brahma into (the world of) Brahma. He comes to the lake Ara and crosses it with his mind, coming to which others who know only the present (world) sink. He reaches the points of time called Yestiha and they flee from him. He comes to the lake Viraja and crosses it with his mind. There he washes away his both good and evil deeds. Of those deeds, his beloved ones receive the results of good deeds and his and his unpleasant relations receive the results of bad deeds. Thus just as a man in a chariot looks at the two wheels so does he look at the day and night, at good deeds and bad deeds and all dualities. thus leaving behind both good deeds and bad deeds, the knower of Brahman goes towards Brahman.

5. sa agacchati tilyam vriksam tam brahmagandhah pravisati sa agacchati salajyam samsthanam tam brahmarasa pravisati agacchaty aparajitam ayatanam tam brahmatejah pravisati sa agacchati indraprajapati dvaragopau tav asmad apadravatah sa agacchati vibhupramitam tam brahmayasah pravisati sa agacchati vicaksanam asandim brihadrathantare samani purvau padau, syaitanaudhase caparau padau vairupavairaje sakvararaivate tirasci sa prajna prajnaya hi vipasyati sa agacchaty

amitaujasam paryankam sa pranastasya bhutam ca bhavishyac ca purvau padau sriscera caparau bhadrayajnayajniye sirsanye brihadrathantare anucye ricas ca samani ca pracinatanani yajumshi tirascinani somam sava upastaranam udgitho'pasras' ca ya srir upabarhanam tasmin brahmaste tam ittham vitpadenaivagra arohati, tam brahmaha prcchati ko'siti tam pratibruyat.

5. *He reaches the tree Ilya, and the fragrance of Brahma enters into him. He comes to the city Salajya, and the essence of Brahma enters into him. He reaches the palace Aparajita, and the radiance of Brahma enters into him. He comes to the two door-keepers, Indra and Prajapati, and they flee from him. He comes to the hall Vibhu, and the greatness of Brahman enters into him (he thinks, I am Brahman). He comes to the throne Vikaksana. The Brihad and Rathantara Samans are its two front feet towards the east. The Syaita and Naudhasa Samans are its two hind feet towards the west. The Vairupa and Vairaja Samans are its lengthwise sides (to the south and north). The Sakvara and Raivata Samans are its crosswise sides (to the east and west). It is intelligence for one sees by intelligence only. He reaches the couch Amitaujas. That is breath. The past and future are its two fore feet. Wealth and the earth are its hind feet. Bhadra and Yajnayajniya are its head piece and the other (the base). Brihad and Rathantara Samans are its lengthwise covers (south and north). The Riks and Samans are its lengthwise covers (north and south). The Yajus the crosswise covers (east and west). The moon beams are the cushions. The High Chant (Udgita) is the coverlet. Wealth is the pillow. On this couch sits Brahma. He who knows this climbs into it with one feet only. Him Brahma asks, "Who are you?" and he should answer..*

6. ritur asmy artavo'asmy akasad yoneh sambhuto bharyayai retah samvatsarasya tejo bhutasya bhutasyatma bhutasya tvam atmasi yas tvam asi soham asmi tam aha ko'aham asmiti satyam iti bruyat kim tad yat satyam iti yad anyad devebhyas ca pranebhyas ca tat sad atha yad devas ca pranas ca tad tyam tad etaya vacabhivyahriyate satyam ity etavad idam sarvam idam sarvam asity evainam tad aha tad etac chlokenapyuktam.

6. *"I am the season. I am of the season. I am born in the space of the womb of a wife through the seed, as the light of the year, and as the embodied self of all beings. You are the self of the beings. That which you are, I am also that."*

He says, "Who am I?"

He should say, "The True."

"What is that called the True?"

"What is other than the gods and the senses, that is Sat (the true). Now, what is the gods and the breaths, that is Tyam. Therefore, that is spoken as SATYAM, all this here, whatever is there. All this is you are." This is also stated in a hymn of the Rigveda.

7. yajudarah samasira asavrinmurtir avyaya sa brahmeti vijneya risir brahmamayo mahan iti: tam aha kena paumsrani namany apnotiti praneneti bruyat kena napumsakaniti manaseti kena strinamaniti vaceti kena gandhaniti praneneti kena rupaniti caksusheti kena sabdaniti srotreneti kenannarasan iti jihvayeti kena karman iti hastabhyam iti kena sukhaduhkhe iti sarireneti kenanandam ratim prajapatim ity upastheneti kenetya iti padabhyam iti kena dhiyo vijnatavyam kaman iti prajnayeti bruyat tam aha apo vai khalu me loko'yam te'sva iti sa ya brahmano jitir ya vyastis tam jitim jayati tam vyastim vyasnute ya evam veda, ya evam veda.

7. The seer, whose belly is Yaju, head is Saman, and form is Rik, he is to be known as the imperishable great Brahma.

He says to him, "By what means did you obtain my masculine names?"

He should say to him, "By breath."

"By what (did you obtain) my neutral names?'

"By mind"

"By what, my feminine names"

"By speech."

"By what, the smells?"

"By breath."

"By what, the forms?"

"By the eye."

"By what, the sounds?"

"By the ear."

"By what, the taste in the foods?"

"By the tongue."

"By what, the actions?"

"By the two hands."

"By what, pleasure and pain?"

"By the body."

"By what, the sounds?"

"By the ear."

"By what, happiness, sexual intercourse and procreation?"

"By the female sex organ."

"By what, the movement?"

"By the two feet."

"By what, thinking, knowing and desires?"

"By intelligence," he should say.

To him, he says, "Water, indeed, is my world. It is (now) yours."

Whatever victory is of Brahma, whatever belongs to Brahma, that victory he wins and that belonging becomes his, he who knows this, yes, he who knows this.

Chapter 2
The Greatness of Breath

1. prano brahmeti ha smaha kausitakih: tasya ha va etasya pranasya brahmano mano dutam caksur goptr srotram samsravayitr vak parivestri; sa yo ha va etasya pranasya brahmano mano dutam veda dutavan bhavati, yas caksur goptr goptraman bhavati, yah srotram samsravayitr samsravayitrman bhavati , yo vacam parivestrim parivestriman bhavati, tasmai va etasmai pranaya brahmana etah sarva devata ayacamanayaiva balim haranti evam evam haivasmai sarvani bhutany ayacamanayaiva balim haranti ya evam veda tasyopanisan na yaced iti tad yatha gramam bhiksitva labdhopavisen naham ato dattam asniyam iti ta evainam upamantrayante ye purastat pratyacaksiran esa dharmo'yacato bhavaty annnadas tevainam upamantrayante dadama ta iti.

1. "Breath is Brahma," thus, indeed, said Kausitaki. Of this breath, which is verily Brahma, the mind is the messenger, the eye is the protector (or the concealer), the ear the announcer, and speech the housekeeper. He who, indeed, knows the mind as the messenger of this breath which is Brahma, becomes endowed with the messenger. He who knows the eye as the protector, becomes endowed with the protector. He who knows the ear as the announcer, becomes endowed with the announcer. He who knows the speech as the housekeeper becomes endowed with the housekeeper. Now, to that breath, which is verily Brahma, all these deities (organs in the body) bring offerings, unasked; and to the same breath, even all beings bring offerings, unasked. For he who knows this, this is the secret teaching, "Do not ask for charity." Just as person who goes through a village begging for alms and receives nothing sits down and says to himself, "I shall never accept any alms given here," and upon saying that those who formerly refused to give him feel obliged to invite him (with offerings), so is the case with him who does not beg. To him, those who make offerings of food, offer an invitation and say, "Here, we give you."

2. prano brahmeti ha smaha paingyas tasya va etasya pranasya brahmano vac parastac caksur arundhate, caksuh parastac chotram arundhate, srotram parastac mana arundhate, mana parastac prana arundhate, tasmai va etasman pranaya brahmana etah sarva devata ayacamanaya balim haranti, evam haivasmat sarvani bhutany ayacamanayaiva balim haranti ya evam veda tasyopaisan na yaced iti, tad yatha gramam bhiksit-va'labdhvopavisen naham ato dattam asniyam iti, ta evainam upamantrayante ye purastat pratyacaksiran esa dharmo'yacato bhavati annadas tv evainam upamantrayante dadama ta iti.

2. "Breath is Brahma," thus, indeed, said Paingya. In this breath, which is verily Brahma, on the upper side of speech the eye is enclosed, on the sides of the eye the ear is enclosed, on the inside of the ear the mind is enclosed, and on the lower side of the mind the organs (breaths) are enclosed. Now, to that breath, which is verily Brahma, all these deities (organs in the body) bring offerings, unasked; and to the same breath, even all beings bring offerings, unasked. For he who knows this, this is the secret teaching, "Do not ask for charity." Just as person who goes through a village begging for alms and receives nothing sits down and says to himself, "I shall never accept any alms given here," and upon saying that those who formerly refused to give him feel obliged to

invite him (with offerings), so is the case with him who does not beg. To him, those who make offerings of food, offer an invitation and say, "Here, we give you."

Notes: Parastat means on the other side, higher than, beyond or after. I have interpreted it differently to denote the location of each of the organ in relation to the other. Arundhate means enveloped, enclosed, or surrounded. Paingya was probably a disciple of Kausitaki. Some commentators have interpreted this verse to mean that the speech is backed by the eye, the eye is backed by the ear, the ear is backed by the mind, the mind is backed by the breath. That is, speech needs the supervision of the eye, the eye needs the supervision of the ear etc.

3. athata eka dhanavarodhanam yad ekadhanam abhidhyayat paurnamasyam vamavasyam va suddhapakse va punye naksatra etesam ekasmin parvani agnim upasamadhaya parisamuhya paristirya paryuksa daksinam janvacya sruvenajyahutir juhoti: van nama devatavarodhini sa me'amusmad idam avarundhyat tasyai svaha: prano nama devatavarodhani. sa me'amusmad idam avarundhyat tasyai svaha: caksur nama devatavarodhani. sa me'amusmad idam avarundhyat tasyai svaha: srotram nama devatavarodhani. sa me'amusmad-idamavarunddham tasyai svaha: mano nama devatavarodhini sa me'amusmad idam avarundhyat tasyai svaha: prajna nama devatavarodhini sa me'amusmad idam avarundhyat tasyai svaha ity: atha dhumagandham prajighayajyalepenangany anuvimrijya vacamyamo'abhipravrijyartham bruyad dutam va prahinuyal labhate haiva.

3. *Now, as to the attainment of the highest treasure. If a man covets this, which is the one treasure, on the night of a full moon day or a new moon day or in the bright half of the moon and under an auspicious star, during any of these times, he should build a fire, after sweeping the ground, spreading the sacred grass and sprinkling water. Bending his right knee, with a ladle or a cup he should pour into the fire the offerings of clarified butter, (saying these words):*

"The deity named speech is the obtainer of boons, may he obtain this for me from him. Svaha."

"The deity named breath is the obtainer of boons, may he obtain this for me from him. Svaha."

"The deity named eye is the obtainer of boons, may he obtain this for me from him. Svaha."

"The deity named ear is the obtainer of boons, may he obtain this for me from him. Svaha."

"The deity named mind is the obtainer of boons, may he obtain this for me from him. Svaha."

"The deity named intelligence is the obtainer of boons, may he obtain this for me from him. Svaha."

Then, after inhaling the smell of the smoke, and smearing his limbs with a layer of clarified butter, in silence, he should declare his wish, or send a messenger, and slowly walk away. He will truly obtain his wish.

4. athato daivah smaro yasya priyo bubhused yasyai va yesam vaitesam evaitasmin parvany etayaivavrtaita ajyahutir juhoti vacam te mayi juhomy asau svaha; pranam te mayi juhomy asau svaha; caksus te mayi juhomy asau svaha; srotram te mayi juhomy asau svaha; manas te mayi juhomy asau svaha; prajnam te mayi juhomy asau svaha; atha dhumagandham prajighayajyalepenangany anuvimrijya vacamyamo'bhipravrijya samsparsam jigamisedapi vatad va sambhasamanah priyo haiva bhavati smaranti haivasya.

4. Now, as to securing love with divine help. If one wants to become the beloved of any man or woman or of any men or women then during any of those period mentioned before (in the previous verse), he should pour in a similar manner oblations of clarified butter into fire, saying:

"Your speech, I pour into myself as an offering. Svaha."

"Your breath, I pour into myself as an offering. Svaha."

"Your eye, I pour into myself as an offering. Svaha."

"Your ear, I pour into myself as an offering. Svaha."

"Your mind, I pour into myself as an offering. Svaha."

"Your intelligence, I pour into myself as an offering. Svaha."

Then after inhaling the smell of the smoke, and smearing his limbs with a layer of clarified butter, in silence. he should slowly walk away and try to come into contact with the wind or stand in the direction of it (so that wind will carry his intention to the person/s he desires). Surely he becomes their beloved, and they do think of him.

5. athatah samyamanam pratardanam antaram agnihotram ity acaksate yavad vai puruso bhasate na tavat pranitum saknoti

pranam tada vaci juhoti yavad vai purusah praniti na tavad bhasitum saknoti vacam tada prane juhoty ete anante amrit ahutir jagrac ca svapan sca santatam juhoty atha ya anya ahutayo'antavatyas tah karmamayyo hi bhavanty taddhasmaitat purve vidvamso'agnihotram na juhavamcakruh.

5. *Now, as to the restraint taught by Pratardana or the internal fire sacrifice, as it is called. As long as a person speaks, for that duration he is unable to breath. Thereby, he pours breath as an offering into his speech. As long as a person breaths, for that duration he cannot speak. Thereby, he pours speech as an offering into his breath. These two unending, immortal oblations he pours always as an offering, whether he is awake or asleep. Now, whatever those other offerings there are, they have an ending for they are desire-ridden actions (karma). Knowing this, verily, the ancient did not pour oblations into the fire sacrifice (out of desires).*

Notes: In the previous verse, the worshippers were told how to realize their desires pouring oblations into fire. Here, lest they would misuse such sacrifices, they are advised to practice restraint (samyama), with the declaration that any sacrifice performed with selfish and base desires would lead to karmic consequences and knowing it ancient people avoided performing fire-sacrifices out of desires.

6. **uktham brahmeti ha smaha suskabhringarah tad rig ity upasita sarvani hasmai bhutani sraisthyayabhyarcyante tad yajur ity upasita sarvani hasmai bhutani sraisthyaya yujyante tat samety upasita sarvani hasmai bhutani sraisthyaya sannamante tac chrir ity upasita tad yasa ity upasita tat teja ity upasita tad yathaitac chrimattamam yasasvitamam tejasvitamam iti sastresu bhavati evam haiva sa sarvesu bhutesu srimattamo yasasvitamas tejasvitamo bhavati ya evam veda, tad etad aistikam karmamayam atmanam adhvaryuh samskaroti tasmin yajurmayam pravayati yajur-mayam rinmayam hota rinmaye samamayam udgata sa esa trayyai vidyayah atmaisa u evaitad indrasyatma bhavati, ya evam veda.**

6. *Uktha is Brahman, thus said Suskabhringara. Let him meditate upon it as Rik. To him all beings offer praise as the best. Let him meditate upon it as Yajus and all beings become united by his greatness. Let him meditate upon it as Saman. Before him, indeed, all beings bow down as the best. Let him meditate upon it as the most powerful, let him meditate upon it as the famous, let him meditate upon it as the radiance. Just as this (ukta) is the powerful, famous and radiant in all the scrip-*

tures, so does he who knows this become the most powerful, famous and radiant among all beings. Thus the Adharvayu priest prepares this self (as the altar) which is meant for performing sacrifices and made up of actions. In that he weaves what is made up of Yajus. In what is made up of Yajus, the Hotri weaves what is made up of Riks. In what is made up of Riks, the Udagatri weaves what is made up of Samans. This (self meant for sacrifices and made up of karmas) is the Self of triple knowledge. He who knows thus becomes the self of Indra.

Notes: Aistikam means what is meant for or related to sacrificial ceremonies. The body is meant for sacrifices means it may be used as offering or it may be used to perform sacrifices. It is made up of works means it is shaped largely by the past karmas. This is the self of triple knowledge, means this body meant for sacrifices and used to perform sacrifices is created by the knowledge contained in the triple Vedas, which are basically our source for performing sacrificial actions.

7. athatah sarvajitah kausitakes triny upasanani bhavanti sarvajiddha sma kausitakir udayantam adityam upatisthate yajnopavitam kritvodakam aniya trih prasicyodapatram vargo'si papamanam me vrndhiti, etayaivavrta madhye santam udvargo'asi papmanam ma udvrindhity etayaivavritastam yantam samvargo'asi papmanam me samvrindhiti tad yad ahoratr-abhyam papam akarot sam tad vrnkte tatho evaivam vidvan etayaivavrtadityam upatishate yad ahoratrabhyam papam karoti, sam tad vrnkte.

7. Now as to the three fold meditation of the all conquering meditation of the Kausitaki. The all conquering Kausitaki worshipped the sun while rising, wearing the sacred thread, having brought the water in a vessel and sprinkled the water thrice from the vessel, saying, "You are the deliverer. Deliver me from my sins." In the same manner, he (worshipped) the midday sun, saying, "You are the highest deliverer. Deliver me from my sins." In the same manner, he worshipped the setting sun, saying, "You are the complete deliverer. Deliver me from my sins." Thus, whatever sin he committed during the day and night, from that he got full deliverance. In the same manner, he who knows this, and worships the sun in a similar manner, whatever sin he commits during day and night, from that he becomes delivered fully.

8. atha masi masy amavasyayam vrttayam pascac candramasam drisyamanam upatisthetaivavrita haritatrine va pratyasyati yan me susimam hridayam divi candramasi sritam, manye'ham mam tad vidvamsam maham pautram agham rudam iti, na hy asmat purvah prajah praititi nu jataputrasyathajata putras-

yapyayasva sametu te sam te payamsi sam u yantu vaja yam aditya amsumapyayayantity etas tisra rico japitva masmakam pranena prajaya pasubhir apyayayisthah yo'sman dvesti yam ca vayam dvismas tasya pranena prajaya pasubhir apyayaya sva aidrim avrtam avrta adityasyavritam anvavarta iti daksinam bahum anvavartate

8. *Now, month after month, when the new moon day comes around, one should worship the moon in the same manner as it appears in the west, or he should throw two blades of grass towards the moon, saying," That subtle heart of mine which rests in the moon in the heaven, I consider myself the knower of that. May I never weep for the misfortune of losing my sons." Verily, his sons will not die before him. This is in case of a man to whom a son is already born. Now, regarding the one to whom a son is not yet born, (he should say), "Increase. May the vigor come to you. May milk and food gather in you. That ray which the Adityas gladden (may that rest in you)." Having uttered these three Riks, he should say, "'Do not increase by our breath, by our offspring, by our cattle. He who hates us and whom we hate, increase by his breath, by his offspring, by his cattle. Then I turn myself with the turn of Indra. I return the turn of Aditya." Saying these words, he raises his right arm and drops it again.*

Notes: The three riks are addressed to the moon. A prayer is made to the moon (symbolized as the wife) asking him to increase (in size and vigor) day by day with the pregnancy, gathering milk and food from the sacrifices and enjoying the rays of the sun. The third Rik is a prayer asking for the rays of Aditya to rest in the moon. The sun is compared to the husband. Hence, his rays will gladden the moon, the wife. It may be noted that there is an implied symbolism in this verse, with the moon representing the wife and the sun the husband. This is suggested in the very beginning of the verse by stating that the heart of the sacrificer (husband) rests in the moon (the wife). The same is implied in the three riks, which are meant to invigorate the moon (or the wife) so that she may deliver a child. The last prayer is to ensure that the moon does not increase in size consuming the breath (life), the children and the cattle of the sacrificer but those of his enemies. The moon is known to consume the bodies of the souls that go there. Hence the suggestion.

9. atha paurnamasyam purastac candramasam drisyamanam upatistheta etayai vavrita somo rajasi vicaksanah pancamukho'asi prajapatir brahmanas ta ekam mukham tena mukhena rajno'atsi tena mukhena mam annadam kuru, raja ta ekam mukham tena mukhena visotsi tena mukhena mam annadam kuru, syenas ta ekam mukham tena mukhena paksino'atsi tena mukhena mam annadam kuru, agnista ekam mukham tenemam lokamatsi tena mukhena mam annadam kuru, tvayi pancamam mukham tena mukhena sarvani bhutany atsi tena mu-

khena mam annadam kuru, masmakam pranena prajaya pasubhir avaksestha yo'asman dvesti yam ca vayam dvismas tasya pranena prajaya pasubhir avaksiyasveti daivim avritam avarta adityasyavritam anvavarta iti daksinam bahum anvavartate.

9. Then, on the night of full moon, one should worship the moon when it appears in the east in the same manner saying, "You are Soma, the King, the discerning, the five-mouthed, and the lord of the beings. The Brahmanas are your one mouth. With that mouth you eat the Kshatriyas. With that mouth, make me an eater of food. The kings are your one mouth. With that mouth you eat the people. With that mouth, make me an eater of food. The hawk is your one mouth. With that mouth, you eat the birds. With that mouth, make me an eater of food. Fire is your one mouth. With that mouth, you eat this world. With that mouth, make me an eater of food. You have a fifth mouth. With that mouth you eat all beings. With that mouth, make me an eater of food. Do not decrease us in respect of our lifespan, progeny and cattle. He who hates us and whom we hate, decrease him in respect of his lifespan, his progeny and his cattle. Thus I turn myself with the turn of the god. I return the turn of Aditya." Saying these words, he raises his right arm and drops it again.

10. atha samvesyan jayayai hridayam abhimriset , yat te susime hridaye hitam antah prajapatau, tenamrtatsyesane ma tvam putryam agham niga iti, na hy asyah purvah prajan praititi.

10. Now, when they are together, he should stoke her heart, saying, "O, well behaved one, who has attained immortal joy by that which has been placed in your heart by Prajapati, may you never fall into sorrow for your children." Then, her children would not die before her."

11. atha prosyan putrasya murdhanam abhijigret, angad angat sambhavasi hridayad adhijayase, atma vai putra namasi sa jiva saradah satam asav iti dadhati asma bhava parasur bhava hiranyam astritam bhava, tejo vai putra namasi sa jiva saradah satam, asav iti namasya grihnati, athainam parigrahnati, yena prajapatih prajah paryagrihnat tad aristyai tena tva parigrihnamy asavity athasya daksine karne japati, asmai prayandhi maghavan rijisin itindra sresthani dravinani dhehiti ma cchetta ma vyathisthah satam sarada ayuso jivasa, putra te namna murdhanam abhijighramiti trirasya murdhanam abhijighred gavam tva hinkarenabhihinkaromiti trir asya murdhanam abhihinkuryat.

11. Now if a man has been away and returns home, he should smell his son's head, saying, "You are born from me, limb by limb; you are born from the heart; you, my son, are myself only. May you live for a hundred autumns." He gives him his name, saying, "May you become like a rock; may you become like an axe; may you be desired everywhere like gold. My son, you are the light itself. May you live for a hundred years. He calls him by his name. Then he embraces him, saying," Just as Prajapati embraces his progeny for their welfare, so do I embrace you (whose name is...)." Then he recites in his right ear, "Give Him, O swift Maghavan," and in his left ear, "O Indra, bestow upon him the most excellent wealth. Do not cut off (our family tree). Do not inflict suffering. Let him live for a span of hundred autumns. I smell your head, O son, with your name" Three times he should make a lowing sound over his head, saying, "I make a lowing sound over you like the cows."

12. **athato daivah parimara etadvai brahma dipyate yadagnirjvalatyathaitanmriyate yanna jvalati tasyadityameva tejo gacchati vayum prana etadvai brahma dipyate yathadityo drisyate'athaitanmriyate yanna drisyate tasya candramasameva tejo gacchati vayum prana etadvai brahma dipyate yaccandrama drisyate'athaitanmriyate yanna drisyate tasya vidyutameva tejo gacchati vayum prana etadvai brahma dipyate yadvidyudvidyotate'athaitanmriyate yanna vidyotate tasya vayumeva tejo gacchati vayum pranasta va etah sarva devata vayumeva pravisya vayau sripta na murcchante tasmadeva punarudirata ityadhidaivatamathadhyatmam.**

12. Now follows Daivah Parimara, the going around death by the gods. This Brahman glows indeed when the fire burns and then this one dies when it does not burn. Of that, to the sun alone goes its light, to the air its breath.

This Brahman glows when the sun is seen and then, when (the sun) not seen, it dies. Of that, to the moon alone goes its light, to the air its breath.

This Brahman glows when the moon is seen and then, when not seen, it dies. Of that, to the lightning alone goes its light, to the air its breath.

This Brahman glows when the lightning is seen and then, when not seen, it dies. Of that, to the to the air alone goes its light, to the air its breath.

Indeed, all these deities enter into air only, and although dead, they do not perish. Thereafter, they do rise again. This is with regard to the deities (in the body). Now, with reference to the self (body).

Notes: Parimara (pari+mara) means going around death, or avoiding death by going around it. When you are going somewhere and you know that there is a certain danger along the path, you travel by an alternate route to avoid it. The deities in the body, who are situated in the organs, do the same thing. They are immortals. But being part of the body, they cannot avoid the mortality of the body. When the body dies and is consigned to flames, what do they do? That process it explained here. They quietly escape into air, which is the absorber, and from there after sometime, they find another abode. The body remains alive as long as there is light in it. When the light is gone, it is time for the deities to escape.

13. etad vai brahma dipyate yad vaca vadaty athaitan mriyate yan na valati tasya caksur eva tejo gacchati pranam prana etad vai brahma dipyate yacc aksusa pasyaty athaitan mriyate yan na pasyati tasya srotram eva tejo gacchati pranam prana etad vai brahma dipyate yacchotrena srinoty athaitan mriyate yan na srinoti tasya mana eva tejo gacchati pranam prana etad vai brahma dipyate yan manasa dhyayaty athaitan mriyate yan na dhyayati tasya pranam eva tejo gacchati pranam pranas ta va etah sarva devatah pranam eva pravisya prane mritva na murchante tasmad eva punar udirate tad yadi ha va evam vidvamsam ubhau parvatav abhipravarteyatam daksinas cottaras ca tustursamanau na hainam striniyatam atha ya enam dvisanti yan ca svayam dvesti ta evainam parimriyante.

13. This Brahman glows indeed when one speaks with speech and then it dies when one does not speak. Of that, to the eye alone goes its light, to the breath its breath.

This Brahman glows indeed when one sees with the eye and then it dies when one does not see. Of that, to the ear alone goes its light, to the breath its breath.

This Brahman glows indeed when one hears with the ear and then it dies when one does not hear. Of that, to the mind alone goes its light, to the breath its breath.

This Brahman glows indeed when one thinks with the mind and then it dies when one does not think. Of that, to the breath alone goes its light, to the breath its breath.

Indeed, all these deities enter into breath only, and although dead, they do not perish. Thereafter, they do rise again. If two mountain from the north and south try to roll together and crush him who knows this, they would not be able to crush. But those who hate him, or whom he hates, they all die around him.

Notes: Breath is absorber in the body, just as the air is outside. All things merge into breath. The body dies, but the deities in the organs of the body (tattvas), they are immortal and do not die. Upon leaving one body, they move on to another to continue their enjoyment and nourishment.

14. athato nihsreyasadanam eta ha vai devata aham sreyase vivadamana asmac charirad uccakramuh tadd hapranat suksham darubhutam sisye'thainad vak pravivesa tad vaca vadac chisya eva athainac caksuh pravivesa tad vaca vadac caksusa pasyac chisya eva athainac chrotram pravivesa tad vaca vadac caksusa pasyac chrotrena srinvac chisya eva, athainan manah pravivesta tad vaca vadac caksusa pasyac chotrena srnvan manasa dhayac chisya eva, athainat pranah pravivesa tat tata eva samuttasthau ta va etah sarva devatah prane nihsreyasam viditva pranam eva prajnatamanam abhisambhuya sahaiv aitaih sarvair asmac charirad uccakramauk te vayupravista akasatmanah svariyuh, tatho evaivam vidvan prane nihreyasam viditva pranam eva prajnatamanam abhisambhuya sahaiv aitaih sarvair asmac charirad utkramati, sa vayupravista akasatma svareti, sa tad gacchati yatraite devas tat prapya yad amrta devas tad amrto bhavati ya evam vadam.

14. Now, as to the attainment of the highest good. All the deities, disputing among themselves, saying, "I am the best," rose up from the body. Then the body lay, without life, withered like a log. Then the speech entered it. Speaking with the speech, it still lay lifeless. Then the eye entered it. Speaking with the speech, and seeing with eye, it still lay lifeless. Then the ear entered it. Speaking with the speech, seeing with the eye and hearing with the ear, it still lay lifeless. Then the mind entered it. Speaking with the speech, seeing with the eye, hearing with the ear and thinking with the mind, it still lay lifeless. Then breath entered it and they, indeed, all arose at once. All the deities, having realized the highest good accruing from the breath, and having understood that breath alone is responsible for the intelligence in the body, went out of the body, all at once. They entered into the air and being subtle in nature like the space, entered the heaven. In the same manner, he who knows this, having realized the highest good of breath, having understood that breath is responsible for the intelligence of the body, when he departs from the body with all these together, he enters into the air and, being subtle in nature like the space, enters into the heaven. He goes to where the gods are. Having reached that, he who thus knows, becomes immortal with that (knowledge) by which gods became immortal.

Notes: The breath and the organs belong to the body, not to the Self. Hence pranam eva prajnanam atma only can mean that breath alone is the consciousness (or intelligence) in the body. It is true because without breath the body becomes lifeless, devoid of intelligence and consciousness. I have also taken some liberties in translating the last few lines of this verse to convey the correct meaning with regard to the fate of the person who knows the supremacy of breath in the body.

15. athatah pitaputriyam sampradanam iti cacaksate pita putram presyannahvayati navais trinair agaram samstirya agnim upasamadhayodakumbham sapatram upanidhayahatena vasasa sampracchannah pita syeta etya putra uparistad abhinipadyata indriyair indriyani samsprisyapi vasma asinayabhimukhayaiva sampradadhyad athasmai samprayacchati vacam me tvayi dadhaniti pita vacam te mayi dadha iti putran pranam me tvayi dadhaniti pita pranam te mayi dadha iti putras caksur me tvayi dadhaniti pita caksuste mayi dadha iti putrah srotram me tvayi dadhaniti pita srotram te mayi dadha iti putrah anna-rasan me tvayi dadhaniti pita annarasan te mayi dadha iti putrah karmani me tvayi dadhaniti pita karmani te mayi dadha iti putrah sukhaduhkhe me tvayi dadhaniti pita sukhaduhkhe te mayi dadha iti putrah anandam ratim prajaim me tvayi dadhaniti pita anandam ratim prajatim te mayi dadha iti putrah ityam me tvayi dadhaniti pita ityam te mayi dadha iti putrah mano me tvayi dadhaniti pita manas te mayi dadha iti putrah prajnam me tvayi dadhaniti pita prajnam te mayi dadha iti putrah yady u va apabhigadah syat samasenaiva bruyat pranan me tvayi dadhanati pita, pranan te mayi dadha iti putrah atha daksinavrid upaniskramati tam pitanumantrayate yaso brahma varcasam kirtis tva jusatam ity athetarah savyam amsam nvaveksate paninantaradhaya vasanantena va pracchadya svargan lokan kaman apnuhiti sa yady agadah syat putrasyaisvarye pita vaset pari va vrajet yady u vai preyat yadevainam samapayeyuh yatha samapayitavyo bhavati yatha samapayitavyo bhavati

15. Now, as to the father's gifting to the son, as they call it. The father, when he is about to depart from this world, calls his son. Having strewn the house with fresh grass, having kindled the fire, having arranged a pot of water with a jug (full of rice), wearing fresh clothes, the father remains lying. He put himself above his son who has arrived and touches his organs with his own organs. Or he may perform the tradition of gifting while he sits before him (if he is in a position to sit). Now, he does the gifting thus:

The father, "I have hereby placed in you my speech."

The son, "I have hereby taken into me your speech."

The father, "I have hereby placed in you my breath."

The son, "I have hereby taken into me your breath."

The father, "I have hereby placed in you my eye."

The son, "I have hereby taken into me your eye."

The father, "I have hereby placed in you my ear."

The son, "I have hereby taken into me your ear."

The father, "I have hereby placed in you my taste for food."

The son, "I have hereby taken into me your taste for food."

The father, "I have hereby placed in you my duties."

The son, "I have hereby taken into me your duties."

The father, "I have hereby placed in you my joys and sorrows."

The son, "I have hereby taken into me your joys and sorrow."

The father, "I have hereby placed in you my pleasure, sexual enjoyment and procreation."

The son, "I have hereby taken into me your pleasure, sexual enjoyment and procreation."

The father, "I have hereby placed in you my walking."

The son, "I have hereby taken into me your walking."

The father, "I have hereby placed in you my mind."

The son, "I have hereby taken into me your mind."

The father, "I have hereby placed in you my intelligence."

The son, "I have hereby taken into me your intelligence."

If the father is very ill and unable to speak, he may say summarily, "I have hereby placed in you my breaths." And the son should say, "I have taken into me your breaths."

Then walking around his father, with his right side towards him, he turns to the east and walks away. His father calls after him, "May my fame, the luster of my face, and my name and honor may always stay with you." Then the other should look back over his left shoulder, and covering his face with his hand or with the hem of his garment, should say, "May you attain the heavenly world and fulfill all your desires."

If the father recovers, he should live under the authority of his son, or wander about like a mendicant. But if he departs, then he should be sacrificed in the final sacrifice, as the final sacrifice ought to be performed, yes, as the final sacrifice ought to be performed.

Notes: The father to son transmission ritual is based on the Vedic belief that a father lives through his son and a son indeed is another birth of the father. In this manner a father transfers all his energies, talents, skills, knowledge, vigor and power to his son. The ceremony also ensures that the son, who has been given the privilege to succeed his father, becomes the head of the household and carries forward the duties and obligations of his father and those of his family until he himself transfers them to his son. The last few lines of this verse are translated differently by different scholars. I have translated it based upon the meaning samapa, which means a sacrifice. In Hindu tradition, funeral is also a sacrifice, the last sacrifice (antyeshti) in which the body is offered as a sacrifice into fire. It has to be done strictly according to the established practice for the soul to find its way to the next world. That is what I believe is implied here and I have therefore translated it accordingly.

Chapter 3
The Superiority of Breath

1. pratardano ha vai daivodasih indrasya priyam dhamopajagama yuddhena paurusena ca tam hendra uvaca pratardana varam te dadaniti sa hovaca pratardanah tvam eva me vrinisva yam tvam manusyaya hitatamam manyasa iti tam hen-dra uvaca na vai varo' varasmai vrinite tvam eva vrinisvety avaro vai kila meti hovaca pratardanah atho khalva indrah satyad eva neyaya satyam hindrah, tam hendra uvaca mam eva vijanathy etad evaham manusyaya hitatamam manye yan mam vijaniyam trisirsanam tvastram ahanam aruanmukhan yatinsalavrikebhyah prayaccham bahvih sandha atikramya divi prahladiyan atrinam aham antarikse pauloman prithivyam kalakanjn tasya kena tatra na loma canamiyate; sa yo mam veda na ha vai tasya kena cana karmanad loko miyate na steyena na bhruna hatyaya na matrvadena na pitrivadhena na nasya papam cakriso mukhan nilam vettiti.

1. *It is said that Prataradana son of Divodasa, verily arrived at the beloved abode of Indra by waging wars and by his valor. To him Indra said, "Pratardana, ask me for any boon." Pratardana said, "You choose me a boon yourself. which you consider is in the best interests of a human being." Indra said, ""No one who chooses actually chooses for another. Choose yourself." Pratardana said, "Then that boon I have to choose would be no boon for me." Now, Indra did not want to swerve from truth, for Indra is truth himself. Indra said to him, "Know me. That alone, I consider is the most beneficial for a human being, which is in knowing me." I slew the three headed son of Tvastri. I delivered the Arunmukhas, and the ascetics (yatis) to the wolves. I broke many agreements and slew the people of Prahlada in the heaven, the people of Paulomas in the mid-region, and the Kalakanjas on earth. Not even a single hair on my body of mine was harmed then. Therefore, he who knows me thus, his world is harmed by no deed of his, not by stealing, not by the destruction of a fetus in the womb, not by the killing of his mother, not by the killing of his father. If he commits a sin, blue color does not depart from his face.*

Notes: Pratardana reached the heaven by dying in the battlefield. He died a warrior's death. Hence, he reached heaven. Upon being asked to seek a boon, he did not ask for it because, proud as he was, he thought any boon he might ask would not be good enough for him. Indra told him that he should try to know him, so that he would become liberated. In this verse, Indra is depicted not as the lord of heaven only, but as Brahman Himself. A liberated person is no more tainted by his actions, even if they are mortal sins. Indra meant it when he said that he who knew him would not suffer from the sins of his actions. He also said that the blue or dark color would not go away from his face if he committed a sin. What it means is that since a knower of Indra is forever free from sin, his face would not turn pale with fear or guilt of committing a sin.

2. sa hovaca prano'asmi prajnatma tam mam ayur amritam ity upasva ayuh pranah prano va ayuh prana yavadd hy asmin sarire prano vasati tavad ayuh pranena hy evamusmin loke'amritatvam apnoti prajnaya satyam samkalpam sa yo ma ayur amritam ity upaste sarvam ayur asmin loka ety apnoty amritatvam aksitim svarge loke tadd haika ahur ekabhuyam vai prana gacchantiti na hi kascana saknuyat sakrid vaca nama prajnapayitum caksusa rupam srotrena sabdam manasa dhyanam ity ekabhuyam vai prana bhutvaaikaikam etani sarvany prajnapayantiti vacam vadantim sarve prana anuvadanti caksuh pasyat sarve prana anupasyanti srotram srnvat sarve prana anusrinvanti mano dhyayat sarve prana anudhyayanti pranam

pranantam sarve prana anupranantity evam u haitad iti hendra uvacasti tv eva prananam nihsreyasm iti.

2. He said, "I am breath (prana). Meditate upon me as the intelligent self, as lifespan, as immortality itself. Lifespan is breath, breath is lifespan. As long as breath dwells in the body, so long is the span of life. By breath only does one obtains immortality in the other world, and by intelligence truth and will. He who worships me as lifespan and immortality, reaches his full span of life in this world and obtains in the heavenly world (svarga) immortality and imperishability. Now, in this regard some say that the breaths (sense-organs) become one, (because otherwise) no one would be able to discern instantly name, form sound and thought by speech, by the eye, by the ear and by the mind. These breaths, by becoming one only, enable us to discern all this one by one. When speech speaks, all the breaths speak after it. When the eye sees, all the breaths see after it. When the ear hears, all the breaths hear after it. When the mind thinks, all the breaths think after it. When the breath breathes, all the breaths breathe after it. Thus it is so, indeed," said Indra. "There is however a greater good among the breaths."

Notes: Ayuh means the lifespan. A person's lifespan is very much dependent upon the breath in the body. A person lives as long as he breathes. That is the purport of Indra's teaching. A person has consciousness or awareness (prajna) as long as he is alive and breathing. And when he has intelligence, only then he can discern truth and exercise his will. Thus these four, breath, intelligence, truth and will are interconnected. Therefore, breath is very much central to our existence. Breath is used in this verse with two different meanings. The first one refers to prana or the life breath that we inhale and exhale. We have seen elsewhere that this prana is of five kinds, such as prana, apana, vyana etc. We have also seen before that this breath is superior to the rest of the deities present in the body because without it none of the organs will function. Now, Prana in plural means the organs in the body, such as the eye, the ear, the nose etc. They are also called breaths because at the time of death, the deities hidden in the organs resort to the departing breath and return to their abode. The latter part of the verse suggests that these breaths or sense-organs act in unison, as if they are one. Because of it, we are able to process all the sensations, such as hearing, seeing, listening simultaneously and perceives names and forms instantly.

3. jivati vagapeto mukan vipasyamo jivati caksur apeto'ndhan hi pasyamah jivati srotrapeto badhiran hi pasyamah jivati mano'peto balan hi pasyama jivati bahucchinno jivaty urucchinna ity evam hi pasyamah, ity atha khalu prana eva prajnat medam sariram parigrihyotyapayati tasmad etam evoktham upasiteti saisa prane sarvaptir yo vai pranah sa prajna ya va prajna sa pranah tasyaisaiva dristir etad vijnanam yatraitat purusah suptah svapnam na kajncana pasyaty athasmin prana evaikadha bhavati tad enam vak sarvai

namabhi sahapyeti caksuh savaihrupaihsahapyeti, srotram sarvai sabdah sahapyet manah sarvaih dhyanaih sahapyeti sa yada pratibudhyate yathagnerjvalato sarva diso visphulinga vipratistherann evam evaitasmad atmanah prana yathayatanam vipratisthante pranebhyo deva devebhyo lokah sa esa prana eva prajnatmedam sariram parigrhyotthapayati tasmad etat evoktham upasiteti saisa prane sarvaptih, yo vai pranah sa prajna ya va prajna sa pranah tasyaisaiva siddhire etad vijnanam yatraitat purusa arto marisyannabalyam etya sammoham eti tam ahur udakramit cittam na srinoti na pasyati vaca vadaty na dhyayati athasmin prana evaikadha bhavati tad enam vak sarvaih namabhih sahapyeti caksuh sarvaih rupaih sahapyeti srotram sarvaih sabdaih sahapyeti manah sarvaih dhyanaih sahapyeti sa yadasmac charirad utkramati sahaivaitaih savaih utkramati.

3. *One lives even without speech. We see the dumb. One lives without sight. We see the blind. One lives without hearing. We see the deaf. One lives without the mind. We see the infants. One lives without the arms. One lives without the legs. This indeed we all see. Now, this breath alone is the intelligence Self that takes hold of this body and make it rise up. Therefore, it is said that it should be worshipped as Uktha only. This one is the all pervading. That which is breath that is intelligence; and that which is intelligence that is breath. This is the view and this is the understanding regarding it. when a person is asleep, does not see any dreams, he becomes one with breath alone. Then speech with all the names goes to him, the eye with all the forms goes to him, the ear with all the sounds goes to him, the mind with all the thoughts goes to him. When he wakes up, just as the sparks fly in all directions from a burning fire, thus breaths proceed from that self to their respective abodes, gods from the breaths and worlds from the gods. Now, this breath alone is the intelligence Self that takes hold of this body and make it rise up. Therefore, it is said that it should be worshipped as Uktha only. This one is the all pervading. That which is breath that is intelligence; and that which is intelligence that is breath. This is the proof and this is the understanding regarding it. When a person is sick, about to die, has become weak and fallen unconscious, they speak of him, "His consciousness has departed, he does not hear, does not see, does not speak with the speech, and does not think." He becomes one with the breath only. Then speech with all names goes to him. The eye with all forms goes to him. The ear, with all sounds goes*

to him. The mind with all the thoughts goes to him. And when he departs from the body, he departs along with all these.

Notes: This verse declares that prana is indeed prajna (yo vai pranah sa prajna). From a scientific perspective this may sound odd, because how can the breath be intelligence? Are not they different? Yes, they are in the gross manifestation, but not so in the subtle world. There are two reasons for this correlation. Firstly, so long as there is breath, there is life and intelligence. When a person dies, intelligence also departs. This obviously suggests a hidden connection. Secondly, the same subtle energy that is present in the breath is also present in the intelligence. Hence, you have body awareness, which is an aspect of intelligence only. The difference between the two is the energy present in the breath is generic because breath has to circulate that subtle energy, which some call astral energy, to all parts of the body; whereas the energy present in the intelligence is suffused with knowing (jna). Hence prajna is that breath (prana) in which knowing (jna) is present. Hence prajna is pra(jn)a.

4. vag evasmin sarvani namany abhivisrijyante vaca sarvani namany apnoti, prana evasmin sarve gandha abhivisrijyante pranena sarvangandhanapnoti caksur evasmin sarvani rupany abhivisrijyante caksusa sarvani rupany apnoti srotram evasmin sarve sabda abhivisrijyante, srotrena savan sabdan apnoti, mana evasmin savani dhyanany abhivisarjyante, manah sarvani dhyanany apnoti, saha hy etavasmin sarire vasatah sahotkramatah atha yuthasyai prajnayai sarvani bhutany ekam bhavanti, tad vyakhyasyamah.

4. To him speech sends forth all names so that by speech he obtains all names. To him breath sends forth all smells so that by breath he obtains all smells. To him the eye sends forth all forms, so that by the eye he obtains all forms. To him the ear sends forth all sounds so that by the ear he obtains all sounds. To him the mind sends forth all thoughts so that by the mind, he obtains all thoughts. Together, indeed, they dwell in the body and together they depart. Now, how in intelligence all the beings become one, that we explain.

Notes: The departing soul obtains the knowledge of names, forms etc., from the sense organs so that he can make use of them in the next world even without the senses. This verse does not explicitly state who are the two who dwell in the body together and depart. From the previous verses, we can deduced that they are breath and intelligence. In some versions, we do find a clear reference to intelligence in the verse itself.

5. vag evasya ekam angam ududham tasyai nama parastat prativihita bhutamatra prana evasya ekam angam ududham tasya gandhah parastat prativihita bhutamatra caksur evasya ekam angam ududham tasya rupam parastat prativihita bhutamatra srotram evasya ekam angam ududham tasya sabdah parastat prativihita bhutamatra jihvaivasya ekam angam ududham tasy

annarasah parastat prativihita bhutamatra hastav evasya ekam angam ududham tayoh karma parastat prativihita bhutamatra sariram evasya ekam angam ududham tasya sukhaduhkhe parastat prativihita bhutamatra upastha evasya ekam angam ududham tasyanando ratih prajatih parastat prativihita bhutamatra padav evasya ekam angam ududham tayor ityah parastat prativihita bhutamatra mana evasya ekam angam ududham tasyai dhih kamah parastat prativihita bhutamatra.

5. *Speech is one part taken out of it. Name is what is expelled from it as its object and placed in the beings. Breath is one part taken out of it. Smell is what is expelled from it as its object and placed in the beings. The eye is one part taken out of it. The form is what is expelled from it as its object and placed in the beings. The ear is one part taken out of it. The sound is what is expelled from it as its object and placed inside the creature. The tongue is one part taken out of it. The taste for food is what is expelled from it as its object and placed inside the beings. The hands are one part take out of it. Duty is what is expelled from it as its object it and placed in the beings. The body is one part taken out of it. The pleasure and pain is what is expelled from it as its object and placed in the beings. The sexual organ is one part taken out of it. Sexual pleasure along with procreation is what is expelled from it as its object and placed in the beings. The two feet are one part taken out of it. Movement is what is expelled from it as its object and placed in the beings. The mind is one part taken out of it. The thoughts and desire is what is expelled from it as its object and placed inside the beings.*

Notes: The verse explains how sense-objects were separated from senses, which are but aspects of the same intelligence, and placed outside of them. Thus names, forms, sounds, smells, tastes and thoughts were separated and placed outside in the world of beings and objects (bhutamatra)

6. prajnaya vacam samaruhya vaca sarvani namanyapnoti prajnaya pranam samaruhya pranena sarvan gandhan apnoti prajnaya caksuh samaruhya sarvani rupany apnoti prajnaya srotram samaruhya srotrena sarvan sabdan apnoti prajnaya jihvam samaruhya jihvaya sarvan annarasan apnoti prajnaya hastau samaruhya hastabhyam sarvani karmany apnoti prajnaya sariram samaruhya sarirena sukhaduhkhe apnoti prajnayopastham samaruhyopasthenanandam ratim prajatim apnoti prajn-aya padau samaruhya padabhyam sarva itya apnoti prajnaya manah samaruhya prajnayaiva manasa sarvani dhyanani apnoti.

6. *Controlling the speech with intelligence, by speech all names are obtained. Controlling the breath with intelligence, all smells are obtained. Controlling the eye with intelligence, all forms are obtained. Controlling the ear with intelligence, all sounds are obtained. Controlling the tongue with intelligence, all tastes of food are obtained. Controlling the hands with intelligence, all duties are obtained. Controlling the body with intelligence, all pleasures and pains are obtained. Controlling the sexual organ with intelligence, happiness, sexual pleasures and procreation are obtained. Controlling the feet with intelligence, all movements are obtained. Controlling the mind with intelligence, all thoughts are obtained.*

Notes: Intelligence is the lord of the organs. Intelligence is again breath only. The objects that have been separated from the deities are obtained by them once again under the control of intelligence. In some texts the last line mentions dhih instead of manas.

7. na hi prajnapeta van nama kimcana prajnapayet anyatra me mano'bhud ity aha naham etan nama prajnasisam iti na hi prajnapetah prano gandham kamcana prajnapayet anyatra me mano'bhud ity aha naham etam gandham prajnasisamiti na hi prajnapetam caksu rupam kamcana prajnapayed anyatra me mano'abhud ity aha naham etad rupam prajnasisam iti na hi prajnapetam srotram sabdam kamcana prajnapayed anyatra me mano'bhud ity aha naham etam sabdam prajnasisam iti na hi prajnapetam jihvannarasam kamcana prajnapayet anyatra me mano'bhud ity aha naham etam annarasam prajnasisam iti na hi prajnapetau hastau karma kimcana prajnapetam anyatra me mano'abhud ity aha naham etat karma prajnasisam iti na hi prajnapetam sariram sukhaduhkham kimcana prajnapayet anyatra me mano'abhud ity aha naham etat sukham na duhkham prajnasisam iti na hi prajnapeta upastha anandam na ratim na prajatim kamcana prajnapayet anyatra me mano'bhud ity aha naham etam anandam na ratim prajatim prajnasisam iti na hi prajnapetau padav ityam kamcana prajna payetam anyatra me mano'abhud ity aha naham etam ityam prajnasisam iti na hi prajnapeta dhih kacana siddhyen na prajnatavyam prajnayet.

7. *For verily, with the departure of intelligence, speech does not make known any names by other means. "My mind was absent," one says, "I was unable to make sense of that name." For verily, with the departure of intelligence, breath does not make known any smells by other means.*

"My mind was absent," one says, "I was unable to make sense of that smell." For verily, with the departure of intelligence, the eye does not make known any forms by other means. "My mind was absent," one says, "I was unable to make sense of that form." For verily, with the departure of intelligence, the ear does not make known any sound by other means. "My mind was absent," one says, "I was unable to make sense of that sound." For verily, with the departure of intelligence, the tongue does not make known any taste of food by other means. "My mind was absent," one says, "I was unable to make sense of that taste of food." For verily, with the departure of intelligence, the hands do not make known any actions by other means. "My mind was absent," one says, "I was unable to make sense of that action." For verily, with the departure of intelligence, the body does not make known any pleasure or pain by other means. "My mind was absent," one says, "I was unable to make sense of that pleasure or pain." For verily, with the departure of intelligence, the sexual organ does not make known any happiness, sexual pleasure, and procreation by other means. "My mind was absent," one says, "I was unable to make sense of that happiness, sexual pleasure and procreation." For verily, with the departure of intelligence, the feet do not make known any movements by other means. "My mind was absent," one says, "I was unable to make sense of that movement." With the departure of intellignece no thought whatsoever is obtained. Nothign is understood that can be understood.

Notes: Prajna is the intelligence which gives us the ability to know or make sense of the world. The world that we experience is verily a medley of perceptions made possible by intelligence. Without Prajna we are cut off from the world and its objects. Perceptions will not register in our minds and we will not know what is going on. Since our very knowing and understanding depend upon this single most important aspect of our existence, our understanding of the world, people and objects differ from one another, just as we differ in the way we make use of our intelligence and make sense of the world. If breath is vital for our existence, intelligence is vital for our knowledge and understanding.

8. na vacam vijijnasita vaktaram vidyat na gandham vijijnasita ghrataram vidyat na rupam vijijnasita drastataram vidyat na sabdam vijijnasita srotaram vidyat nannarasam vijijnasi tannarasasasya vijnataram vidyat na karma vijijnasita kartaram vidyat na sukhaduhkhe vijijnasita sukhaduhkhayor vijnataram vidyat nanandam na ratim na prajatim vijijnasitanandasya rateh prajater vijnataram vidyat netyam vijijnasitaitaram vidyat na mano vijijnasita mantaram vidyat tava eta dasaiva bhutamatra adhiprajnam dasa prajnamatra adhibhutam yadd bhutamatra na syur na prajnamatrah syur

yad va prajnamatra na syurna na bhutamatrah syuh na hyanyatarato rupam kimcana siddhyen no etan nana tad yatha rathasyaresu nemir arpito nabhav ara arpita evam evaita bhutamatrah prajnamatrasv arpitah prajnamatrah prane arpitah sa esa prana eva prajnatmanando'ajaro'amritah na sadhuna karmana bhuyan bhavati no evasadhuna kaniyan esa hy eva sadhu karma karayati tam yam ebho lokebya unninisata esa u evasadhu karma karayati tam yam adho ninisate, esa lokapala esa lokadhipatih, esa lokesah, sa ma atmeti vidyat sa ma atmeti vidyat.

8. One should not desire to know the speech, one should know the speaker beyond that speech. One should not desire to know the smell, one should know the grasper of that smell beyond that. One should not desire to know the form, one should know the seer beyond that. One should not desire to know the sound, one should know the grasper of that sound beyond that. One should not desire to know the taste of food, one should know the taster of the food beyond that. One should not desire to know the action, one should know the doer beyond that. One should not desire to know pleasure and pain, one should know the knower of the pleasure and pain beyond that. One should not desire to know happiness, sexual pleasure and procreation, one should know the knower of happiness, sexual pleasure and procreation beyond that. One should not desire to know the movement, one should know the mover beyond that. One should not desire to know the mind, one should know the thinker of the mind beyond that. These are the ten parts of the (objective) material manifestation with regard to (subjective) intelligence and these are the ten parts of the (subjective) manifestation of intelligence with regard to the (objective) material world. Truly, if there are no material manifestations (objects) there will be no manifestations of intelligence (subjects). Similarly, if there are no manifestations of intelligence (subjects), there be no material manifestations (objects). Truly, with one or the other alone no from (or knowing) whatsoever can be experienced and none of this manifold diversity. Just as the rim of a chariot wheel is fixed on the spokes and the spokes on the hub, even so the parts of the material manifestation are fixed on the aspects of intelligence and the aspects of the intelligence are fixed on the breath. This breath, verily, is intelligent self, which is blissful, without aging and immortal. He does not flourish by good actions nor decrease by bad actions. This one, indeed, prompts him to do good actions whom he wants to uplift from this world. This one also, indeed, prompts him to indulge in bad actions whom he want to bring down. He is the protector of the world. He is the ruler of the world. He is the lord of the world. He is, my Self only, thus one should know. He is my Self only, thus one should know.

Notes: "One should not desire to know the speech, one should know the speaker beyond that speech," means one should not focus upon the perceptions or the objects, but upon the seer (self) who experiences them and who is above or beyond (taram) all the senses. By moving in the objective world with the senses, one gets caught in the materiality, whereas by knowing the Self or the seer one becomes liberated. This is the message. There are three aspects to our knowing, namely the knower, which is the subject, the knowing, and the known, which is the object. In a state of duality, there can be no knowing when either of the subject or the object are missing. This is what is meant by the statement that there is no material manifestation (known) without intelligence (knower) and vice versa. The self is not described here as something other than what one is in relation to the empirical world. He is the knower, the experiencer, the perceiver, the seer, or the subjective element in the objective world. He is ageless, but in the body he is subject to the modifications of the mind and body. Upon the death of the body, depending upon his deeds, that is whether he caused the good deeds to happen or the bad deeds, he goes to different worlds.

Chapter 4
Partial Definitions of Brahman

1. atha ha vai gargyo balakir anucanah samspasta asa so'vasad usinaresu savasan matsyesu kurupancalesu kasividehesv iti sa hajatasatrum kasyame abrajyovaca: brahma te bravaniti tam hovaca ajatasatruh sahasram dadma iti etasyam vaci janako janaka iti va u jana dhavantiti.

1. Now, Gargya Balaki was renowned as a famous person of great erudtion, for it was said of him that he lived among the people of Usinara, Matsya, Kurupancala and Kasivideha. He once went to Ajatasatru and said, "Let me speak about Brahman to you." Ajatasatru said, "A thousand I give you. For that (gift), people would rush forward saying, "O king, O king."

Notes: The same story is also found in the Brihadaranyaka Upanishad (2.1) with some variations. Although Balaki was an erudite scholar who lived among many people and participated in many discussions, tradition identifies him as proud (drpta) Balaki because of his vanity and limited knowledge of Brahman.

2. aditye brhac candramasy annam vidyuti satyam stanayitnau sabdo, vayav indro vaikuntha akase purnam, agnau visahir it, apsu teja ity adhidaivatam; athadyatmam, adarse pratirupaschayayam dvitiyah, pratisrutkayam asur iti sabde mrtyuh sva-

pne yamah sarire prajaptih daksine aksini vacah sarve'ksini satyasya.

2. In the sun which is great, in the moon, in food, in lightning, in truth, in the sound of the thunder, in wind, in Indra Vaikuntha, in the space which is full, in the fire which is the vanquisher, in the water, in the light, this is with reference to the deities. Now, regarding the Self, in the reflection of the mirror, in the shadow the second, in the echos of life, in the sounds of death, in the body which is Prajapati, in the right eye which is speech and in the left eye which is truth.

Notes: This verse provides a summary of the discussion that is to follow between Balaki and Ajataasatru.

3. sa hovaca balakih ya evaisa aditye purusas tam evaham upasa iti tam hovac ajatasatruh ma maitasmin samavadayisthah brihatpandaravasa atisthah sarvesam bhutanam murdheti va aham etam upasa iti sa yo haitam evam upaste'atisthah sarvesam bhutanam murdha bhavati.

3. Then Balaki said, "That person in the sun, him I worship (as Brahman)." Ajatasatru said, "Please do not make me to debate on him. I meditate upon him who is the great, who wears white garments, the highest and the head of all beings. He who meditates upon him thus, becomes the highest and the head of all beings."

Notes: In some texts, the expression "tam evaham upasa" is substituted with "tam evaham upasa brahmopasa" meaning I worship him as Brahman. In the text used here the reference to Brahman is omitted. However the implication is the same.

4. sa hovaca balakih ya evaisa candramasi purusas tam evaham upasa iti tam hovaca ajatasatruh, ma maitasmin samavadayisthah somo raja annasyatmeti va aham etam upasa iti sa yo haitam evam upaste'annasyatma bhavati.

4. Then Balaki said, "That person in the moon, him I worship." Ajatasatru said, "Please do not make me to debate on him. I meditate upon him as the King Soma, the self of all food. He who meditates upon him thus, becomes the Self of all food."

Notes: In some texts the reference to the moon as Soma raja is not mentioned. However, I decided to keep it since the moon is popularly known in the Vedic tradition as Soma.

5. sa hovaca balakih ya evaisa vidyuti purusas tam evaham upasa iti tam hovaca ajatasatruh ma maitasmin samavadayisthah satyasyatmeti va aham etam upasa iti sa yo haitam evam upaste satyastma bhavati.

5. Then Balaki said, "That person in the lightning, him I worship." Ajatasatru said, "Please do not make me to debate on him. I meditate upon him as the self of truth. Whoever meditates upon him thus becomes the Self of truth."

Notes: In some texts the lighting is described as the self of light (tejasyatma)

6. sa hovaca balakih ya evaisa stanayitnau purusa etam evaham upasa iti tam hovaca ajatasatruh ma maitasmin samavadayisthah sabdasyatmeti va aham etam upasa iti sa yo haitam evam upaste sabdasyatma bhavati.

6.. Then Balaki said, "That person in the thunder, him I worship." Ajatasatru said, "Please do not make me to debate on him. I meditate upon him as the self of the sound. Whoever meditates upon him thus becomes the Self of sound."

7. sa hovaca balakih ya evaisa vayau purusas tam evaham upasa iti tam hovaca ajatasatruh ma maitasmin samavadayisthah indro vaikuntho'aparajita seneti va aham etam upasa iti sa yo haitam evam upaste jisnur ha va aparajayisnur anyatastyajayi bhavati.

7. Then Balaki said, "That person in the air, him I worship." Ajatasatru said, "Please do not make me to debate on him. I meditate upon him as Indra Vaikuntha, the unvanquished army. Whoever meditates upon him thus becomes victorious, invincible and conquerors of his enemies."

8. sa hovaca balakih ya evaisa akase purusas tam evaham upasa iti tam hovaca ajatasatruh ma maitasmin samavadayisthah purnam apravarti brahmeti va aham etam upasa iti sa yo haitam evam upaste puryate prajaya pasubhir yasasa brahmavarcasena svargena lokena sarvam ayur eti.

8. Then Balaki said, "That person in the space, him I worship." Ajatasatru said, "Please do not make me to debate on him. I meditate upon him as full, transcendental Brahman. Whoever meditates upon him thus becomes filled with progeny, cattle, fame, the luster of Brahman and the heavenly world. He lives for the full span of his life."

Notes: Apravarti means beyond nature. Hence it is translated here as transcendental. Some translated it as inactive, meaning non-reacting.

9. sa hovaca balakih ya evaiso'agnau purusas tam evaham upasa iti tam hovaca ajatasatruh ma maitasmin samavada-

yisthah visasahiriti va aham etam upasa iti sa yo haitam evam upaste visasahirva esa bhavati.

9. Then Balaki said, "That person in the fire, him I worship." Ajatasatru said, "Please do not make me to debate on him. I meditate upon him as the all conquering. Whoever meditates upon him thus becomes the all conquering among others."

10. sa hovaca balakih ya evaiso'apsu purusas tam evaham upasa iti tam hovaca ajatasatruh ma maitasmin samavadayisthah tejasa atmeti va aham etam upasa iti sa yo haitam evam upaste tejasa atma bhavati iti adhidaivatam athadhyatmam.

10. Then Balaki said, "That person in the worship, him I worship." Ajatasatru said, "Please do not make me to debate on him. I meditate upon him as the self of light. Whoever meditates upon him thus becomes the self of light." Thus with reference to the deities. Now with reference to the body.

Notes: In some texts "tejasatma" is replaced by "namniasyatma" meaning the Self of the name.

11. sa hovaca balakih ya evaisa adarse purusas tam evaham upasa iti tam hovaca ajatasatruh ma maitasmin samavadayisthah pratirupa iti va aham etam upasa iti sa yo haitam evam upaste pratirupo haivasya prajayamajayate napratirupah.

11. Then Balaki said, "That person in the mirror, him I worship." Ajatasatru said, "Please do not make me to debate on him. I meditate upon him as the reflection. Whoever meditates upon him thus, to him is born a splitting image of him among his offspring, not one who is not his splitting image."

12. sa hovaca balakih ya evaisa cchayayam purusas tam evaham upasa iti tam hovaca ajatasatruh ma maitasmin samavadayisthah dvitiyo'anapaga iti va aham etam upasa iti sa yo haitam evam upaste vindate dvitiyat dvitiyavan bhavati.

12. Then Balaki said, "That person in the shadow, him I worship." Ajatasatru said, "Please do not make me to debate on him. I meditate upon him as the double. Whoever meditates upon him thus, begets a double and becomes a possessor of his double."

Notes: The double may be a son, a loyal disciple or follower, who follows him dutifully like his shadow.

13. sa hovaca balakih ya evaisa pratisrutkaya purusas tam evaham upasa iti tam hovaca ajatasatruh ma maitasmin samavadayisthah asur iti va aham etam upasa iti sa yo haitam evam upaste na pura kalat sammoham iti.

13. Then Balaki said, "That person in the echo, him I worship." Ajatasatru said, "Please do not make me to debate on him. I meditate upon him as the life. Whoever meditates upon him thus, does not pass into unconsciousness before his time."

Notes: In some texts, it is stated that Ajatasatru worshipped echo as wife who would never leave or fail to respond. And thus who ever worshipped him thus got a second from his second (wife).

14. sa hovaca balakih ya evaisa sabde purusas tam vaham upasa iti, tam hovaca ajatasatruh ma maitasmin samavadayisthah mrtyur iti va aham etam upasa iti sa yo haitam evam upaste na pura kalat praititi.

14. Then Balaki said, "That person in the sound, him I worship." Ajatasatru said, "Please do not make me to debate on him. I meditate upon him as death. Whoever meditates upon him thus, does die before his time."

15. sa hovaca balakih ya evaisa purusah suptah svapnaya carati tam evaham upasa iti, tam hovaca ajatasatruh ma maitasmin samavadayisthah yamo rajeti va aham etam upasa iti sa yo haitam evam upaste sarvam hasma idam sraisthyaya yamyate.

15. Then Balaki said, "That person who when asleep moves about in the dreams, him him I worship." Ajatasatru said, "Please do not make me to debate on him. I meditate upon him as King Yama. Whoever meditates upon him thus, all that is here is conquered for his wellbeing."

16. sa hovaca balakih ya evaisa sarirah purusas tam evaham upasa iti tam hovaca ajatasatruh ma maitasmin samavadayisthah prajapatir iti va aham etam upasa iti sa yo haitam evam upaste prajayate prajaya pasubhir, yasasa brahma varcasena svargena lokena sarvam ayur iti.

16. Then Balaki said, "That person in the body, him I worship." Ajatasatru said, "Please do not make me to debate on him. I meditate upon him as Prajapati. Whoever meditates upon him thus, flourishes with offspring, cattle, fame, the luster of Brahman, the heavenly world and reaches the full span of his life."

17. sa hovaca balakih ya evaisa daksine'ksini purusas tam evaham upasa iti tam hovaca ajatasatruh ma maitasmin samavadayisthah vaca atmagner atma jyotista atmeti va aham etam upasa iti sa yo haitam evam upasta etesam sarvesam atma bhavati.

16. Then Balaki said, "That person in the right eye, him I worship." Ajatasatru said, "Please do not make me to debate on him. I meditate upon him as the self of speech, as the self of fire and as the self of light. Whoever meditates upon him thus, becomes the self of all these."

18. sa hovaca balakih ya evaisa savye'ksani purusas tam evaham upasa iti tam hovaca ajatasatruh ma maitasmin samavadayisthah satyasyatma vidyuta atma tejasa atmeti va aham etam upasa iti sa yo haitam evam upasta etesam sarvesam atma bhavatiti.

18. Then Balaki said, "That person in the left eye, him I worship." Ajatasatru said, "Please do not make me to debate on him. I meditate upon him as the self of truth and as the self of the lightning. Whoever meditates upon him thus, becomes the self of all these."

19. tata u ha balakih tusnimasa tam hovac ajatasatruh etavann u balaka iti etavad iti hovaca balakih tam hovaca ajatasatruh mrisa vai kila ma samvadistha brahma te bravaniti hovaca yo vai balaka etesam purusanam karta yasya vai tat karma sa veditavya iti tata u ha balakih samitpanih praticakrama upayaniti tam hovaca ajatasatruh pratiloma rupam eva tan manye yat ksatriyo brahmanam upanayetaihi vyeva, tva jnapayisyamiti tam ha panav abhipadya pravavraja tau ha suptam purusam ajamatuh tam hajatasatruh amantrayamcakre brihatpandaravasah somarajann iti sa u ha sisya eva tata u hainam yastya viciksepa sa tata eva samuttasthau tam hovaca ajatasatruh kvaisa etad balake puruso'sayista kvaitad pabhut kuta etad agad iti hita nama purusasya yatraitad uritatam abhipratanvanti, tad yatha sahasradha keso vipatitas tavad anvyah pingalasyanimna tisthanti, suklasya krsnasya pitasya lohitasya ca tasu tada bhavati yada suptah svapnam na kancana pasyati.

19. Thereafter, Balaki became silent. To him Ajatasatru said, "Balaki, is that all?" "That is all," replied Balaki. To him Ajatasatru said, "Vainly, did you engage me in this discussion, saying, 'Let me tell you about

Brahman.' Truly, O Balaki, who is the doer among the persons, whose work all this is, he alone should be known." Thereupon, Balaki approached with fuel in his hand, saying, "I approach you as student." To him Ajatasatru said, "It is against the tradition for a Kshatriya to initiate a Brahmana as a student. Come, I will make you know it clearly." Then, holding his hand, he walked him to a person who was sleeping. Then Ajatasatru addressed him saying, "O great white robed one, O King Soma" He remained asleep. Then, he nudged him with a stick and he woke up immediately. Ajatasatru said, "Where was this person when he was asleep, O Balaki? What happened to him? And from where did he return?" Balaki had no answers. Then Ajatasatru said to him, "Where this person was, where it happened and from where he returned, which I asked, that place is the arteries named hita, inside a person, spreading from the heart into the body. As small as a hair divided into a thousand fold, they consist of a subtle matter which is white, black, yellow and red. In them one remains while sleeping and sees no dreams whatsoever."

20. athasmin prana evaikadha bhavati tad enam vak sarvair namabhih sahapyeti caksuh sarvaih rupaih sahpyeti srotram sarvaih sabdaih sahapyeti, manah sarvair dhynaih sahapyeti sa yada pratibudhyate yathgner jvalatah sarva dis visphulinga vipratistherann evam evaitasmad atmamanah prana yathayatanam vipratisthante pranebhyo deva devebhyo loka sa esa prana eva prajnatmedam sariram atmanam anupravista atomabhya anakhebhyah tad yatha ksurah ksura dhane'vopahito visvabharo va visvambharakulaya evaisa prajnatme-dam sariram atmanam anupravista alomabhya anakhebhyah tam etam atmanam eta atmano'nvavasyante: yatha sresthinam svas tad yatha sresthsvair bhunkte yatha va svah sresthinam bhunjanty evam evaisa prajnatmaitair atmabhir bhunktam evam evaita atmana etam atmanam bhunjanti sa yavaddha va indra etam atmanam na vijajne tavad enam asura abhibahuvuh sa yada vijajne'tha hatvasuran vijitya sarvesam ca devanam sarvesam ca bhutanam srayisthyam svarajyam adhipatyam paryait tatho evaivam vidvan sarvan papmano'pahalya sarve-sam ca bhutanam sraisthyam svarajyam adhipatyam paryeti ya evam veda, ya evam veda.

20. Now, in this breath only he becomes one. The speech along with all names goes to it. The eye with all forms goes to it. The ear with all

sounds goes to it. The mind with all thoughts goes to it. When he wakes up, just as the sparks from a blazing fire fly in all directions, so do the breaths (organs) rush to their respective positions, from the breaths to the deities and from the deities to their worlds. This breath and so also the intelligent self enter into the body up to the end of the hairs and nails. Just as a barber's knife might be hidden in a case, or as fire in a fire place, so is the self of intelligence spread in the body up to the very end of hairs and nails. All these many organs are located inside the Self only. They depend upon it just as his men depend upon the chief. Just as the chief enjoys the services of his men, or just as they render him service, so does the intelligent self enjoy the services of these organs while they render service to the intelligent self. Truly, so long as Indra did not know the Self (which is intelligence), the demons were able to overwhelm him. When he understood it, he destroyed them and conquered them. He achieved greatness, sovereignty and lordship among all gods and all beings. He who knows this, also overcomes all evils, and attains eminence, sovereignty and lordship among all beings, he who knows this, yes he who knows this.

Kena Upanishad

Editor's Note

Like the Isavasya Upanishad, the Kena Upanishad derives its name from the starting word, 'kena,' meaning by whom. It belongs to the Talvakara or Jaiminiya Upanishad Brahmana of the Samaveda. Hence, it is also known as the Talvakara Upanishad. It is divided into four sections. The first two sections are in verse, containing fourteen verses and the next two are in prose, with 21 passages. The latter contains a story that brings to light not only the supremacy of Brahman in relation to the Vedic gods but also their comprehensive ignorance of Him. The following are the important teachings of the Upanishad

- No one can be sure of Brahman

- Any contact with Brahman will be very brief and indeterminate. Even the gods Agni, Vayu and Indra got but a brief glimpse of Him as much as what one can see in a flash of lightning or in the wink of an eye.

- You can reach Brahman or the Self not through the senses but by remembering Him constantly.

- The contemplative practice should be augmented by other practices, namely austerities, restraints, sacrificial actions, knowledge of the Vedas and truth

Presented here is a revised translation of the Kena Upanishad by Jayaram V, published originally on Hinduwebsite.com.

Invocation

apyayantu mamangani vak pranas caksuh srotram atho balam indriyani ca sarvani. sarvam brahmopanisadam ma'ham brahma nirakuryam ma ma brahma nirakarot anirakaranam astu anirakaranam me'stu. tad atmani nirate ya upanisatsu dharmas te mayi santu. aum santih, santih, santih.

Aum, may my limbs, speech, breath, eyes, ears, as also my strength and all my senses grow well. All is Brahman as declared in the Upanishads. May I not refute Brahman. May Brahman does not forsake me. May there be no rejection (of me by Brahman). May there be no rejection (by me of Brahman). May the duties enshrined in the Upanishads live through me as I am engaged in the pursuit of the Self.

Translation

Section 1

Who is the True Lord of the Body?

1. kenesitam patati presitam manah kena pranah prathamah praiti yuktah; kenesitam vacamimam vadanti caksuh srotram ka u devo yunakti.

1. By whose will and commands does this mind work? By whose commands does the breath proceeds first? By whose will does one utters the speech? Who is that deity who prompts the eyes and the ears?

Notes: Who is responsible for our bodily functions? This is a simple question, indeed, which can evoke different answers from different people and perspectives. Asking questions and drawing conclusions should be part of learning and knowing, which our Vedic seers practiced with great persistence. Self-knowledge arises from self-enquiry followed by self-study. In this verse, the teacher of the Upanishad raised these questions to provoke his students and make them think. Our seeing, hearing, speaking and other bodily functions seem to be natural and mechanical motor functions of the body. We do not normally think about them, because we take them for granted. The truth is they do not happen automatically. All our actions arise from an inner source. The next verse answers this question.

2. srotrasya srotram manaso mano yad vaco ha vacam sa u pranasya pranah; caksusas caksur atimucya dhirah prety asmal lokad amrta bhavanti.

2. Since He is the ear of the ear, the mind of the mind, the speech of the speech, the life of all life, and the eye of the eye, wise men after giving up (sensory pleasures) and departing from here, become immortal.

Notes: The question raised in the previous verse has been answered here. It is by the commands of the Self does the organs work. However, for the sake of liberation, one should renounce all sensory pleasures.

3. na tatra caksur gacchati na vag gacchati no manah; na vidmo na vijanimo yathaitad anusisyat.

3. There the eye goes not, nor the speech, nor the mind. We do not know, we cannot determine how to teach this.

Notes: How can you explain the inexplicable. Here the teacher is honestly explaining the difficulty of teaching something that cannot be seen, heard, spoken about or thought of. Transcendental truths cannot be easily explained because the mind is incapable of expressing that which is inexpressible.

4. anyad eva tad viditad atho aviditad adhi; iti susruma purvesam ye nastad vyacacaksire.

4. It is other than the known and it also beyond the unknown. Thus we have heard from those who were here before who explained it to us.

Notes: The known and the unknown are with regard to the empirical knowledge, what has been perceived and known and what has not yet been perceived or experienced, but not unknowable. The known is also the wakeful consciousness. The unknown is the deep sleep state because we know nothing about it. The transcendental state is beyond the unknown.

5. yad vaca nabhyuditam yena vag abhyudyate; tad eva brahma tvam viddhi nedam yad idam upasate.

5. That which is not spoken by speech, but by which speech is spoken, know that alone to be Brahman, not what people worship here.

Note: Brahman is not the deities (sense organs) whom people worship and nourish through internal and external sacrifices. In the body, the Self is not the same as the organs. He is beyond them. The Vedic hymns are uttered by speech and used in the invocation of gods. Therefore, as per the criteria expressed here, their source is Brahman, but they are not Brahman. Brahman or the Self, is beyond them.

6. yan manasa na manute yenahur mano matam; tad eva brahma tvam viddhi nedam yad idam upasate.

6. That which is not conceived by the mind, but by which, they say that the mind does conceive, know that alone to be Brahman, not what people worship here.

Notes: The Self is not only beyond the bodily organs but also beyond the mind, which is considered the king among the senses (deities). However, he is the support for both of them.

7. yac caksusa na pasyati yena caksumsi pasyati; tad eva brahma tvam viddhi nedam yad idam upasate.

7. *That which is not seen by the eye, but by which the eye is able to see, know that alone to be Brahman, not what people worship here.*

8. **yac cchrotrena na srnoti yena srotram idam srutam; tad eva brahma tvam viddhi nedam yad idam upasate.**

8. *That which is not heard by the ear, but by which the ear can hear, know that alone to be Brahman, not what people worship here.*

9. **yatpranena na praniti yena pranah praniyate; tadeva brahma tvam viddhi nedam yadidamupasate**

9. *That which is not breathed, but by which breath is breathed, know that alone to be Brahman, not what people worship here.*

Notes: The Self is the knower, the enjoyer, the perceiver, and the indweller of the body. He is the reason why the body remains alive and the organs function. That indwelling Self is true Brahman, not the gods whom we worship in the sacrifices. Why this is so is illustrated in the third section.

Section 2
The Difficulty of Knowing Brahman

1. **yadi manyase suvedeti dabhramevapi nonam tvam vettha brahmanorupam; yadasya tvam yadasya devesvatha nu mimamsyameva te manye viditam.**

1. *If you think, "I have known Brahman well enough," indeed you have known but very little of He who is established in you or in gods. Therefore you should still enquire about Brahman.*

"I think (he) is known."

Next: The Self is not known by knowing the body or the bodily parts. Very little indeed can be known about the Self by knowing these two. The teacher implied this in his instruction when he suggested to the student that knowing Brahman was indeed difficult and he should continue to contemplate upon Him even if he thought that he had known Him sufficiently by gaining whatever little knowledge he could by knowing his body and bodily parts. The student, went back, deliberated upon Brahman and returned saying, "I think, I have known Him now." This means that the student had not yet fully grasped the transcendental nature of the Self or the true purport of this teacher's words.

2. **naham manye suvedeti no na vedeti veda ca; yo nastadveda tadveda no na vedeti veda ca.**

2. *I do not think, "I know (Him) perfectly well," nor (do I think), "I do not know Him at all." He who amongst us understands this, "Not that I do not know at all. I know but I do not know perfectly well," he alone knows (that Brahman).*

Notes: The teacher explained to the student who thought that he had known Brahman that it was not possible to know Him fully well. At the same time, he qualified his statement saying that it might not be correct to say that He was not entirely unknowable. A true knower of Brahman knows the possibility and the impossibility of knowing Brahman. He knows that Brahman is reachable, but none can claim to have a perfect knowledge of Him not only because He is vast and infinite but also because such knowledge cannot be obtained by study or contemplation. One cannot remember well what happens in a transcendental state because in that state the mind and the senses remain withdrawn and asleep. Hence, they do not participate in that experience just as we do not know what happens in a deep sleep state. When the mind is awake, the Self is unknown and when the Self is known the mind is asleep. Thus, the mind has little awareness of the Self. However, one may retain a vague idea of what happened in a transcendental state. Hence, the knowledge of Brahman is always indistinct or indeterminate. Yet one cannot say one has gained nothing at all from such experiences. When one wakes up, there is always a residual feeling of knowing and experiencing the deeper states.

3. yasyamatam tasya matam matam yasya na veda sah; avijnatam vijanatam vijnatam avijanatam.

3. To whomsoever it is unknown, to him it is known. To whomsoever it is known, he does not know. It is unknown to those who know it and known to those who do not know.

Notes: We know the Self when we are in deep sleep, but when we wake up do not know or remember what happened in that sleep. Therefore, although we think we do not know the Self, we may know it unconsciously. The Self is also experienced in a state of self-absorption, when there is no duality and distinction between the knower and the known and when our mind and senses are fully withdrawn. Thus when, there is an awareness of the knower it is unknown and when the knower is absent it is known. Hence, it is unknown to those whose mind and senses are active and who experience duality and known to those whose mind and senses are asleep and who enter into a state of unity without the distinction between the knower and the known. Thus we are consciously unconscious of the Self, but unconsciously conscious of it. Yet we are never sure whether we know it at all, because our experience of the transcendental Self is always indeterminate.

4. pratibodhaviditam matam amrtatvam hi vindate; atmana vindate viryam vidyaya vindate'mrtam.

4. It is known only by entering into an awakened state. When it is known one gains immortality. He gains luster within his body and with knowledge (of the Self) he gains immortality.

Notes: Pratibhodha means an awakened state. One can know the Self only by becoming a witness to it. That is, he must be awake even when his body is asleep and he enters into the transcendental state. Only then he will be rightly aware of the Self. The knowledge of the Self brings luster to his body and makes him immortal.

5. iha ced avedid atha satyam asti na ced iha vedin mahati vinasoih; bhotesu bhotesu vicitya dhirah pretyasmallokadamrta bhavanti.

5. In this world if one knows It, one gains truth. If one does not know it, great is the loss. Seeing the Self clearly in all, the wise ones become immortal, when they depart from this world.

Section 3

A Brief Encounter Between Brahman and Gods

1. brahma ha devebhyo vijigye tasya ha brahmano vijaye deva amahiyanta; ta aiksantasmakam evayam vijayo'smakam evayam mahima iti.

1. Once Brahman said to have achieved victory for the gods. But not knowing this, the gods took pride in their victory. In that victory which truly belonged to Brahman, the gods rejoiced. They thought, "Ours, indeed, is this victory, our indeed is the greatness."

Notes: Just like our senses, the gods have a limitation in knowing the Self or Brahman. Because of their ignorance, they assumed that they were responsible for the results of their actions. Therefore they attributed the success of their actions to themselves. They were unaware that the doer of all deeds was Brahman only, which led to the assumption that they achieved victory in a battle against the demons on their own.

2. tadd haisam vijajnau tebhyo ha pradur babhova tan na vyajanata kim idam yaksam iti,

2. Knowing this (conceit of gods), He appeared before them. They did not know who that Guardian Spirit was.

Note: Brahman appeared before the gods as a Yaksha. The Yakshas are a class of celestial beings or guardian spirits who inhabit the mid-region. Kubera, the richest of all beings in all the worlds, is also a Yaksha. The Yakshas are described in the scriptures as shape shifters who often protect hidden treasures as guardian angels.

3. te'gnim abruvan jataveda etad vijanihi kim etad yaksam iti tatheti.

3. The said to Agni," O Jataveda, find out in detail what this spirit is." "Yes," (he said).

4. tad abhyadravat tam abhyavadat ko'sity agnir va aham asmity abravii jataveda va aham asmiti.

4. He hastened towards him, and He said to him, "Who are you?"

"I am Agni indeed, I am Jataveda, the knower of all."

Notes: Agni has been specifically described here as Jataveda, which means knower of all things in creation. Truly, fire is hidden in the objects of the universe. Therefore the title is very appropriate for him. This incident illustrates that even a deity like Agni, who has complete knowledge of creation, has little understanding of Brahman.

5. tasmims tvayi kim viryam ity apidam sarvam daheyam yad idam prthivyam iti.

"What power do you have?"

"I can burn all this, whatever is there upon this earth."

6. tasmai trnam nidadhau etad daheti tad upapreyaya sarvajavena tan na sasaka dagdhum sa tata eva nivavrte naitad asakam vijnatum yad etad yaksamiti.

6. Before him, (He) placed a straw and said, "Burn this." Agni rushed towards it with all his might, but could not burn it. He came back from there (and said),"I am unable to know what this spirit is."

Notes: To understand this you can use your own body as an analogy. None of the bodily organs in your body can function on their own without your will. Your sense organs powerless with your commands. You are the true enjoyer and the lord of your body, while your senses act under the impetus of your will. The same is illustrated here at the cosmic level. The Person who appeared before the gods was the indweller of the cosmic body. The gods derived their strength from Him and were helpless without His will.

7. atha vayum abruvan vayave tad vijanihi kim etad yaksam iti tatheti.

7. Then, they said to Vayu, "O Vayu, find out what this spirit is."

"Yes."

8. tad abhyadravat tam abhyavadat ko'siti vayur va aham asmity abravin matarisva va aham asmiti.

8. He hastened towards him and he said to him, "Who are you?"

Vayu said, "I am indeed Vayu, I am Matariswan, traveler of the mid-region."

9. tasmims tvayi kim viryam ity apidam sarvam adadiyam yad idam prthivyam iti.

9. "What power do you have?"

"I can blow away all this, whatever is there upon earth."

10. tasmai trnam nidadhau etad adatsveti tad upapreyaya sarvajavena tan na sasakadatum; sa tata eva nivavrte naitad asakam vijnatum yad etad yaksam iti.

10. *Before him, (He) placed a straw and said, "Blow this." Vayu rushed towards it with all his might, but could not blow it away. He came back from there (and said),"I am unable to know what this spirit is."*

11. athendram abruvan maghavann etad vijanihi kim etad yaksam iti tatheti tad abhyadravat tasmat tirodadhe.

11. *Then, they said to Vayu, "O Maghavan, find out what this spirit is."*

"Yes."

As he rushed towards Him, He moved away from him and disappeared

12. sa tasminn evakase striyam ajagama bahusobhamanam umam haimavatim tam hovaca kim etad yaksam iti.

12. *Then, in the same region of the sky, appeared Uma, extremely dazzling, the daughter of Himavat. He said to her, "What is this Spirit?"*

Note: The Self is ungraspable and unreachable by the divinities and yet cannot function without Him. Neither fire nor air nor Indra, gods of immense strength and potency and leaders of the heaven, could use their powers before Brahman; nor could they understand who He was. By this mysterious action Brahman established firmly who controlled the entire creation and from where everyone derived their strength and actions. The story clearly illustrated that we can restrain our senses, who are the deities in our bodies, with our will and we can become stabilized in the contemplation of the Self. We also learn from it that we should not worship the gods, but only Brahman or our indwelling Self. The gods are not the highest beings. They are just one step above us. Even with all their powers, they depend upon us for nourishment. In the human body, the three deities, namely fire, air and Indra, are represented by the eye, the breath and the mind respectively. They are powerless without our will. They are not the real doers. Only the Self is. They are also incapable of helping us to realize the inner Self. The body is an instrument of Nature. It does not know the Self. The mind may go nearer to it, but it does not reach it or grasp it, as in case of Indra. Lastly, from the reference to Uma Haimavathi in this verse, we may conclude that the Yaksha, who appeared before the gods was none other than Lord Siva Himself.

Section 4

Brahman, the Highest and the Supreme

1. sa brahmeti hovaca brahmano va etad vijaye mahiyadhvam iti tato haiva vidamcakara brahma iti.

1. *She said, "It was Brahman. In Brahman's victory only, indeed, you felt joy." From that only, (Indra) learned that it was Brahman.*

2. tasmad va ete deva atitaramivanyan devan yadagnir vayur indras te; hy enan nedistham pasparsus te hy enat prathamo vidamcakara brahma iti.

2. *Therefore, these gods, Agni, Vayu and Indra, stand above all the other gods, for it was they who had come into closest contact with Brahman, and they were the first ones to know that He was Brahman.*

3. tasmad va indro'titaramivanyan devan sa hy enan nedishtam pasparsa sa; hy enat prathamo vidamcakara brahma iti.

3. *Therefore Indra stands above all the other gods for he went nearest to Brahman, and indeed he was the first to know (from Uma Haimavathi that it was) Brahman.*

4. tasyaisa adeso yad etad vidyuto vyadyutada itin nyamimisada ity adhidaivatam.

4. *Of this, there is this instruction, as in the flash of lighting or as in the wink of an eye. These (descriptions of Brahman) are in reference to the gods.*

Note: The teacher here applied an analogy to explain his students how brief was the encounter between gods and Brahman and how they perceived Him. Although they went closest to Him, they saw but little of Him because He appeared to them briefly and that also in the form of a celestial being (Yaksha), not as Himself. Therefore their knowledge of Brahman was as limited and inconclusive as any knowledge one might gain by perceiving an object in a flash of lightning or in the wink of an eye. In other words, the gods could get but a brief glimpse of Brahman even from close proximity. It was not sufficient enough for them to know Him completely. Their knowledge was so inadequate and vague that until they were told by Uma Haimavathi, they did not even know whom they saw and who He was.

5. athadhyatmam yad etad gacchativa ca mano'nena caitad upasmaraty abhiksnam samkalpah

5. *Now concerning the Self. It is that which can be verily reached, when the mind keeps remembering repeatedly with firm intention.*

Notes: The Self can be known only when the mind is riveted upon it constantly and keeps remembering it. The same is emphasized in the Yogasutras also. Isvara the Lord of the body can be known only by constant remembrance and through devotion (paridhana). The gods (organs of the body) do not know much about Brahman. Therefore, the organs of the body are not very useful in our search for the Self or Brahman. To know the Self, we have to withdraw them into our minds and practice self-restraint (pratyahara). Then, we have to focus our minds upon our inmost Selves with firm resolve (samkalpa), until they are fully silenced and stabilized in deep contemplation. This is the proven way to achieve Self-realization or achieve union with Brahman. The mind facilitates this union, especially through the sustained practice of yoga. When it is withdrawn from the external world, the mind returns to the Self and remain focused on it, which culminates in self-realization. Hence this instruction.

6. tadd ha tadvanam nama tadvanam ity upasitavyam sa ya etad evam; vedabhi hainam sarvani bhutani samvanchanti

6. *The name of That is said to be tadvanam. It should be worshipped (meditated) with this very name tadvanam only. Whoever thus worships (Him) in this manner, all beings seek Him.*

Notes: Tadvanam means dearer to all or adored by all. Brahman is adored by all because He is the indwelling Self of all. Now, whoever realizes Brahman, becomes the Self of all. Therefore, a self-realized yogi is sought by all.

7. upanisadam bho bruhi ity ukta ta upanisad brahmim va va ta upanisadam abruma iti

7. *"Sir teach me the Upanishad."*

"The secret knowledge has been taught to you. Indeed, I have spoken to you the secret knowledge of Brahman."

Notes. Previously, a student told his teacher that he knew Brahman. Then, the teacher admonished him, explaining the difficulties of knowing Him. Next, he told him who was the lord of the body and by whose commands the organs in the body functioned. Then, through a legend, he illustrated the supremacy of Brahman over the gods also. Even after learning about Brahman from his teacher, the student was not sure whether he received complete instruction. So he asked him whether there was anything else to know, to which the teacher replied here that he taught him whatever he knew

8. tasyai tapo damah karmeti pratistha vedah sarvangani satyam ayatanam.

8. *Of that (knowledge of Brahman), austerity, restraint, and sacrificial actions are the support. The Vedas are its limbs. Truth is its abode.*

Notes. Five means to know Brahman are suggested here, namely austerities, restraints, sacrificial actions, knowledge of the Vedas and truth. The austerities consists of fasting, abstinence and other observances, which produce pain as well as bodily heat (tapas). The restraints include non-injury, non-stealing, truthfulness, celibacy and non-covetousness. Sacrificial actions means both external and internal sacrifices. Truth is the abode of Brahman because falsehood, ignorance and delusion do not exist in the realm of the highest Brahman. They may exist in His creation, but He does not exist in them.

9. yo va etamevam vedapahatya papmanamanante svarge loke jyeye pratitisthati pratitisthati

9. *Whoever knows this thus, having destroyed all his sins becomes firmly established in the endless highest heaven. Yes he remains firmly established.*

Tattiriya Upanishad

Editor's Note

The Taittiriya Upanishad belongs to the Taittiriya School of the Yajurveda and hence the name. It is divided into three chapters and 32 sections, of which the first chapter, Sikhshavalli, containing 13 sections deals with siksha or the study of phonetics or pronunciation, which is an important branch of the Vedic studies. The second chapter, Brahmandavalli is divided into nine sections. It deals with various aspects of Brahmand, the Universal Egg or manifest Brahman, such as the course of evolution, matter and life, life and mind, Brahman as the source of creation and so on. The third chapter is named Bhriguvalli. It is divided into 10 sections, which deal with an enquiry into Brahman by sage Bhrigu, in a conversation with his father, Varuna.

Following is a new translation of the Upanishad by Jayaram V.

Chapter 1 - Siksa Valli

Section 1

Invocation

1. aum sam no mitrah sam varunah; sam no bhavaty aryama; sam na indro brihaspatih; sam no visnururukramah; namo brahmane; namaste vayo; tvam eva pratyaksam brahmasi; tvam eva pratyaksam brahma vadisyami; ritam vadisyami; satyam vadisyami; tanmamavatu; tadvaktaramavatu; avatu mam; avatu vaktaram; aum santih santih santih.

1. *May Mitra be favorable to us. May Varuna be favorable. May Aryaman be favorable to us. May Indra and Brihaspati be favorable to us. May Vishnu, of wide strides, be favorable to us. Salutation to Brahman. Salutations O Vayu. You, verily, are the visible Brahman. You alone I declare as the visible Brahman. I declare (you) as the controller. I declare (you) as the truth. May It protect me. May It protect the teacher. May It protect me. May It protect the teacher. Aum. Peace. Peace. Peace.*

Notes: Sam means calm, peaceful, kind, favorably disposed, or satisfied. The Vedic sacrifices are meant to propitiate the gods with the offerings of food which they require, and make them peaceful, calm and favorably inclined towards the worshippers so that having become gratified with the offerings they receive, they shower their blessings upon them and help them achieve their desired goals. Ritam (rtam) means order and regularity found in creation. It refers to the smooth and orderly progression of events commonly found in Nature such as the passing of time or movements of days and nights, seasons, planets, and the universal laws of Nature. Vayu, as the mover of the mid-region, is invoked in this verse as the controller of that orderly flow of events. He is also invoked as Brahman because he is invisible, expansive, carrier of things such as sound and speech and the source of breath (prana).

Section 2

The Study of Pronunciation

1. aum siksam vyakhyasyamah: varnah svarah, matra balam, sama santanah, ityuktah siksadhyayah.

1. *Aum, we shall now explain the subject of pronunciation. The letters, tone, emphasis, articulation, and combination. Thus, is explained as the study of pronunciation.*

Notes: The study of these has a lot of significance in Vedic education, because the success of a priest who participates in the Vedic ceremonies depends upon his ability to pronounce the words in the chants correctly, for which he needs to know how to articulate the words, where to stress them, where to pause and how to use the correct pitch to create the right vibrations and produce the right combination of sounds and conditions for the divinities to descend from the heaven and accept the offerings.

Section 3

The Great Combinations

1. saha nau yasah, saha nau brahmavarcasam atha tat samhitaya upanisadam vyakhyasyamah, pancasv adhikaranesu, adhilokam, adhijyautisam, adhividyam, adhiprajam, adhyatmam, ta mahasam hita ityacaksate.athadhilokam prithivi purvarupam, dyauruttararupam; akasah sandhih, vayuh sandhanam, ityadhilokam.

1. May fame come to us both. May the radiance of Brahman come to us both. Now, we shall explain the secret knowledge of the combinations under five headings: with reference to the world, the shining objects, knowledge, progeny and the body. They are the great combinations, they say. Now, with regard to worlds. The earth is the prior form. The heaven is the later form. The space is the their meeting place, the air is the connector. This is with regard to the worlds.

Notes: The teacher wished for the success of everyone in the group. He did so because Vedic society valued correct pronunciation of the hymns chanted during the sacrifices. The reputation of a teacher depended very much upon the success of his students. Since this was a class about pronunciation, the teacher rightly prayed for the success of both. This section is about samhitas or combinations the connection that exists between the individual objects and what connects them.

2. athadhijautisam, agnih purvarupam, aditya uttararupam, apah sandhih, vaidyutah sandhanam, ityadhijyautisam.

3. Now, with regard to the shining objects. Fire is the prior form, the sun is the later form, the water is their meeting place, lightning is their connector. This is with regard to the heavenly lights.

3. athadhividyam, acaryah purvarupam, antevasy uttararupam, vidya sandhih, pravacanam sandhanam, ityadhividyam.

3. Now with regard to knowledge. The teacher is the prior form, the student is the later form, knowledge is their meeting place, the teaching is the connector. This is with regard to knowledge.

4. athadhiprajam, mata purvarupam, pitottararupam, praja sandhih, prajananam sandhanam, ity adhiprajam.

4. Now, with regard to progeny. The mother is the prior form, the father the later form, the progeny is their meeting place. The act of procreation is the connector This is with regard to progeny.

5. athadhyatmam, adhara hanuh purvarupam, uttara hanuruttararupam, vaksandhih, jihva sandhanam, ityadhyatmam.

5. *Now with regard to the body. The lower jaw is the prior form. The upper jaw is the later form. Speech is the meeting place. Tongue is the connector. This is with regard to the body.*

6. itima mahasamhitah, ya evam eta mahasamhita vyakhyata veda, sandhiyate prajaya pasubhih, brahmavarcasenannadyena suvargyena lokena.

6. *These are the great combinations. Whoever knows these combinations thus explained, is united with progeny, cattle, the splendor of Brahman, food and the heavenly world.*

Section 4

A Teacher's Prayer for Knowledge and Prosperity

1. yas candasam risabho visvarupah, candobhyo, adhyamritat sambabhuva, sa mendro medhaya sprinotu, amritasya deva dharano bhuyasam, sariram me vicarsanam, jihva me madhumattama, karnabhyam bhuri visruvam, brahmanah koso, asi medhaya pihitah, srutam me gopaya.

1. *He who is the bull among the desires, who assumes all forms, who is born from the immortal Vedic meters, may that great Indra cheer me with his intelligence. O divinity, may I be a possessor of immortality. May my body be vigorous; may there be exceeding sweetness in my tongue; may I hear profusely with my ears. You are the sheath of Brahman, covered by intelligence, protect my knowledge of the sruti (Vedas).*

Notes: Srutam means what is heard, usually with regard to the hymns of the Vedas. This prayer seeking protection against loss of that knowledge through memory lapse.

2. avahanti vitanvana, kurvana, aciramatmanah, vasam si mama gavasca, annapane ca sarvada, tato me sriyamavaha, lomasam pasubhih saha svaha, a ma yantu brahmacarinah svaha, vi ma, a, ayantu brahmacarinah svaha, pra ma, a, ayantu brahmacarinah svaha, damayantu brahmacarinah svaha, samayantu brahmacarinah svaha

2. *Thereafter, may you bring to me the goddess of fortune, who is the carrier, the multiplier (of riches), and the long lasting maker for herself and for me of clothes, cows, food and drink for all times. May you bring*

her to me together with wool and cattle. Svaha. May students of chaste conduct come to me from every side. Svaha. May students of chaste conduct come to me variously. Svaha. May students of chaste conduct come to me in a proper manner. Svaha. May students of chaste conduct come to me restraining their bodies. Svaha. May students of chaste conduct come to me restraining their minds. Svaha.

Notes: This is a prayer to Indra seeking his help in obtaining favors from Sri Mahalakshmi, the goddess of prosperity. It is a continuation of the previous verse and presents some difficulty in translating it literally. The seeker first extols the goddess as the carrier, multiplier and accomplisher of all good things in life. She does it not only for herself but for her devotees also at all times. Having made that observation, the seeker then asks Indra to help him in getting her favors. A teacher's prosperity depends upon having more students. Therefore he is seeking the help of Indra to propitiate the goddess and obtain wealth in the form of cattle, wool, clothes, food and drink and students. Svaha means "personally (sva) I am (aha)," a word uttered for emphasis with each offering dropped or poured into the sacrifice.

3. yaso jane, asani svaha, sreyan vasyaso, asani svaha, tam tva bhaga pravisani svaha, sa ma bhaga pravisa svaha, tasmin sahasrasakhe ni bhagaham tvayi mrije svaha, yatha apah pravata ayanti, yatha masa aharjaram, evam mam brahmacarinah, dhatarayantu sarvatah svaha, prativeso'si pra ma bhahi pra ma padyasva.

3. May I become famous among people. Svaha. May I become renowned among the wealthy. Svaha. May I enter into you, O Abode of Light. Svaha. May you, O Abode of Light, enter into me. In You, that river of thousand branches, O Abode of Light, may I wash away my sins. Svaha. As water flows down a slope, as months into a year so, O Giver, may students of chaste conduct come to me from all directions. Svaha. You are the resting place. For me you shine. You come to me again and again.

Section 5

The Four Mystic Utterances

1. bhur bhuvah suvah iti va etah tisro vyahritayah, tasam u ha smaitam caturthim, mahacamasyah pravedayate, maha iti, tat brahma, sa atma, anganyanya devatah, bhuriti va ayam lokah, bhuva ityantariksam, suvarityasau lokah maha ityadityah, adityena vava sarve loka mahiyante.

1. Bhur, bhuvah, suvah, these, verily, are the three mystic utterances. Besides them, there is the fourth, Mahah, made know by the son of Mahacamasa. That is Brahman, that is the Self, its limbs are other gods. Bhur is this world; bhuva is the mid-region; suvah is that world above, maha is sun. By the sun indeed all worlds become great.

Notes: Vyahritis are the mystic utterances used in daily prayers by the Vedic householders, while invoking the divinities. This in brief is the structure of the universe in the Vedic cosmology, the earth, the mid world, the higher world of heaven and the great world of the immortals. This division is with regard to the worlds (adhiloka).

2. Bhur iti va agnih, bhuva iti vayuh, suvarityadityah, maha iti candramah, candramasa vava sarvani jyotimsi mahiyante.

2. Bhur, verily is this fire; bhuva verily is this air; suvah verily is the sun; maha verily is the moon. By the moon indeed all the shining objects become great.

Notes: This interpretation of the four utterances is with regard to the shining objects (adhijyotisa).

3. bhur iti va ricah, bhuva iti samani, suvariti yajumsi maha iti brahma, brahmana vava sarve veda mahiyante,

3. Bhur, verily is the Rigveda hymn; bhuva verily is the Saman; suvah verily is the Yaju formula; maha verily is Brahman. By the Brahman indeed all the Vedas become great.

Notes: This interpretation of the four worlds is with regard to knowledge (adhividya).

4. bhuriti vai pranah, bhuva ityapanah, suvariti vyanah, maha ityannam, annena vava sarve prana mahiyante.

3. Bhur, verily is the incoming breath; bhuva verily is the downward breath; suvah verily is the diffused breath; maha verily is the food. By food indeed all the breaths become great.

Notes: This interpretation of the four worlds is with regard to the body (adhyatma).

5. ta va etas catasras caturdha, catasras catasro vyahritayah, ta yo veda, sa veda brahma, sarve, asmai deva balim avahanti.

5. These verily are the four of the four. Four (explanations) of the four utterances. He who knows them, he knows Brahman. To him all gods bring offerings.

Section 6

Meditating Upon Brahman

1. sa ya eso, antarahridaya akasah, tasminnayam puruso manomayah, amrito hiranmayah, antarena taluke, ya esa stana ivavalambate, sendrayonih, yatrasau kesanto vivartate, vyapohya sirsakapale, bhurityagnau pratitisthati, bhuva iti vayau.

1. This space that is inside the heart, in that is the Person, who is enveloped by mind, immortal and golden hued. Between the two palates that which hangs down like the nipple (of a cow), where (from outside) the roots of the hair divides the head into two, that is the source of Indra. He (the departing Purusha) saying,"Bhur," rests in fire, and saying, "Bhuva," (rests) in air.

2. **suvar ity aditye, maha iti brahmani, apnoti svarajyam, apnoti manasaspatim, vakpatis caksus patih, srotrapatih vijnanapatih, etat tato bhavati, akasa sariram brahma, satyatma pranaramam mana anandam, santisamriddham amritam, iti pracinayogyopassva.**

2. Saying,"Suvah," (he) rests in the sun; saying, "Maha," he rests in Brahman, attains self-rule, attain the lordship of the mind, attains the lordship of speech, lordship of sight, lordship of hearing, lordship of wisdom. Thereafter he becomes Brahman whose body is the space, whose nature is truth, in whom the breaths come to rest, whose mind is blissful, who flourishes with peace and immortality. Thus, O Pracinayogya, you should meditate (upon Brahman).

Section 7

The Fivefold Aggregates

1. **prithivy antariksam dyaur diso, va avantaradisah, agnir vayur adityas candrama naksatrani, apa osadhayo vanaspataya akasa atma, ity adhibhutam, athadhyatmam, prano vyano, apana udanah samanah, caksuh srotram mano vak tvak, carma mamsam snavasthi majja, etad adhividhaya risir avocat, panktam va idam sarvam, panktena iva panktam sprinoti.**

1. The earth, the mid-region, heaven, the quarters and the intermediate quarters; fire, air, the sun, the moon and the stars; water, plants, trees, space and the body; this is with regard to the elements (present in a being). Now, with regard to the bodily parts: prana, vyana, apana, udana, and samana; the eye, the ear, the mind, the speech and touch; skin, flesh, muscle, bone and marrow. Having seen this arrangement, a seer said: "All this is fivefold. With these the fivefold (aggregates) the fivefold (being) is filled up.

Notes: Adhibhtua is the physical or the material universe consisting of all the objects that are made up of the five elements. Adhyatma is what constitutes one's physical self or the mind and body. The last sentence is translated differently by different interpreters. The correct meaning is by these five aggregates, the body of the fivefold being is filled up.

Section 8
The Significance of Aum

1. aum iti brahma, aum itidam sarvam, aum ity etad anukritir ha sma va apyo sravayetyasravayanti, aum iti samani gayanti, aum somiti sastrani sam santi, aum ity adhvaryuh pratigaram pratigrinati, aum iti brahma prasauti, aum ity agnihotram anujanati, aum iti brahmanah pravaksyann aha brahmopapna vaniti, brahmaivopapnoti.

1. This Aum is Brahman. This Aum is all this. This word, which is Aum, invokes obedience. Moreover, when told, "Aum, recite," they recite. Uttering Aum, they sing the Samans. Uttering, "Aum, Som," they recite scriptures. Uttering Aum, the Adharvayu priest responds with praise. Uttering Aum, the Brahman priest indicates approval. Uttering Aum the Agnihotri priest gives permission (to the sacrificer) to make offerings (in the fire sacrifice). A Brahmana says Aum when he was about to begin the recitation (of the Vedas), wishing, "May I attain Brahman." Thus (wishing) he attains Brahman.

Notes: This verse explains both the ritual and spiritual significance of Aum. Aum is chanted in the beginning of various types of recitation and ritual chanting. Aum is chanted to indicate the beginning of rituals as well as compliance. Aum is chanted to know the Self and realize Brahman.

Section 9
The Order and Regularity of Life

1. ritam ca svadhyaya pravacane ca, satyam ca svadhyaya pravacane ca, tapas ca svadhyaya pravaca-ne ca, damas ca svadhyaya pravacane ca, samas ca svadhyaya pravacane ca, agnayas ca svadhyaya pravacane ca, agnihotram ca svadhyaya pravacane ca, atithayas ca svadhyaya pravacane ca, manu-sam ca svadhyaya pravacane ca, praja ca svadhyaya pravacane ca, prajanas ca svadhyaya pravacane ca, prajatis ca svadhyaya pravacane ca, satyam iti satyava ca rathitarah, tapa iti taponityah paurusi-stih, svadhyaya pravacane eveti nako maudgalyah, taddhi tapas taddhi tapah.

1. Practice order and regularity (of your life) by self-study and teaching, truth by self-study and teaching, austerity by self-study and teaching, restraint of the body by self-study and teaching, sameness by self-study and teaching, the upkeep of daily fire sacrifices by self-study and teaching, the fire sacrifice by self-study and teaching, honoring the guests by self-study and teaching, serving the people by self-study and teaching, raising the offspring by self-study and teaching, procreation by self-study and teaching, and training the grandchildren by self-study and teaching. This is the truth, says Satyavacas, the son of Rathitara. This is austerity says Taponitya son of Parusisti. This is nothing but self-study and teaching says Naka, the son of Mudgala. That, indeed, is austerity. That, indeed, is austerity.

Notes: Svadhyaya means learning the Vedas by self-effort through recitation, remembrance and contemplation. Rtam means the order and regularity of the world or the orderly flow of time and events as willed by God. Rtma is maintained by God by enforcing divine laws through duty. It is possible only when everyone, from the highest to the lowest in the hierarchy of creation perform their obligatory duties selflessly. Duty (dharma) and order go hand in hand. And it has to be upheld in every aspect of life by a person who is bound to his duty (dharma) by means of self-study and teaching. Other aspects of dharma like truth, austerity, sacrifices, procreation, raising a family should also be practiced with the help of these two, self-study and teaching. Self-study increases one's own knowledge and awareness of dharma. Teaching increases the knowledge and awareness of others. When everyone in society has right knowledge, divine laws flourish and the order and regularity of the world is ensured. This is the essence of this verse. This is the truth. This is an austerity in itself. Nothing else is required to uphold dharma, other than self-study and teaching.

Section 10
Trisanku on Knowledge and Wisdom

1. aham vriksasya reriva, kirtih pristham gireriva, urdhvapavitro vajiniva svamritam asmi, dravinam savarcasam, sumedha amritoksitah, iti trisankor vedanuvacanam.

1. I am the mover of the tree (of my family). My fame is like the peak of a mountain. My mind is pure. I verily have as my food the nectar of immortality found in the sun. I am bright with the wealth (of knowledge). I am endowed with the right wisdom which is eternal and imperishable. Thus proclaimed Trisanku after knowing (the Self).

Notes: This verse is interpreted variously. According to some the tree is the tree of creation or the universe. I believe it is the reference to the family tree. When a person achieves liberation, he not only liberates himself, but also helps his ancestors immensely by uplifting them to the immortal world by his very achievement. Thus, Trisanku declared in this verse that he helped his ancestors to move to the higher world. Urdhvam is interpreted by some as the source. I believe the reference to the head or the mind, which constitute the uppermost part of the body is very clear.

Section 11
Farewell Advise to Students

1. vedam anucyacaryontevasinamanusasti, satyam vada, dharmam cara, svadhyayan ma pramadah, acaryaya priyam dhanam

ahritya prajatantum ma vyavaccetsih, satyan na pramaditavyam, dharman na pramaditavyam, kusalan na pramaditavyam, bhutyai na pramaditavyam, svadhyaya pravaca-nabhyam na pramaditavyam.

1. *After teaching the Vedas, in the end, the teacher instructs the pupil. Speak the truth. Perform your duty. Do not neglect the self-study of the Vedas. After giving the gift desired by the teacher, do not break the chain of your progeny. Do not neglect truth. Do not neglect duty. Do not neglect your health. Do not neglect your material wellbeing. Do not neglect the self-study and the teaching of the Vedas.*

2. devapitrikaryabhyam na pramaditavyam, matri devo bhava, pitri devo bhava, acarya devo bhava, atithi devo bhava, yany anavadyani karmani, tani sevitavyani, no itarani, yany asmakam sucaritani, tani tvayopasyani, no itarani.

2. *Do not neglect your duties to gods and ancestors. May your mother be honored as a goddess by you; may your father be honored as a god by you; may your teacher be honored as a god by you; may your guest be honored as a god by you. Whatever actions are free from egoism, they should be practiced, not others. Whatever good conduct you find among us (teachers), that alone should be practiced, not others.*

Notes: Anava means egoism or acting like a particle (anu) distinct from God. Actions arising out of egoism should be discarded since they lead to karmic consequences and bondage. Actions should be performed as an offering. A teacher should be a role model, but the teacher himself is suggesting here that students should not follow their teachers blindly. They should follow only that conduct of the teachers which is considered good (sucarita).

3. ye ke casmaccreyamso brahmanah, tesam tvayasanena prasvasitavyam, sraddhaya deyam, asradd-haya'deyam, sriya deyam, hriya deyam, bhiya deyam, samvida deyam, atha yadi te karmavicikitsa va vrittavicikitsa va syat.

3. *Those brahmanas among us who are praiseworthy, their fatigue should be removed by offering them a seat. What is given should be given with sincerity, not to be given with insincerity, given plentifully, given with modesty, given with obedience, given with kindness. Now, if there is any doubt in you with regard to duties or if there is any doubt in you with regard to your profession.*

4. ye tatra brahmanah sammarsinah, yukta ayuktah, aluksa dharmakamah syuh, yatha te tatra varteran, tatha tatra vartthah; athabhyakhyatesu, ye tatra brahmanah sammarsinah,

yukta ayuktah, aluksa dharmakamah syuh, yatha te tesu varteran, tatha tesu vartethah, esa adesah, esa upadesah, esa vedopanisat, etadanusasanam, evamupasitavyam, evamu caitadupasyam.

4. You should conduct yourself in such and such manner as those brahmanas who are competent to occupy the seat of a judge, who can discern the right from the wrong, who are not cruel, who are interested in performing actions for the sake of dharma would behave in such situations. Now with regard to those who have been accused, you should conduct yourself in such and such manner as those brahmanas who are competent to occupy the seat of a judge, who can discern the right from the wrong, who are not cruel, who are interested in performing actions for the sake of dharma would behave in such situations. This is the command. This is the teaching. This is the secret teaching of the Vedas. This is the instruction. This one should follow. This alone should be followed.

Notes: Yuktayukta means right and wrong or what is appropriate and inappropriate and used in reference to discerning knowledge (vicaksana jnanam). This is an important quality for any person who performs the functions of a judge. Sammarsina means to be qualified to sit upon the seat of a judge to deliver judgment. The suggestion given in this verse to the young students is if they have to judge any actions or speak against anyone who has been accused of doing wrong, they have to follow the best practices followed by wise people in society and uphold the values they uphold.

Section 12

A Joint Invocation for Divine Help

1. aum sam no mitrah sam varunah; sam no bhavaty aryama; sam na indro brihaspatih; sam no visnururukramah; namo brahmane; namaste vayo; tvam eva pratyaksam brahmasi; tvam eva pratyaksam brahma vadisyami; ritam vadisyami; satyam vadisyami; tanmamavatu; advaktaramavatu; avatu mam; avatu vaktaram; aum santih santih santih.

1. May Mitra be favorable to us. May Varuna be favorable. May Aryaman be favorable to us. May Indra and Brihaspati be favorable to us. May Vishnu, of wide strides, be favorable to us. Salutation to Brahman. Salutations O Vayu. You, verily, are the visible Brahman. You alone I declare as the visible Brahman. I declare (you) as the controller. I declare (you) as the truth. May It protect me. May It protect the teacher. May It protect me. May It protect the teacher. Aum. Peace. Peace. Peace.

Chapter 2 - Brahmananda Valli

Section 1

Brahman and Creation

sa ha nav avatu saha nau bhunaktu saha viryam karavavahai tejasvi nav adhitam astu; ma vidvisavahai; aum, santih, santih, santih.

May He protect us both; may He nourish us both together; may we both become energetic by working together; may our study illumine (our minds); may there be no hatred between us. Aum, peace, peace, peace.

1. aum brahmavid apnoti param, tad esa, abhyukta, satyam jnanam anantam brahma, yo veda nihitam guhayam parame vyoman, so, asnute sarvan kaman saha, brahmana vipasciteti, tasmadva etasmadatmana akasah sambhutah, akasadvayuh, vayoragnih, agnerapah, adbhyah prithivi, prithivya osadhayah, osadhibhyo, annam, annatpurusah, sa va esa puruso, annnarasamayah, tasyedameva sirah, ayam daksinah paksah, ayamuttarah paksah, ayamatma, idam puccham pratistha, tadapyesa sloko bhavati.

1. Aum, the knower of Brahman attains the Supreme. Of this there is the saying: He who knows Brahman as truth, knowledge, infinite, who is hidden in the cave (of the heart) and in the supreme space, enjoys all desires and becomes one with Brahman, the omniscient. From that (Brahman) who is this Self manifested space, from space air, from air fire, from fire water, from water the earth, from the earth the plants, from the plants food, from the food the being. This, verily, is the being who is made up of food. This, indeed, is his head. This (right side) is the southern quarter. This (left side) is the northern quarter. This (the middle part) is the body. This (lower side) is the tail, the foundation. Regarding this there is also this verse.

Section 2

The Importance of Food

1. annadvai prajah prajayante, yah kasca prithivim sritah, atho annenaiva jivanti, athainadapi yantyantatah, annam hi bhutanam jyestham, tasmat sarvausadhamucyate, sarvam vai te'annamapnuvanti, ye, annam brahmopasate, annam hi bhutanam

jyestham, tasmat sarvausadhamucyate, annad bhutani jayante, jatanyannena vardhante, adyate, atti ca bhutani, tasmadannam taducyata iti, tasmadva etasmadannarasamayat, anyo, antara atma pranamayah, tenaisa purnah, sa va esa purusavidha eva, tasya purusavidhatam, anvayam purusavidhah, tasya prana eva sirah, vyano daksinah paksah, apana uttarah paksah, akasa atma, prithivi puccam pratistha, tadapyesa sloko bhavati

1. From food only are produced all beings, whatsoever that dwell upon earth. Further, by food only they live and in the end to food only they return. Food alone is the eldest of the living beings. Therefore it is called the universal medicine. Those who worship food as Brahman, they obtain all food. Food alone is the eldest of the living beings. Therefore it is called the universal medicine. From food all beings are born; having born, by food they grow. It is eaten (by beings) and its eats beings. Therefore, it is called food. Now, different from this (body) which is made up of food is another body inside, which is made up of breath. By that (breath) is filled this (food body). This one is also in the shape of the being. As is the shape of that form of the being so is the shape of this form of the being. Of him, the in breath is its head, the diffused breath the right side, the downward breath is the left side, the space is the body, the earth is the tail, the foundation. Regarding this there is also this verse.

Section 3

Breath and Mind

1. pranam deva anu prananti, manusyah pasavasca ye, prano hi bhutanamayuh, tasmat sarvayusamucyate, sarvameva ta ayuryanti, ye pranam brahmopasate, prano hi bhutanamayuh, tasmat sarvayusamucyata iti, tasyaisa eva sarira atma, yah purvasya, tasmadva etasmat pranamayat, anyo' antara atma manomayah, tenaisa purnah, sa va esa purusavidha eva, tasya purusavidhatam, anvayam purusavidhah, tasya yajureva sirah, rigdaksinah paksah, samottarah paksah, adesa atma, atharvangirasah puccam pratistha, tadapyesa sloko bhavati.

1. The organs act by following the breath; so do humans and the animals. Breath, indeed, is the life of beings. Therefore, it is called the life of all. Those who worship Brahman as breath they attain full life, for breath, indeed, is the life of beings. Therefore, it is called the life of all. This, indeed, is the soul of that prior (food) body. Now, different from

this (breath body) which is made up of breath is another body inside, which is made up of mind. By that (mind) is filled this (breath body). This one is also in the shape of the being. As is the shape of that form of the being so is the shape of this form of the being. Of him, the Yajurveda is its head, the Rigveda the right side, the Samaveda is the left side, the teaching is the body, the hymns of Atharvan and Angirasa are the tail, the foundation. Regarding this there is also this verse.

Section 4

Mind and Intelligence

1. yato vaco nivartante, aprapya manasa saha, anandam brahmano vidvan, na bibheti kadacaneti, tasyaisa eva sarira atma, yah purvasya, tasmadva etasmanmanomayat, anyo, antara atma vijnanamayah, tenaisa purnah, sa va esa purusavidha eva, tasya purusavidhatam, anvayam purusavidhah, tasya sraddhaiva sirah, ritam daksinah paksah, satyamuttarah paksah, yoga atma, mahah puccam pratistha, tadapyesa sloko bhavati.

1. From where the words return, along with the mind, unable to attain it, that blissful Brahman he who knows does not fear even a little. This, indeed, is the soul of the that prior one (breath body). Now, different from this which is made up of mind is another body inside, which is made up of intelligence. By that (intelligence) is filled this (mental body). This one is also in the shape of the being. As is the shape of that form of the being so is the shape of this form of the being. Of him, faith is its head, the order and regularity of the world the right side, truth the left side, yoga the body, the great one (intelligence) the tail, the foundation. Regarding this there is also this verse.

Notes: Mind is usually considered a receptacle of thoughts. It does not produce thoughts. Thoughts are believed to exist in the space of Brahman and they enter the mind of a person according to his desires and inclinations in which intelligence said to play an important role. Intelligence gives us the ability to exercise our will. It is therefore considered superior to the mind.

Section 5

Intelligence and Bliss

1. vijnanam yajnam tanute,karmani tanute, api ca, vijnanam devah sarve, brahma jyesthamupasate,vijnanam brahma cedveda, tasmaccenna pramadyati, sarire papmano hitva, sarvankamansamasnuta iti, tasyaisa eva sarira atma, yah pur-

vasya, tasmadva etasmadvijnanamayat, anyo, antara atma, anandamayah, tenaisa purnah, sa va esa purusavidha eva, tasya purusavidhatam, anvayam purusavidhah,tasya priyameva sirah, modo daksinah paksah, pramoda uttarah paksah, ananda atma,brahma puccam pratistha, tadapyesa sloko bhavati.

1. *Intelligence sets in motion the sacrifice. It sets in motion all obligatory duties. All the gods worship intelligence as Brahman, the eldest. He who knows Brahman as intelligence does not neglect (his duties). Getting rid of all the sins of his body, he attains all desires. This, indeed, is the soul of the that prior one (mental body). Now, different from this which is made up of intelligence is another body inside, which is made up of bliss. By that (bliss) is filled this (Self). This one is also in the shape of the being. As is the shape of that form of the being so is the shape of this form of the being. Of him, pleasure is its head, happiness the right side, joy the left side, bliss the body, Brahman the tail, the foundation. Regarding this there is also this verse.*

Section 6
Brahman, the Self in the Body

6. asanneva sa bhavati, asadbrahmeti veda cet, asti brahmeti cedveda, santamenam tato viduriti, tasyaisa eva sarira atma, yah purvasya, athato, anuprasnah, utavidvanamum lokam pretya, kascana gaccati u, aho vidvanamum lokam pretya kascitsamasnuta u, so, akamayata, bahu syam prajayeyeti, sa tapo, atapyata, sa tapastaptva, idam sarvamasrijata, yadidam kinca, tatsristva, tadevanupravisat, tadanupravisya, sacca tyacca abhavat, niruktam caniruktam ca, nilayanam canilayanam ca, vijnanam cavijnanam ca, satyam canritam ca satyamabhavat, yadidam kinca, tatsatyamityacaksate, tadapyesa sloko bhavati.

1. *Non-existent, verily, becomes, when one knows thus, "Non-existence is this Brahman." Existent becomes by that knowing, when one knows thus, "Brahman does exist." This (Brahman), indeed, is the soul of the that prior one (bliss body). Now, (the answer) as to the following question. Whether anyone who knows not upon departing from this life go to the other world; or does anyone who knows upon departing from here attains that world? He desired, "May I become many; may I be born." He performed austerity. Having performed the austerity, out of that austerity, He created all this, whatever that is here. Having created it, he entered into it. Having entered into it, he became both the mani-*

fested (gross) and the unmanifested (subtle), the definable and the indefinable, the supporting and the non-supporting, the intelligent and the not-intelligent, the true and the untrue. The true became all this, whatever. This is what they call the true. Regarding this there is also this verse.

Notes: This verse has been interpreted variously by different scholars. For me the correct meaning seems to be that Brahman who is both manifested and unmanifested, existence and non-existence (sat and asat), becomes existent for those who believe that He exists and becomes non-existent for those who believe that He does not exist. Thus God does not force the atheists and non-believers to think otherwise. As declared in the Bhagavadgita, He strengthens their faith in their non-belief according to their predominant thoughts (samskaras).

Section 7
The Blissful Nature of Brahman

1. asadva idamagra asit, tato vai sadajayata, tadatmanam svayamakuruta, tasmattatsukritamucyata iti, yadvai tat sukritam, raso vai sah, rasam hyevayam labdhvanandi bhavati, ko hyevanyatkah pranyat, yadesa akasa anando na syat, esa hyeva, a, anandayati, yada hyevaisa etasminnadrisye, anatmye, anirukte, anilayane, abhayam pratistham vindate, atha so, abhayam gato bhavati, yada hyevaisa etasminnudaramantaram kurute, atha tasya bhayam bhavati, tatveva bhayam viduso, amanvanasya, tadapyesa sloko bhavati.

1. *Non-existent, verily, this (world) was in the beginning. From that verily was born existence. It made itself as the Self (of the existence). Therefore it is called a virtuous act. Verily, that which is well made is the delight of existence; for truly on obtaining the delight of existence one becomes blissful. Indeed, who can breathe in and breathe out , if this bliss does not exist in the space? This one alone is That which brings blissfulness. When this one (the existence) becomes established in That which is invisible, incorporeal, inexpressible and fearless, then does indeed one becomes fearless. When this one (existence) finds even the smallest distinction, then he becomes fearful. That, indeed, is the fear of the impure arising from the thoughts of separation (anava).*

Notes: Fear and insecurity arise when we think we are distinct and different from the rest of creation. It makes us distrustful of the world and people around us and protect ourselves from them. This notion of distinction also drives us into selfish and egoistic thinking whereby we indulge in desire-ridden actions and become bound to the cycle of births and deaths, which in itself is the cause of great fear. However, fear does not exist for those who find God everywhere and in everything. If you genuinely believe that Brahman exists in everyone and in everything, including yourself, that identification alone makes your fearless and assured. Anava means egoism or living like a small particle (anu) in the cosmic sea of creation. When this feeling prevails, one is bound to suffer from fear and insecurity, fear of the unknown, fear of gain and loss, fear of death, sin and suffering.

Section 8

Progressive States of Bliss

1. bhisa, asmadvatah pavate, bhisodeti suryah, bhisa, asmadagniscendrasca, mrityurdhavati pancama iti, saisanandasya mimamsa bhavati,

yuva syatsadhuyuva, adhyayakah, asistho dridhistho balisthah, tasyeyam prithivi sarva vittasya purna syat, sa eko manusa anandah, te ye satam manusa anandah, sa eko manusyagandharvanamanandah, srotriyasya cakamahatasya,

te ye satam manusyagandharvanamanandah, sa eko devagandharvanamanandah, srotriyasya cakamahatasya,

te ye satam devagandharvanamanandah, sa ekah pitrinam ciralokalokanamanandah, srotriyasya cakamahatasya,

te ye satam pitrinam ciralokalokanamanandah, sa eka ajanajanam devanamanandah, srotriyasya cakamahatasya,

te ye satam ajanajanam devanamanandah, sa ekah karmadevanam devanamanandah, ye karmana devanapiyanti, srotriyasya cakamahatasya,

te ye satam karmadevanam devanamanandah, sa eko devanamanandah, srotriyasya cakamahatasya,

te ye satam devanamanandah, sa eka indrasya, a, anandah, srotriyasya cakamahatasya,

te ye satamindrasya, a, anandah, sa eko brihaspateranandah, srotriyasya cakamahatasya,

te ye satam brihaspateranandah, sa ekah prajapateranandah, srotriyasya cakamahatasya,

te ye satam prajapateranandah, sa eko brahmana anandah, srotriyasya cakamahatasya,

sa yascayam puruse, yascasavaditye, sa ekah, sa ya evamvit, asmallokatpretya, etamannamayamatmanamupasankramati, etam pranamayam atmanam upasankramati, etam manomayam atmanam upasankramati, etam vijnanamayam atmanam

upasankramati, etam anandamayam atmanamupasankramati, tadapyesa sloko bhavati.

1. *From fear of Him Vatah (the wind) blows, from fear of Him the sun rises. From fear of Him the five divinities such as Agni (fire), Indra, and Mrityu (death) work. Now regarding the bliss of this one this is the (conclusion drawn from) philosophical enquiry.*

If there were a young man, a good young man, well versed in the Vedas, efficient in action, with steady mind and senses, strong and if the wealth of the earth were entirely for him only, that is one measure of human bliss. A hundred times of that bliss is one measure of the bliss of celestial humans known as the Gandharvas, so also (the bliss) of a person well versed in the Vedas and who is not stricken with desires. A hundred times of the bliss of celestial humans is one measure of the bliss of the divine celestials known as Deva Gandharvas, so also (the bliss) of a person well versed in the Vedas and who is not stricken with desires.

A hundred times the bliss of ancestors (pitrs) in their long-lasting world is one measure of the bliss of those who become gods by birth in the divine world of Ajana, so also (the bliss) of a person well versed in the Vedas and who is not stricken with desires.

A hundred times the bliss of those who become gods by birth in the divine world of Ajana is one measure of the bliss of those who become gods by duty known as karmadevas, who reach the gods by their sacrifices, so also (the bliss) of a person well versed in the Vedas and who is not stricken with desires.

A hundred times the bliss of those who become gods by duty is one measure of the bliss of the (immortal) gods, so also (the bliss) of a person well versed in the Vedas and who is not stricken with desires.

A hundred times the bliss of the (immortal gods) is one measure of the bliss of Indra, so also (the bliss) of a person well versed in the Vedas and who is not stricken with desires.

A hundred times the bliss of Indra is one measure of the bliss of Brihaspati, so also (the bliss) of a person well versed in the Vedas and who is not stricken with desires.

A hundred times the bliss of Brihaspati is one measure of the bliss of Prajapati, so also (the bliss) of a person well versed in the Vedas and who is not stricken with desires.

A hundred times the bliss of Prajapati is one measure of the bliss of Brahma, so also (the bliss) of a person well versed in the Vedas and who is not stricken with desires.

He who is in this person, and who is in the sun above, He is one only. Whoever knows this, upon departing from this world, attains the body made up of food, attains the body made up of breath, attains the body made up of mind, attains the body made up of intelligence and attains the body which is made up of bliss.

Notes: Different types of men, gods and celestial beings are mentioned in this verse. The Gandharvas are celestial beings who inhabit the mid-region. They are endowed with ethereal bodies and exceptional artistic talents. They are classified here as human gandharvas, who assume human form at will and visit the earth frequently, and as godly gandharvas, who inhabit Indra's heaven and entertain the gods. Three types of gods are mentioned. Those who are born as gods by virtue of the merit of their past lives, those who become equal to gods upon earth by virtue of their obligatory duties and sacrifices and the real gods who are immortal, who said to be thirty three. The last part of the verse signifies that whoever knows the nature of Brahman will have all the bodies in his next birth when he returns from the ancestral world.

Section 9
Offering Actions to the Self Within

1. yato vaco nivartante, aprapya manasa saha, anandam brahmano vidvan, na bibheti kutascaneti, etam ha vava na tapati, kimaham sadhu nakaravam, kimaham papamakaravamiti, sa ya evam vidvanete atmanam sprinute, ubhe hyevaisa ete atmanam sprinute, ya evam veda, ityupanisat.

1. From where the words return, along with the mind, unable to attain it, that blissful Brahman who knows, he does not fear even a little. Such a person, verily, is not tormented by the thought, "Why did not I perform good deeds? Why have I indulged in sinful actions?" Whoever knows this offers them to his Self. Indeed, he offers both to himself, who knows thus. Such is the secret teaching.

Notes: The knower of the Self is not troubled by the nature of his actions since he knows that the Self is the source of his action. Accordingly he offers all his actions to his Self, without desiring their fruit and thereby escapes from their consequences. Therefore, he is not troubled by the nature of his actions. Fear rules our minds. We fear for various reasons and philosophically speaking, our fear stems from the realization or the understanding that we are lonely and helpless in this world. This fear is normal because we learn from our experience and perceptions that we are limited in many ways and against the forces of Nature we cannot prevail for long. Fear also arises, if you are a religious person, from the idea of sin and its consequences. Our actions are rooted in our desires and our desires lead to attachment and the continuation of our existence in the cycle of births and deaths. All these produce fear and that fear is our constant experience. This fear disappears only when we realize our eternal Nature and experiences oneness with Brahman.

Chapter 3 – Bhrigu Valli

Section 1

Varuna's Teachings to Bhrigu

aum, sa ha nav avatu saha nau bhunaktu saha viryam karavavahai tejasvi nav adhitam astu; ma vidvisavahai; aum, santih, santih, santih.

Aum, may He protect us both; may He nourish us both together; May we both become energetic by working together; may our study illumine (our minds); may there be no hated between us. Aum, peace, peace, peace.

1. bhrigurvai varunih, varunam pitaramupasasara, adhihi bhagavo brahmeti, tasma etatprovaca, annam pranam caksuh srotram mano vacamiti, tam hovaca, yato va imani bhutani jayante, yena jatani jivanti, yatprayantyabhisamvisanti, tadvijijnasasva, tad brahmeti, sa tapo, atapyata, sa tapastaptva

1. Bhrigu, the son of Varuna, went near his father and said, "Godman, teach me Brahman." To him, he said this, "Food, breath, eye, ear, mind, speech." He said (further), "That from which these beings are born, that by which, when born, these beings live, that into which they enter upon departing, That you should know, That is Brahman. He performed austerities. Having performed austerities...

Section 2

Food is Brahman

1. annam brahmeti vyajanat, annaddhyeva khalvimani bhutani jayante, annena jatani jivanti, annam prayantyabhisamvisantiti, tadvijnaya, punareva varunam pitaramupasasara, adhihi bhagavo brahmeti, tam hovaca, tapasa brahma vijijnasasva, tapo brahmeti, sa tapo, atapyata, sa tapastaptva.

1. He realized that food was Brahman. From food, verily, beings are born here. Being born, they live by food, and upon departing they enter into food and become one with it. Having realized this, he again went near his father and said, "Godman, teach me Brahman."To him, he said this, "Know Brahman through austerities. Austerity is Brahman." He performed austerities. Having performed austerities...

Section 3
Breath is Brahman

1. prano brahmeti vyajanat, pranaddhyeva khalvimani bhutani jayante, pranena jatani jivanti, pranam prayantyabhisamvisantiti, tadvijnaya, punareva varunam pitaramupasasara, adhihi bhagavo brahmeti, tam hovaca, tapasa brahma vijijnasasva, tapo brahmeti, sa tapo, atapyata, sa tapastaptva.

1. He realized that breath was Brahman. From breath, verily, beings are born here. Being born, they live by breath, and upon departing they enter into breath and become one with it. Having realized this, he again went near his father and said, "Godman, teach me Brahman."To him, he said this, "Know Brahman through austerities. Austerity is Brahman." He performed austerities. Having performed austerities...

Section 4
Mind is Brahman

1. mano brahmeti vyajanat, manaso hyeva khalvimani bhutani jayante, manasa jatani jivanti, manah prayantyabhisamvisantiti, tadvijnaya, punareva varunam pitaramupasasara, adhihi bhagavo brahmeti, tam hovaca, tapasa brahma vijijnasasva, tapo brahmeti, sa tapo, atapyata, sa tapastaptva.

1. He realized that mind was Brahman. From mind, verily, beings are born here. Being born, they live by mind, and upon departing they enter into mind and become one with it. Having realized this, he again went near his father and said, "Godman, teach me Brahman."To him, he said this, "Know Brahman through austerities. Austerity is Brahman." He performed austerities. Having performed austerities...

Section 5
Intelligence is Brahman

1. vijnanam brahmeti vyajanat, vijnanaddhyeva khalvimani bhutani jayante, vijnanena jatani jivanti, vijnanam prayantyabhisamvisantiti,tadvijnaya, punareva varunam pitaramupasasara,adhihi bhagavo brahmeti, tam hovaca, tapasa brahma vijijnasasva,tapo brahmeti, sa tapo, atapyata,sa tapastaptva.

1. He realized that intelligence was Brahman. From intelligence, verily, beings are born here. Being born, they live by intelligence, and upon departing they enter into intelligence and become one with it. Having realized this, he again went near his father and said, "Godman, teach me Brahman."To him, he said this, "Know Brahman through austerities. Austerity is Brahman." He performed austerities. Having performed austerities...

Section 6

Bliss is Brahman

1. anando brahmeti vyajanat, anandadhyeva khalvimani bhutani jayante, anandena jatani jivanti, anandam prayanty abhisamvisantiti, saisa bhargavi varuni vidya, parame vyoman pratisthita, sa ya evam veda pratitisthati, annavan annado bhavati, mahan bhavati prajaya pasubhir brahmavarcasena, mahan kirtya.

1. He realized that bliss was Brahman. From bliss beings are born here. Being born, they live by bliss and upon departing they enter into bliss and become one with it. This then is the knowledge taught by Varuna to (his son) Bhrigu, which (starting from food) becomes established in the highest (bliss). He who knows this becomes established (in the bliss). He becomes a possessor of food, and an eater (of food). He becomes great in offspring, in cattle, in the vigor of Brahman and in very great fame.

Section 7

Food and Breath

1. annam na nindyat, tadvratam, prano va annam, sariram annadam, prane sariram pratisthitam, sarire pranah pratisthitah, tad etad annam anne pratisthitam, sa ya etad annam anne pratisthitam veda pratitisthati, annavan annado bhavati, mahan bhavati prajaya pasubhir brahmavarcasena, mahan kirtya.

1. Do not speak ill of food, that should be the vow. Breath verily is food, the body is the eater of food. In the breath does the body rest. In the body does the breath rest. Thus food is established in food. He who knows that this food is established in the (other) food becomes established. He becomes a possessor of food, and an eater (of food). He becomes great in offspring, in cattle, in the vigor of Brahman and in very great fame.

Section 8
Food and Water

1. annam na paricaksita, tad vratam, apo va annam, jyotir annadam, apsu jyotih pratisthitam, jyotisy apah pratisthitah, tad etad annam anne pratisthitam, sa ya etad annam anne pratisthitam veda pratitisthati, annavan annado bhavati, mahan bhavati prajaya pasubhir brahmavarcasena, mahan kirtya.

1. Do not reject food. That should be the vow. Water, verily is food, fire is the eater of food. In water does fire rest. In fire does water rest. Thus food is established in food. He who knows that this food is established in the (other) food becomes established. He becomes a possessor of food, and an eater (of food). He becomes great in offspring, in cattle, in the vigor of Brahman and in very great fame.

Section 9
Food and Earth

1. annam bahu kurvita, tadvratam, prithivi va annam, akaso, annadah, prithivyam akasah pratisthitah, akase prithivi pratisthita, tad etad annam anne pratisthitam, sa ya etad annam anne pratisthitam veda pratitisthati, annavan annado bhavati, mahan bhavati prajaya pasubhir brahmavarcasena, mahankirtya.

1. Make food plentiful. That should be the vow. The earth, verily is food, space is the eater of food. In space does the earth rest. In the earth does space rest. Thus food is established in food. He who knows that this food is established in the (other) food becomes established. He becomes a possessor of food, and an eater (of food). He becomes great in offspring, in cattle, in the vigor of Brahman and in very great fame.

Section 10
The Importance of Offering Food

1. na kancana vasatau pratyacaksita,tadvratam, tasmadyaya kaya ca vidhaya bahvannam prapnuyat, aradhyasma annamityacaksate, etadvai mukhato, anam raddham, mukhato, asma annam radhyate, etadvai madhyato, anam raddham, madhyato, asma annam radhyate, edadva antato, annam raddham, antato, asma annam radhyate.

1. *Do not refuse lodging to anyone. That should be the vow. Therefore, by any method whatsoever, one should gather plenty of food, so that people can say, "There is food readily available to him." If this food is given early, food comes to the giver early. If the food is offered in the middle, food comes to the giver in the middle. If the food is given in the end, food comes to the giver in the end.*

Notes: If the food is given early means if the food is offered to the guest quickly and readily at the very beginning without letting the guest wait for it. If the food is offered in the middle means if the food is offered with some delay or hesitation after letting the guest wait for it. If the food is offered in the end means, if the food is offered with great reluctance after everyone in the house ate or offering the left overs at the end of a long wait.

2. **ya evam veda, ksema iti vaci, yogaksema iti pranapanayoh, karmeti hastayoh, gatiriti padayoh, vimuktiriti payau, iti manusih samajnah, atha daivih, triptir iti vristau, balamiti vidyuti.**

2. *He who knows this, as preservation in speech, as keeping what is acquired in the in breath and downward breath, as action in the hands, as movement in the feet, as release in the anus, these are the signs (of Brahman) in humans. Now, as to (the signs) in the deities, satisfaction in rains, strength in the lightning.,*

3. **yasa iti pasusu, jyotiriti naksatresu, prajatiramritamananda ityupasthe, sarvamityakase, tatpratisthetyupasita, pratisthavan bhavati, tanmaha ityupasita, mahanbhavati, tanmana ityupasita, manavanbhavati**

3. *As fame in cattle, light in the stars, procreation, immortality and bliss in the sexual organs, as everything in space (one should meditate upon Brahman). One should contemplate upon That as the support, then one is supported. One should contemplate upon that as greatness, then one becomes great. One should contemplate upon That as the mind, then one becomes a thinker.*

4. **tannama ityupasita, namyante, asmai kamah, tadbrahmetyupasita, brahmavanbhavati, tadbrahmanah parimara ityupasita, paryenam mriyante dvisantah sapatnah, pari ye, apriya bhratrivyah, sa yascayam puruse, yascasavaditye, sa ekah.**

4. *One should worship That bowing down, then for him all desires bow down. One should worship That as supreme, then one becomes endowed with the Supreme. One should worship That as Brahman's*

means of destruction, then one's rivals who envy him will perish, so also those rivals whom he dislikes.

5. sa ya evam vit, asmallokat pretya, etam annamayam atmanam upasankramya, etam pranamayam atmanam upasankramya, etam manomayam atmanam upasankramya, etam vijnanamayam atmanam upasankramya, etam anandamayam atmanam upasankramya, iman llokankamanni kamarupyanuancaran, etat sama gayannaste, ha vu ha vu ha vu.

5. He who knows this, upon departing from this world, attains this self made of food, attains the self made of breath, attains the self made of mind, attains the self made of intelligence, attains the self made of bliss. In these worlds, he goes up and down, eating the food he desires, assuming the forms he desires. He sits singing this chant (of great joy), "Aha, oho, aha, oho, aha, oho."

6. aham annam aham annam aham annam, aham annadah, aham annadah, aham annadah, aham slokakrit aham slokakrit aham slokakrit, aham asmi prathamaja ritasya, purvam devebhyo, amritasya nabhayi, yo ma dadati sa ideva ma, vah, aham annam annam adantamadmi, aham visvam bhuvanam abhyabhavam, suvarna jyotih, ya evam veda, ityupanisat.

6. I am food, I am food, I am food, I am the eater of food. I am the eater of food. I am the eater of food. I am the binding agent, I am the binding agent, I am the binding agent. I am the first born of the cosmic order, before the gods and the center of Immortality. He who offers me, he alone protects me. He who eats food (without offering), I, as food, eat him. I, as the Supreme Lord, overpower the whole world. I am the golden light like that of the sun. Whosoever knows this (becomes so). This is the secret teaching.

The Peace Chant

aum sa ha nav avatu saha nau bhunaktu saha viryam karavavahai tejasvi nav adhitam astu; ma vidvisavahai; aum, santih, santih, santih.

Aum, may He protect us both; may He nourish us both together; May we both become energetic by working together; may our study illumine (our minds); may there be no hated between us. Aum, peace, peace, peace.

Isavasya Upanishad

Editor's Note

Isa Upanishad or Isavasya Upanishad derives its name from "Isa," the word with which it begins, which means by the Lord, a reference to the Manifested Brahman or Isvara, the Lord of the Universe and the entire creation. It belongs to the 40th chapter of the Vajasaneya Samhita of the White Yajurveda. The Upanishad makes an emphatic declaration that Brahman pervades the whole universe and all this belongs to Him. Hence, we have a claim to enjoyment of life through renunciation, but not to the ownership of the things or our actions. To overcome our ignorance and escape from the darkest hells, we need to know the true nature of our hidden selves and achieve oneness with Brahman. Thus, the Upanishad is theistic in its approach, and foundational to the devotional practices of Hinduism. The verses may even point to a growing tendency in the Vedic tradition to the devotional worship of an unitary, universal and personal God. It also contains prayers for people in the final moments of their dying with supplications to the gods to lead them on the righteous path to the higher worlds, in view of their good deeds.

The following is a revised translation of the Isavasya Upanishad by Jayaram V.

Invocation

aum purnamadah purnamidam purnat purnam udacyate; purnasya purnam adaya purnam eva vasisyate. aum santih santih santih.

Aum! That is full. This also is full. From that full arises this full. Taking the full from the full, the full remains full. Aum, peace, peace, peace.

Notes: Adah, meaning That, refers to Brahman, the soul, transcendental reality, the Sun, heaven and the immortal world. This refers to the phenomenal world, the body and the earth. Purnam means complete, full or satisfied. It is wrongly translated by many as infinite. The Rigvedic Indians considered the Sun as the symbol of Brahman and the world, which housed the abode of the immortals. The sun, which appears as a bright circle in the sky, is the big shining zero high above. It is bright, always full and visible to all. Its power and effulgence is not diminished by the light that comes out of it. It remains full throughout days, months and years, unlike the moon, which wanes and waxes. So is the case with Brahman and His creation. His power is not diminished by the things that are manifested by Him in creation. Everyone shares His power and glory and yet He remains full. He remains full within the worlds He manifests and remains full beyond them also. He is the true inhabitant of everything that we know and do not know. There is nothing we can do or take away from Him. That fullness or infinity exists in each of us also, which cannot be diminished by our thoughts or actions. Therefore, there is not cause for us to be selfish or self-centered.

Technically you can say something is full, only when you know its limits. Brahman is infinite, without a beginning and an end. Therefore, He is indeterminate. However, you can speculate or logically argue that infinity cannot be infinite without being full. You may draw an analogy between Brahman and zero. No other number represents Brahman so perfectly as the zero. Like Brahman, the zero number is both the support for all other numbers and indeterminate. It is the source of all diversity. A zero remains zero, whether you add or subtract anything from it. The zero is both emptiness and fullness. You can fit into it everything and you can add it to anything without altering its value.

This verse is a peace invocation (santimantram). Peace is invoked thrice with the utterance of Aum; first in reference to the Sun where the immortals live; second time in reference to the ancestral world where the ancestors live; and the third time in reference to the earth where the mortals live.

Translation
All This Belongs to Brahman

1. **Aum Isavasyamidam sarvam yatkinca jagatyam jagat; tena tyaktena bhunjitha ma grdhah kasyasvid dhanam.**

1. All this, whatever that moves here in this moving world, is covered by God. Therefore, by renunciation alone is enjoyment. Do not covet, for whose is the wealth?

Notes: Isa means the Lord or God. Jagat means the moving or movable world of ours, the world which is lighted up or awakened by the rays of the sun. It is a reference to the nature of our existence, which is transient and always in a state of churning. Everything in the world is transient. Everything is subject to change. Everything that exists here is also pervaded and enveloped by God. What this means is that we live inside God. We are part of His universal body. He is the womb of this world. Since He is omnipresent, we cannot live outside of Him or without Him. Living inside Him, enveloped by Him and pervaded by Him, we have to depend upon Him for our existence and our wellbeing. He provides food to all earthly beings. He provides breath. He provides bodies and the resources that are necessary for our living and surviving. We may claim ownership of things, but in truth their source is Isvara and He is their true owner. This verse reminds us of this fundamental truth about our existence and correctly suggests that we should not claim ownership of anything, but live with an attitude of detachment and renunciation. We have a moral and religious obligation (dharma) to live here selflessly, doing our duties with devotion and humility as servants of God since He is the provider of everything. We live in Him, depend upon Him and enjoy the things that truly belong to Him. As the true inhabitant of the world, He alone has the claim to enjoy the pleasures of the world. In a world upon which we can make no claim of ownership, a world that does not belong to us however rich and powerful we may be, amidst things that we cannot rightfully claim as ours, there is no better way to live freely than renouncing the world and its things and living with humility, detachment and selflessness.

Covetousness is an obstacle. Claiming what does not belong to you prevents you from achieving liberation. If you claim ownership of things which belong to God, you will be subject to the law of karma and you will suffer from the consequences of claiming what does not belong to you. Therefore the right approach is to give up attachment and the desire for things and life freely in a state of renunciation. *Bhunjita* means protection, eating and enjoyment. All the three meanings are relevant in the context of this verse.

Renunciation is not a rejection of life. It is not some form of morose and lifeless solution meant for a few reclusive people who want to numb their feelings or harden their hearts in search of an antithetic and exhilarating existence. Renunciation is basically a mental practice, which protects you, if you resort to it, from growing roots into your own thinking. It is an attitude of staying free mentally from the things that make you a prisoner of your own mind. Renunciation helps you to remain light and nimble and live freely in the midst of duties and responsibilities. It is the best way to keep your mind and heart free and open to the endless possibilities of life, without fear, guilt, anxiety and uncertainty.

We should not renounce life because of despair or depression arising out of our fears, frustrations or personal failures. You should not take recourse to it because you do not like this world or your obligations. True renunciation arises out of intense longing for the divine, in a state of mind in which attachment to God alone makes sense and in which freedom from want and fearlessness stem from unflinching faith in God and His supreme will. You should do it because you acknowledge God's ownership of it and your sense of morality, which tells you that you should not claim what does not belong to you.

Renunciation is the solution to overcome the problem of karma. Life has to be enjoyed, but without seeking, without coveting, and without struggling to get things done or get things for oneself. It is the renunciation of seeking and of desiring things, which leads to true enjoyment and liberation. In fact, those who renounce the world enjoy life better than those who do not, because they are not troubled by the fear of loss or the possibility of gain. They accept life unconditionally, taking what is given to them and remaining indifferent to what does not happen. This is flowing with the flow, following the Way, or living unconditionally as described in Taoism.

2. kurvanneveha karmani jijivisecchatam samah; evam tvayi nanyatheto'sti na karma lipyate nare.

2. Indeed by doing duty only should there be the wish to live here for a hundred years. For a human being like you, there is no existence other than this by which karma does not cling to you.

Notes: Duty is the reason why we are here. Enjoyment is not the purpose. However, we can enjoy our lives by doing our duties and renouncing our attachments. Enjoyment belongs to the domain of God. All this manifestation is primarily meant for His enjoyment, not for ours. Our duty is to facilitate His enjoyment and make it possible through our selfless and dutiful actions. You have been assigned a role in creation and that role is to enjoy life as an eternal Self through your mind and body by performing selfless actions that are necessary to make that enjoyment possible. True enjoyment belongs to the domain of God. But you can be part of that enjoyment if you center yourself in your eternal Self rather than your mind and body. Those who enjoy their lives considering themselves mere physical beings, without identifying themselves with their inner souls, will become responsible for their actions and suffer from their consequences. This is the simple truth explained several times in many scriptures in various ways. This is also the central theme of the Bhagavadgita. We can take inspiration from this one verse and change our lives in such a way that we can be part of a vast existence and all the enjoyment it offers without being tainted by it.

Human beings cannot avoid their duties. Indeed, mortal or immortal, none can avoid their duties, because in creation everyone has a role and responsibility and certain obligations to fulfill, the purpose of which has already been explained. The same holds true in case of even the tiniest of creatures in the subterranean ground or the laziest of beings in the darkest hells. Today, if you go to some countries, you will find the cities, the towns and the streets filthy. It is because people do not do their part in keeping their streets and surroundings clean. They throw garbage in the streets and public places. If everyone follows the rules and do their part, the world would be a perfect place to live. A country is rich or poor to the extent its people live responsibly doing their part in keeping it prosperous and healthy. The same holds true with regard to our existence in the world and the universe. If we live our lives responsibly, there would be order and regularity in the worlds. There would be peace, prosperity, knowledge and wisdom in every aspect of our lives.

Individually as well as collectively, we have an obligation to perform certain duties to keep the world in good order, such as educating ourselves, performing household duties, protecting our families, giving birth to children and bringing them up, helping others, serving gods and ancestors, and working for our enlightenment. These duties are obligatory, meaning you cannot avoid them, even if they are difficult to perform. They are obligatory because they have been assigned to you by God and you cannot go against His will. If you do, then you will incur karma for the sin of disobeying His command and not doing your duty. The duty is the price you pay to live here upon earth as one of the tenants in the House of God. You cannot be irresponsible when you live in His House. That is what the demons do. Hence, their worlds are always in turmoil and chaos. Our world as well as our lives becomes heavenly or hellish to the extent we perform or ignore our duties. We have a world within each of us and even that is subject to this law.

The duties manifested by God are meant to ensure order and regularity of our lives and establish balance and order in our world. You have duties from God because you are an aspect of God. These are not entrusted to you. They are yours by virtue of your being a divine person. Yet, you will not recognize it as such because of your forgetfulness or what we call delusion. Your duties are meant to keep the worlds going and keep you in harmony and balance with yourself and the world in which you live. Truly speaking, Karma is not a mechanism of punishment, but a way of keeping you in harmony with the environment in which you will feel at home. Evil people, therefore, rest in evil worlds and good people in good worlds. That is the idea. If your actions create confusion, disorder, fear or terror, they will lead you to the darkest hells, because that is where you will find your harmony with others. A snake is safe and comfortable in its little underground hole. A scholar is comfortable in the company of enlightened minds. Gods are comfortable in heaven, and the demons in their hells. Nature does its best to sort things out and put them in their respective compartments to create balance and harmony. Through thoughts and actions you send out a message to the universe what you need and what suits you best and the universe willingly lends you a helping hand in making that available to you. Thus, this verse rightly suggests that we should live responsibly and do our obligatory duties with renunciation and detachment so that we remain in harmony with the divine order established in the entire manifestation and with Brahman Himself.

3. asurya nama te loka andhena tamasa'vrtah; tamste pretyabhigacchanti ye ke catmahano janah.

3. *The worlds of the demons are enveloped in blinding darkness. To them go after departing from the body those who harm themselves.*

Notes: The ideal presented previously was to live dutifully, practicing renunciation. However, what about those who do not follow it? It is answered here. Those who give themselves away to the demons by performing actions for themselves go to the demonic worlds because the demons live for themselves and perform actions solely for their enjoyment. They live selfishly and egoistically, disrespecting the law of God. Since they are filled with the darkness of *tamas* and subject to delusion and ignorance, they abandon their duties in pursuit of their own interests.

The Bhagavadgita lists (16.7-20) the demonic qualities of such people who are cast repeatedly into demonic wombs by God because they are unwilling to change. In today's world, you see a lot of people with the predominance of demonic qualities. They disturb others; they disturb peace; they disturb the world; and they disturb themselves with evil thoughts and perverted actions. They develop so much evil in them that they become inhuman and turn themselves into virtual hells, allowing demonic behavior to take possession of them and dictate their lives and actions.

The demonic people are self-destructive (*atmahana*) because they act indiscriminately against their own spiritual welfare and chances of liberation. In the Bhagavadgita, Lord Krishna says that the self is the friend of the self as well as an enemy of the self. It is a friend when one lives virtuously and an enemy when one acts foolishly and ignorantly. Many people harm themselves and others when they neglect their duties and live irresponsibly. By their irresponsible thoughts and actions, they waste many opportunities to escape from the cycle of births and deaths.

The Transcendental Self

4. anejadekam manaso javiyo nainaddeva apnuvanpurvamarsat taddhavato'nyanatyeti tisthattasminnapo matarisva dadhati.

4. *Unmoving, yet (it is) swifter than the mind. The gods (senses) cannot overtake it because it is always ahead of them. It overruns those who run, remaining seated. Because it is there, the all-pervading Matarisvan supports the activities of beings.*

Notes: The Self is unmoving and unchangeable. Yet it is swifter than the mind because it is everywhere and present wherever the mind goes. Since it is universal and all pervading, it is always ahead of the mind and the senses. So is the case with Brahman in relation to the gods of the heaven. Both remain seated and constant and yet are present everywhere, without moving. Matarisvan is the breath in the body and air in the atmosphere, but Brahman in the entire creation. Like Brahman, both the breath and the air envelop the things they support. By pervading the whole body, breath supports the activities of various bodily parts. By pervading the whole atmosphere, air supports all beings; and by pervading the entire creation, Brahman upholds the worlds and their regularity.

5. tadejati tannaijati taddure tadvantike;tadantarasya sarvasya tadu sarvasya bahyatah.

5. *That moves and That moves not. That is far and That is very near. That is inside of all this and That is also outside of all this.*

Notes: Tat refers to the Self or Brahman in contrast to this (*iha*) meaning the body or this world. "That" is used to denote both because both are indefinable and indistinguishable. The Self is unchangeable and constant, yet in the embodied state it moves from place to place and from one body to another during rebirth. It is far because it is transcendental and beyond the grasp of the mind and the senses. It is also near because it is hidden inside all beings as their very Selves. Inside the body, it is the Witness and the Enjoyer and outside it is the resplendent universal Self. Even mentally, we live in the consciousness of people as images and memories, but when we meet them physically, we are outside of them. The opposite qualities and contradiction of life, which we experience through objectivity and duality represent different facets of life and yet represent a fundamental about our existence upon earth, which is that truth is relative to the context and the standpoint from which it is perceived. For a person who is aware of this paradox, verses such as these make perfect sense; but for those who lack discretion, they may look perplexing and contradictory.

6. yastu sarvani bhutanyatmanyevanupasyati; sarvabhutesu ca'tmanam tato na vijugupsate.

6. *He who sees all beings in himself and himself in all beings does not suffer from any aversion by that experience.*

Notes: You experience attraction and aversion when you have desires and pursue them in your search for fulfillment, peace and happiness. Unfortunately, you will not experience either of these lastingly when you pursue materialistic goals. When you use your senses and rely upon them you are subject to duality and pairs of opposites. You see things differently from yourself and do not experience oneness with creation. However, when you erase the boundaries that separate you from the rest of creation and cultivate a universal vision in which everything becomes a manifestation or extension of yourself, all your seeking and striving will come to an end. When there is nothing else other than you, when everything is an extension of yourself, what else is there for you to seek? If you are in the midst of a deluge, you are not going to seek the water in a well. That is the state of God, which Lord Krishna explains very clearly in the Bhagavadgita, when He says that since He is complete and He is everything, there is nothing that He has to do or not to do, and yet for the sake of the worlds and beings He engages in actions. Cultivating such a universal vision, however, is not easy. It happens only after a prolonged spiritual effort spanning over several life times, when one transcends human limitations and rises above all duality and distinction to see oneself as the Supreme Self. When one reaches this state, one experiences complete cessation of all mental modifications, which leads to peace, stability, equanimity and sameness.

7. yasminsarvani bhutanyatmaivabhudvijanatah; tatra ko mohah kah soka ekatvamanupasyatah.

7. To that person who has realized that all beings have become his very Self what delusion or sorrow can there be, for him who has seen the oneness of all.

Notes: When you find yourself in others, you share their joys and sorrows and stop being selfish or self-centered. Even if your identification is not complete, you will still feel others' pain and empathize with them. When we think about ourselves and our own problems always, even small problems become bigger and our suffering intensifies. Studies in human behavior prove that those who help others have greater chances of experiencing peace and happiness. In feeling the pain of others, our own pain becomes less significant and troublesome. When a yogi sees himself in all and all in himself, he becomes equal to all. That expansive feeling frees him from egoism and delusion, and the suffering that arises from egoistic thinking. The difference between an ordinary person who believes that the physical self is all and an enlightened yogi who see everything as one, lies in their thinking and focus. An ordinary person does not extend his identity beyond his physical personality. He views others as different and in relation to himself. The yogi sees the diversity in life as a manifestation of God and identical to himself. Therefore he does not compete with others for his happiness or desire anything beyond the basic needs of his body. Since he sees himself as the eternal Self , he becomes detached from the dualities of life. However, this happens only when there is sufficient inner transformation and purification of his mind and body.

8. Sa paryagac chukram akayam avranam asnaviram suddham apapaviddham; kavir manisi paribhuh svayambhu yathatathyato'rthan vyadadhac chasvatibhyah samabhyah.

8. He is spread in all directions, bright, without body, without debility, without muscles, pure, untouched by sin, omniscient. The seer, ruler of the mind, the transcendental Lord, self-created, He duly allotted duties to the endless years.

Notes: In the very beginning of creation, Brahman through Brahma assigned duties to all beings including humans. In our case, these duties change with time. Our scriptures identify four stages of human life, namely, studentship (*brahmancarya*), life of a householder (*grihastha*), retirement (*vanaprastha*) and renunciation (*sansyasa*). The Self is untouched by all these. It has no duties. It remains in the body as the enjoyer and witnessing Self without becoming involved with any of the functions and actions of the body. This duality between God and His manifestation, between the Self and the body is suggested here. *Paryagat* means he who travels or moves freely or who is all pervasive. It is in reference to Brahman and His power, which moves freely through the space and manifests as everything in creation. *Sukram* refers to the purity and brilliance of *Saguna* Brahman arising from pure (*suddha*) *sattva*. It refers to the radiance of the Sun, whom the scriptures equate symbolically with Brahman. *Akayam, avranam* and *asnaviram* refer to the transcendental aspect or the absence of body, which is characteristic of Brahman as well as the individual Self. Kavi means the seer or the knower of all. *Manasi* refers to the supreme intelligence, since it rules over the mind. It also refers to the Self, which is considered the Lord (Isvara) of the body. *Svayambhuh* mean self-created or self-existing. It refers to the eternal nature of Brahman, since He is without a beginning and an end.

9. andham tamah pravisanti ye'vidyam upasate; tato bhuya iva te tamo ya u vidyayam ratah,

9. Those who worship knowledge of sacrifices enter into blinding darkness and into greater darkness enter those who worship knowledge of the Self alone.

Notes: Vidya, true knowledge, is the spiritual knowledge of the Self and avidya is that which leads to ignorance and bondage. All material knowledge, including the knowledge of sacrificial ceremonies, falls into this category since they lead to attachments and rebirth. The Vedas are divided into two parts, the ritual part (karmakanda) and the spiritual part (jnanakanda). The Samhitas and the Brahmanas of the Vedas constitute the ritual part. The next two sections, the Aranyakas and the Upanishads, constitute the spiritual part. Corresponding with these two divisions are the two schools of (Darshanas) Hindu philosophy, namely Purva Mimansa and the Uttara Mimansa, also known as Vedanta. The former deals with the rituals and their significance and the latter with the knowledge of the Self and Brahman. The ritual part of the Vedas is lower knowledge. It is considered ignorance (avidya) since it leads to attachment and bondage rather than liberation. This verse states that we must have knowledge of both since both are essential for our liberation. Our obligatory duties during the four stages of our lives are linked to both and require both types of knowledge. Ritual knowledge is important during the first stages, namely studentship and the life of a householder, and spiritual knowledge is important during the next two phases, namely retirement and renunciation. This verse correctly advices us to pursue both types of knowledge since without them we cannot fulfill our obligatory duties. This is the essence of this verse.

What is emphasized here is balance in life. We can neither ignore our worldly responsibilities nor spend our lives entirely in the pursuit of worldly goals. We have to meet our family obligations and once they are done, we have to focus upon our liberation by pursuing the knowledge of the Self. There is a time for both and our scriptures suggested an orderly life divided into four phases for this particular reasons only. Even the four aims of human life, namely dharma, wealth, pleasure and liberation are ordained for us on the basis of this principle only. Neglecting either of them leads to suffering only in the form of bondage and karmic consequences. Renunciation does not mean escape from the material world. Those who do not pursue asceticism, but lead worldly lives should remember this Vedic dictum particularly.

knowledge and Ignorance

10. Anyad evahur vidyaya'nyad ahura vidyaya; iti susruma dhiranam ye nas tad vicacaksire.

10. *Different they say is the result of knowledge of the Self and different they say is the result of the knowledge of sacrifices. Thus, we have heard from the wise men who have explained that (distinction) to us.*

Notes: There are basically two main paths in life, that which leads to wealth and that which leads to knowledge. Both have different implications. Pursuit of wealth by performing sacrifices and other means makes you rich and wealthy; and pursuit of knowledge by studying the scriptures and mastering the knowledge of Self makes you wise and scholarly, but on their own neither of them lead to liberation or permanent peace and happiness. Both may lead to success and happiness upon earth, but by themselves they do not guarantee liberation, unless you use them for a higher purpose. In fact, without proper spiritual foundation, and devoid of a higher purpose they may even lead to pride, arrogance and other evils. One should pursue wealth and knowledge as a part of one's obligatory duties and to establish order and regularity in the world, not for one's own selfish enjoyment. Until they achieve perfection, those who perform sacrificial ceremonies and pursue knowledge as part of their obligatory duties go to the world of ancestors, where their subtle bodies become food to the gods. Once they exhaust their karmas, they return to the earth and take another birth. Thus, life after life, until they are fully transformed, they continue to serve the gods and participate in creation as responsible human beings. The gods want human beings to serve them and feed them continuously, just as we want our domestic animals to serve us and remain under our control. They do not want us to pursue knowledge and achieve liberation because it means fewer people to serve them. Hence, when you pursue knowledge and practice yoga, you will encounter many difficulties on the path. You will have physical and mental discomforts. Your senses and other bodily organs refuse to cooperate with you in the initial stages, until you gain enough control. This is because when you pursue liberation, the gods turn against you and refuse to cooperate with you. However, if you persist, eventually gods will relent and leave you to yourself At the end of the practice, when you reach perfection, you will travel by the path of gods (*devayana*) to the world of immortal and never return. Thus, *karma* and liberation are the two distinct results achieved by human beings by pursuing *avidya* and *vidya* respectively. Our endeavor should be to pursue them both until we achieve liberation.

11. vidyam cavidyam ca yas tad vedobhayam saha; avidyaya mrtyum tirtva vidyaya"mrtam asnute.

11. *He who knows both the knowledge of the Self and the knowledge of sacrifices together crosses death through the knowledge of sacrifices and attains immortality through the knowledge of the Self.*

Notes: To achieve liberation one has to lead a balanced and holistic life. One should pursue both the knowledge of the sacrifices and the knowledge of the Self. In the early stages of life, knowledge of sacrifices and worldly knowledge helps one to perform one's obligatory duties and prepare for the rigors of spiritual life that will come later. All the obligations should be met and all debts should be cleared as far as possible during this phase, which is more or less a preparatory phase. Having taken care of these responsibilities and discharged all obligations, one should then retire from active duty and focus upon one's liberation. According to our tradition, we cannot ignore our duties and we cannot also ignore our liberation. Pursuing knowledge for knowledge sake, ignoring one's duties and obligations is deemed selfish and demonic. It leads to rebirth, bondage and suffering.

12. Andham tamah pravisanti ye'sambhutim upasate; tato bhuya iva te tamo ya u sambhutyam ratah.

12. Into blinding darkness enter those who worship the Unmanifested and into still greater darkness those who take delight in the Manifest.

Notes: Sambhuti means the entire creation, what has manifested or issued forth from Brahman and Nature. The manifested aspect of Nature is part of the manifested aspect of Brahman only. The entire creation is a manifested reality. It is part of Brahman and includes Manifested Brahman, His aspects, Manifested Nature and its aspects, the worlds, the entire pantheon of gods, beings of other worlds, objects, energies and symbols that are used in worship and rituals. All the splendors (*vibhutis*) enumerated in the *Bhagavadgita* fall into this category. Worshippers of the manifest pursue *avidya* or ritual knowledge, since they perform sacrifices and ritual worship in their households or temples as per the procedures established in the scriptures. The body is a manifested aspect,

In contrast, the Self is unmanifested because it is subtle, cannot be perceived and free from duality. *Asambhuti* means that which has not happened, manifested, become, come into existence in the world or differentiated into existence. It includes both the unmanifested Brahman and the unmanifested primordial Nature. The individual Self, the Supreme Self and the primordial Nature in which aspects are not differentiated are unmanifested. Asambhuti also means that which has not become, differentiated, activated or not entered into a state of beingness. Becoming and unbecoming, manifesting and not manifesting, creation and dissolution, these are the twin aspects of life or fundamental modifications of existence. Death is a temporary unbecoming because it does not destroy everything concerning life. In death, past life karmas, dominant desires and latent impressions are carried forward to the next life. Therefore, death does not qualify as a true unbecoming, but certainly, liberation is. There is another interpretation, the one suggested by Shankara. According to this, sambhuti means Nature and asambhuti means the Supreme Self.

All the gods, ancestors, animals, spirits and other beings in all the worlds constitute the manifest. According to this verse, one should not worship names and forms ritually, ignoring the internal worship of Brahman or the pursuit of Self. Worshippers of manifested Brahman through rituals and sacrifices remain bound to the world as they cannot overcome their ignorance, delusion and duality. Worshippers of the unmanifested Brahman, who do not perform their obligatory duties, will not attain immortality as they incur the sin of neglecting their duties and the gods. Both are therefore equally important.

13. Anyad evahuh sambhavad anyad ahur asambhavat; iti susruma dhiranam ye nastad vicacaksire.

13. Different they say is the result from the Manifested and different they say is the result from the Unmanifested. Thus, we heard from the wise who explained that to us.

Notes: Just as the methods of worship are different, the results arising from two aspects of existence are also different. Not all methods of worship are effective. Some may even harm us. In the Bhagavadgita, Lord Krishna declares firmly that those who worship the gods go to them while those who worship Him come to Him only. He also states that even when people do not worship Him directly, He stabilizes their faith in the objects of worship they choose. Here, the verse states that the results arising from the worship of the manifested and the unmanifested are different.

Those who worship the manifested aspects of God, such as the gods and celestial beings, through rituals and sacrifices obtain, wealth, peace, powers, boons and the blessings from them. Upon their death they go to the world of ancestors and where they exhaust their karmas and return to the earth to take another birth. However, those who pursue Brahman and the Self through the practice of yoga, attain liberation. However, as the Bhagavadgita declares, painful is the path of those who worship the unmanifested.

14. sambhutim ca vinasam ca yas tad vedobhayam saha; vinasena mrtyum tirtva sambhutya amrtam asnute.

14. He who understands both the manifest and the destruction together, through destruction crosses death and through the manifest attains immortality.

Notes: Whatever advise that is given here and in the preceding verses is not for the ascetics, but for those who lead worldly lives and go through the four stages of human life. During the first two stages, they should pursue the ritual and spiritual knowledge of the Vedas and worship the deities through rituals and sacrifices. During the next two stages, they should focus on the spiritual teachings of the Vedas and practice detachment and renunciation, keeping their minds firmly fixed upon Brahman or Atman. Thus by following both ritual knowledge and spiritual knowledge and worshipping both the deities and the Self, they succeed in attaining the four goals of human life, namely righteousness, wealth, pleasure, and liberation. This is the holistic life, which prescribed for a devout Hindu who is interested in meeting his obligations and attaining liberation.

The Prayers of a Dying Person

15. hiranmayena patrena satyasyapihitam mukham; tat tvam pusannapavrnu satyadharmaya drstaye.

15. The face of Truth is concealed by a golden vessel. That you Pusan please remove so that I who love truth and duty may see it.

Notes: This is a prayer to the Sun, Pusan, by a person who has spent his whole life, until the end, performing obligatory duties and abiding by truth. Only those who are dutiful and truthful qualify for the world of Brahman, located in the Sun. Pusan is addressed here as That (tat tvam Pusan), meaning Brahman. He is the golden vessel (hirnmayi patra), in which is hidden the immortal world, and to which only the truthful and dutiful beings, such as the one who is praying here, can go. This is a prayer made by a person on the deathbed. He is requesting the Sun to open the doors of the immortal world so that he may enter into that radiant world and attain liberation. Alternatively, he is also requesting the Sun to reveal Himself from behind the radiant disc and show him the way to that world. The golden vessel may also mean the heart, or the subtle body, in which the Self is hidden. Ordinarily, the Self cannot be seen until the mind and body are completely purified and transformed with selfless actions and liberating knowledge, letting the brilliance of the soul shine through.

16.Pusann ekarse yama surya prajapatya vyuha rasmin samuha tejah; yat te rupam kalyanatamam tat te pasyami yo'savasau purusah so'hamasmi.

16. *O Pusan, O one traveler, O controller, O Sun, O son of Prajapati, remove your rays, withdraw your vigorous heat, so that I may see your most benign and auspicious form. The person who is there in the Sun, that I am also.*

Notes: The dying person is now requesting the Sun to show him his most benign form so that he can enter His world without getting burned. Sinners cannot enter the world of Brahman, just as darkness cannot take refuge in the Sun. Besides, the Sun does not yield the path to them as they have unfinished work upon earth. Only those who have become pure and resplendent like the Sun, with the predominance of sattva, are qualified to enter His world. They are the one who possess both ritual knowledge (avidya) and spiritual knowledge (vidya) and who worship both the manifested and the unmanifested aspects of Brahman. Through the study of the scriptures and the practice of yoga, they know that the light hidden in them is the same as the light that they see high above in the sky. For an ordinary person, the sun is a mere planet or a shining disc. He cannot even look at the sun during the day without burning his eyes. The dying person who has spent his whole life pursuing truth and doing his duties, has come to the conviction that the Sun is indeed his destination upon death and he is qualified to reach Him. Why is he qualified? It is because, he has realized his oneness with Him. Therefore, he affirmed this fact to Pusan (so'ham asmi) and requested Him to make his journey easier by withdrawing his rays and reducing his vigor.

17. vayur anilam amrtam athedam bhasmantam sariram; aum krato smara krtam smara krato smara krtamsmara.

17. *May this breath reach the immortal breath! Now, let this body end in ashes. Aum, O mind remember, remember what has been done. O mind remember, remember what has been done.*

Notes: This is not a prayer under ordinary circumstances. This is prayer uttered for the sake of a dying person by a person well versed in the Vedas. He is requesting the gods to separate the soul from the body and return the body to its elements, breath to breath, and body to ashes. At the same he is asking the departing soul to remember all the good deeds that he has done upon earth during his lifetime, because the memories with which one leaves the world is important. This is a very solemn prayer for a soul on the verge of departure from the body. It is preparing the soul for its ascent to the next world. Cremation is the final sacrifice in the life of a mortal being in which the body is sacrificed as an offering to the gods in return for ensuring a safe passage to the soul to reach the next world.

18. agne naya supatha raye asman visvani deva vayunani vidvan; Yuyodhyasmaj juharanam eno bhuystham te nama-uktim vidhema.

18. *O Agni, O god, knower of all our thoughts and deeds, lead us along the auspicious path by virtue of the fruit of our good karma. Remove from us all crooked and deceitful sins. We offer you many words of obeisance.*

Notes: The body is now on the funeral pyre and the fire is lit. The soul has left the body and is now ready to go to the next world. The worshippers are requesting Agni, the fire god to lead him by the auspicious path that goes to the immortal world. The death of that person is a reminder to others that one should live dutifully and truthfully and stay away from crooked and deceitful actions. One has died and gone. The others have to remember that death is going to happen to all of them sooner or later and they must be prepared for that. Therefore, they are praying for proper guidance to escape from the consequences of their actions, so that when the time comes they too can travel by the immortal path to the world of Brahman. The last three verses of this Upanishad are uttered during the funeral rites. The prayers by themselves may not guarantee a place for everyone in the world of Brahman because of individual karmas and past life impressions. However, they certainly provide solace to the descendents of the departed and give them a chance to think about their own lives and the need to stay on the path of righteousness.

Katha Upanishad

Editor's Note

The Katha Upanishad or the Kathakopanishad is an important and major Upanishad in our understanding of Hinduism. It has great philosophical and spiritual significance. The Upanishad is also important to understand the gradual evolution of Upanishadic philosophy and the effort of the Vedic seers to grapple with the problem of death and its value to human life. The Upanishad presently belongs to the Tattiriya section of the Yajurveda. However, prior to that, it formed part of the Kathaka school of the Black Yajurveda. Some scholars also believe that for some time the Upanishad might have been part of the Samaveda and even Atharvaveda.

As the name implies, the Upanishad presents a story (katha) in the form of a significant conversation between Naciketas, a young Brahmana boy sacrificed by his father to Death, and Lord Yama, the Lord of death, on life, death and liberation. Upon being gifted to Yama by his father, Naciketas proved to Yama that he was worthy of learning the higher knowledge to overcome rebirth. In three chapters, Lord Yama taught him the mysteries of life and death and the means to immortality.

You will find in it some early concepts of Hinduism, including a reference to yoga. More importantly, the Upanishad deals with the important subject of Death, how to understand it, how we may deal with it and how we may overcome it. It has 118 verses divided into three chapters and six sections. The legend upon which the Upanishad is based is probably more ancient than the Upanishad itself; and the Upanishad itself might have been a remnant of a previous Upanishad, probably dating back to the Rigveda. It is believed that its original version was lost or forgotten and later recovered. Hence some of its symbolism is too cryptic to understand. A reference to the story of Naciketas is found in the Rigveda itself.

The following is a translation of the Upanishad by Jayaram V

Invocation

sa ha nav avatu saha nau bhunaktu saha viryam karavavahai tejasvi nav adhitam astu; ma vidvisavahai; ai, santih, santih, santih.

May He protect us both; may He nourish us both together; may we both become energetic by working together; may our study illumine (our minds); may there be no hatred between us. Aum, peace, peace, peace.

Notes: This is a peace invocation chanted by both the teacher and his student at the beginning and often at the end of a teaching session. A peaceful mind is essential for learning and practicing yoga. From knowledge comes peace and from peace comes liberation. In this invocation, both teacher and his students pray for unity, harmony, knowledge and illumination. In the welfare of the teacher lies the welfare of the students and vice versa. A teacher benefits from the merit of good teaching and the service he renders to the divine cause, when his students acquire knowledge and themselves serve the cause of dharma. It is through teacher-student relationship that spiritual knowledge is preserved and propagated from generation to generation. Hence, it makes sense that both the teacher and student should pray together and seek the blessings of God.

Chapter 1

Section 1

Naciketas' Death and Journey to Yama's World

1. Aum, usan ha vai vajasravasah sarvavedasam dadau; tasya ha naciketa nama putra asa.

1. Aum, out of desire, Vajasravasa gave away all he had. He had a son whose name was Naciketas.

Notes: Vajasravasa performed the sacrifice not as an obligatory duty or as a sacrificial action, but out of desires for the fruit of the sacrifice. He gave away his wealth out of desire. Therefore, it was not a charitable act in the true sense of the word.

2. tam ha kumaram santam daksinasu niyamanasu sraddha vivesa so'manyata

2. As the gifts were being carried away, faith (sincerity) entered into him who was still in his early adolescence; he thought.

3. pitodaka jagdhatrna dugdhadoha nirindriyah; ananda nama te lokastan sa gacchati ta dadat.

3. They (the cows) have done drinking water, eating grass, and giving milk and they are without vitality and energy. Joyless are the worlds to which goes he who gives away such (worthless cows) in charity.

Notes: Naciketas, the son of Vajasravasa, was pained by the selfishness of his father, who chose to give away in charity some old and almost lifeless cows rather than young and healthy ones. Giving old cows meant, those who received them would be burdened with the responsibility of looking after them even though they were useless, because it was customary for a Brahmana not to kill the cows or get rid of them. In other words, Vajasravasa's act of charity was not a true charity but a ploy to get rid of worthless cattle and avoid the inconvenience of looking after them in their old age. Ideally, he should have given worthy gifts. Therefore, Naciketas was concerned that his father might incur the sin of committing an uncharitable act.

4. sa hovaca pitaram tata kasmai mam dasyasiti; dvitiyam trtiyam tam hovaca mrtyave tva dadamiti

4. He said, "Father, to whom will you gift me for servitude? He (said it) twice or thrice. He (father) said, "To death I will give you."

Notes: By asking the same question twice or thrice, Naciketas angered his father, who was busy otherwise as the host of the sacrifice. Vajasravasa's decision to sacrifice his son was not probably spontaneous or impulsive. He might have already decided to sacrifice him as part of an ancient custom. The story belonged to a period during which human sacrifices (naramedha yajna) were not uncommon. In fact, the very concept of bhakta, meaning a devotee, is rooted in human sacrifices. Originally, a bhakta was offered in a sacrificial ceremony as an offering (food) while the deity, to whom he was offered was the bhokta or the enjoyer of the sacrifice.

5. bahunamemi prathamo bahunamemi madhyamah;kim svidyamasya kartavyam yanmayadya karisyati

5. Among many I stand first; among many I stand in the middle. What duty towards Yama does my father intend to accomplish by my giving away?

Notes: Among many I stand first means among the adult or the older people I stand first. Among the many I stand in the middle means among the younger and the older, I stand in the middle. The comparison may also be with regard to knowledge, intelligence, sincerity, or purity. The thought occurred to him because Naciketas saw his father giving away worthless, old cows. It made sense to see a man given to empty rituals giving away worthless things in charity; but it made no sense to his son why the same person would give away in sacrifice his own son, who was neither old nor worthless. Therefore, Naciketas was perplexed by his father's decision.

6. anupasya yatha purve pratipasya tathapare; sasyamiva martyah pacyate sasyamivajayate punah

6. See how the ancestors lived before and those who came after them. A mortal being dies and decays like corn and is reborn again like corn.

Notes: These words show that young Naciketas was thinking beyond his age and intelligence. Vajasrava might be a selfish father, but he did not seem to have ignored the education of his son. It prepared him well for both death and liberation. It seems as these words imply, the thought of death did not frighten him. It was as if he was prepared for the moment and determined to see death as a passing phase in the recurring cycle of births and deaths. He thought that just as his ancestors went through the cycle of deaths and rebirths, he too would die and would be reborn again. Thus, mentally he prepared himself for the coming of death, accepting it as a recurring phenomenon like the ripening of corn year after year.

7. vaisvanarah pravisatyatithirbrahmano grhan; tasyaitam santim kurvanti hara vaivasvatodakam

7. A Brahmana guest enters the house like Vaisvanarah fire. To cool him down, O son of Vaivasvan, bring him water.

Notes: We have no account of how Naciketas died and went to the world of Yama. We have to presume that he somehow died after his father's decision and reached that world. There the attendants asked Yama, the Lord of the Death, to honor the Brahmana boy, who had come to their house as a guest. When he entered that place, the subtle body of Naciketas dazzled with the purity of sattva. In the darkness of hell it must have shined even more brilliantly, drawing the attention of the attendants to his presence. Seeing him, they were concerned that his brilliance might set the place ablaze. Therefore, they implored Lord Yama, to cool him down with water and treat him like a houseguest rather than a sinner. Even in hell the rules of dharma had to be observed and as per norms a houseguest should be well treated like God Himself. These words of the attendants clearly show that Naciketas was meant to stay in the world of Yama as a guest only for a short time, not as a sinner in which case his stay would have commiserated with his sins. Our scriptures suggest that pious men, who have lived virtuously and performed good deeds may still go to hell on their way to heaven to wash off their old and unresolved sins. Naciketas was clearly destined to go to the ancestral heaven, but on his way he had to spend some time with Death because his father offered him in a sacrifice to Death only.

8. asapratikse samgatam sunrtam cestapurte putrapasumsca sarvan; etad vrnkte purusasyalpamedhaso yasyanasnan vasati brahmano grhe.

8. All his hopes and expectations, all the merit gained by coming into contact with the pious, good speech, good deeds, all his sons and cattle are destroyed for a man of low intelligence, in whose house a Brahmana dwells as a guest of honor without food.

9. tisro ratriryadavatsirgrhe me"nasnan brahman na tithirnam asyah; namaste'stu brahman svasti me'stu tasmatprati trinvaranvrnisva

9. O Brahmana, since you have spent three nights in my house without food, you being a guest of honor and venerable, salutations to you and let good accrue to me by this (expiation). Ask for three boons, one for each (i.e. each night I failed to honor you).

10. santasamkalpah sumana yatha syad vitamanyurgautamo mabhi mrtyo tvatprasrstam mabhivadetpratita etat trayanam prathamam varam vrne.

10. May my father become peaceful in his thoughts without anxiety for the fruit of his actions, pleasant minded and without anger towards me;

and when I am freed by you, may he recognize me and greet me warmly. O Yama, this is the boon I choose as the first out of the three.

Notes: Even in death, Naciketas did his duty as a son towards his father. He kept no ill will towards him even though he sacrificed him to Death. Instead, he requested Yama to transform him into good person. He also desired to return to the same family in his next birth as the son of Vajasravas and that his father should recognize him and treat him well.

11. yatha purastad bhavita pratita auddalakirarunir matp-rasrstah; sukham ratrih sayita vitamanyustvam dadrsivan mrt-yu mukhat pramuktam

11. As before he will be (with affection), your father Auddalaka Aruni, by my will, when he recognizes you. When he happens to see you freed from the face of death, he will be free from anger and he will rest happily in the night.

12. svarge loke na bhayam kimcanasti na tatra tvam na jaraya bibheti ubhe tirtvasanayapipase sokatigo modate svargaloke.

12. In heaven, there is no fear at all, (because) you (death) are not there; and no one is terribly afraid of old age. Transcending both hunger and death, and leaving behind sorrow, one rejoices in the heavenly world.

13. sa tvamagnim svargyamadhyesi mrtyo prabruhi tvam sraddadhanaya mahyam svargaloka amrtatvam bhajanta etad dvitiyena vrne varena

13. Since, you, O Death, know that fire which leads to heaven, and those in the heaven attain immortality, speak to me, who is endowed with the wealth of faith, of that fire. This I have chosen as my second boon.

14. pra te bravimi tadu me nibodha svargyamagnim naciketah prajanan anantalokaptimatho pratistham viddhi tvametam nihitam guhayam

14. Listen to me and understand, O Naciketas, with attention, as I declare to you that very fire that leads to heaven, which I know well. That fire, which is the means to attain the infinite world and which is also the foundation (of all), know that it is hidden in the secret cave (of the heart).

15. lokadim agnim tam uvaca tasmai ya istaka yavatir va yatha va sa capi tat pratyavadad yathoktam athasya mrtyuh punar evaha tustah

15. *To him he (Yama) spoke about the fire and the beginning of the world, what type and number of bricks (were required for the altar of fire sacrifice), and how they should be arranged. And he (Naciketas) repeated them exactly as he was told. Then, Death being satisfied (with the response) said again.*

Note: Either the teacher of this Upanishad intentionally kept out the details of the fire sacrifice which Yama taught to Naciketas, due to their intricate nature or the knowledge was lost. The version of the Katha Upanishad which we have is said to be a condensed form of an ancient and lost Upanishad, which might be as old as the Rig-Veda. The sacrifice was probably an ancient ritual or some kind of Agnicayana sacrifice.

16. tam abravit priyamano mahatma varam tavehadya dadami bhuyah tavaiva namna bhavitayam agnih srnkam cemamane-karupam grhana

16. *His mind filled with appreciation, the great soul spoke to him, "Now, I give you another boon. Henceforth, the fire will be known by your name. Also, accept this chain of multiple forms."*

Notes: Lord Yama made Naciketas' name immortal by naming an important fire sacrifice after him. He also gave him a chain of multiple forms to signify his conquest of death. Mortal beings are chained to death. Lord Yama is a wielder of chains (yama pasas) with which he binds the sinners at the time of their death and drags them fiercely to the gates of hell. By giving Naciketas one of the chains (srnkam) he gave him a commanding power over rescuing the sinners from hell itself.

17. trinaciketas tribhir etya sandhim trikarmakrt tarati janma mrtyu brahmajajnam devam idyam viditva nicayyemam santim atyantam eti

17. *Through the three fires of Naciketa, threefold union and threefold work, one crosses over birth and death. Knowing Him who is born of Brahman, the radiant and adorable deity, and realizing him, he attains endless peace.*

Notes: We do not know what Naciketa fires actually signify, since the teacher of the Upanishad left out the details of the fire sacrifice taught by Yama to Naciketa. Whatever sacrifice Yama taught to Naciketa went by the name Naciketa fire. Sankara interpreted it as one who knows Naciketa fire, studies it and practices it. He also interpreted the union with the three as union with father, mother and teacher; and, alternatively, as union with the knowledge of the Vedas, Smritis and wise men. He mentioned the three types of work as sacrifice, study and charity.

18. trinaciketas trayam etad viditva ya evam vidvams cinute naciketam sa mrtyupasan puratah pranodya sokatigo modate svargaloke.

18. *After knowing the three and making offerings thrice to the Naciketa fires, having known thus and made the offerings to Naciketa fires, he*

casts off the snares of death, and leaving sorrow behind, rejoices in heaven.

19. esa te'gnir naciketah svargyo yam avrnitha dvitiyena varena etam agnim tavaiva pravaksyanti janasas trtiyam varam naciketo vrnisva

19. This is the fire, O Naciketas, which leads to heaven, which you have chosen for your second boon. This fire people will speak of as yours indeed. O Naciketas, you can now ask for the third boon.

20. yeyam prete vicikitsa manusye'stity eke nayam astiti caike etad vidyam anusistas tvayaham varanam esa varas trtiyah.

20. There is this doubt when a man dies. Some say, he is; and some say, he is not. I want to be instructed in this knowledge by you. This is the third in the boons (you have offered me).

Notes: Naciketas was aware that a man would be born again after death; but he did not know the condition in which the soul exists, that is whether it exists with its distinction and individuality or not. He had this doubt because he heard about both possibilities from others.

21. devairatrapi vicikitsitam pura na hi suvijneyam anuresa dharmah anyam varam naciketo vrnisva ma moparotsir ati ma srjainam.

21. Even the gods had doubt about this in the past. Indeed, incomprehensible is the nature of this (Self), being subtle. Ask for another boon, O Naciketas. Do not press me further. Release me from this (obligation).

22. devair atrapi vicikitsitam kila tvam ca mrtyo yan na suvijneyam attha; vakta casya tvadrganyo na labhyo nanyo varastulya etasya kascit.

22. Even the gods, indeed, had doubt about this; and you say, O Yama, that it is not easily understood. Also, I am not going to have another excellent teacher like you. Therefore, for me there is no other boon that is equal.

23. satayusah putrapautran vrnisva bahun pasun hasti hiranyamasvan; bhumer mahadayatanam vrnisva svayam ca jiva sarado yavad icchasi.

23. Ask for sons and grandsons each having a life span of hundred years, many cattle, elephants, gold and horses. Ask for an expansive stretch of land and a life for yourself for as many years as you wish.

Note: Knowledge of the Self cannot be given unless one has overcome attachment to worldly objects. Lord Yama tested Naciketas by tempting him with this offer to see whether he could be distracted by it.

24. etat tulyam yadi manyase varam vrnisva vittam cirajivikam ca; mahabhumau naciketas tvam edhi kamanam tva kama bhajam karomi

24. If you think of any boon that is equal to this, ask for it. Ask for wealth and long life. O Naciketas, become the ruler of a large land. I make you an enjoyer of all desires.

25. ye ye kama durlabha martyaloke sarvan kamams chandatah prarthayasva. ima ramah sarathah saturya na hidrsa lambhaniya manusyaih. abhir matprattabhih paricarayasva naciketo maranam manupraksih.

25. All such enjoyments that are hard to attain in this mortal world, ask for them at your will. Here are the most beautiful maidens with chariots and musical instruments who are hard to win by men. Let yourself be entertained by these, whom I am offering you. However, O Naciketas, do not ask about (overcoming) death.

26. svobhava martyasya yad antakaitat sarvendriyanam jarayanti tejah; api sarvam jivitam alpam eva tavaiva vahas tava nrtyagite.

26. Transient, O Death, are these; besides, they wear away the vigor of a man's organs. All life, indeed, is short. Let yours be the chariots and yours be the singing and dancing.

27. na vittena tarpaniyo manusyo lapsyamahe vittam adraksma cet tva; jivisyamo yavad isisyasi tvam varastu me varaniyah sa eva.

27. Man cannot be happy with wealth alone. Now that we have seen you, we possess wealth, and live as long as you rule over us. That alone is the boon chosen by me that is worth asking for.

28. ajiryatam amrtanam upetya jiryan martyah kvadhahsthah prajanan; abhidhyayan varnaratipramodan atidirghe jivite ko rameta.

28. After coming into the presence of the imperishable and immortal beings, which perishable mortal person who lives upon the earth below, having realized the true nature of music, lovemaking and earthly joys, will take delight in a long life?

Notes: The meaning is this. After seeing the transience of worldly pleasure and Death himself face to face, which person will take delight in a mortal life that is not going to last forever even if it is long and that is not going to offer permanent peace.

29. yasminn idam vicikitsanti mrtyo yat samparaye mahati bruhi nas tat yo'yam varo gudham anupravisto nanyam tasman naciketa vrnite.

29. Of that about which people have this doubt, O Death, tell us, even that which leads to the great hereafter. Naciketas does not choose any boon other than this boon, which goes deep into this hidden secret.

Section 2

The Two Paths

1. anyac chreyo'nyad utaiva preyaste ubhe nanarthe purusam sinitah; tayoh sreya adadanasya sadhu bhavati hiyate'rthadya u preyo vrnite.

1. Different, indeed, is that which arises from the excellent and different also that which arises from the pleasant. Both bind a person for different reasons. Of them, good happens to him who resorts to virtuous deeds; but he who resorts to pleasures falls from the ultimate goal of life.

Notes: Sreyah is the good which arises from performing obligatory duties with detachment and as a sacrificial offering. It is the highest and the most excellent of all the states we are supposed to pursue in life as householders. In contrast, those who indulge in pleasures for selfish enjoyment (preyah) may achieve wealth (artha) and pleasure (kama), but they fail to achieve the highest goal (purushartha) which is liberation.

2. sreyas ca preyas ca manusyam etas tau samparitya vivinakti dhirah; sreyo hi dhiro'bhi preyaso vrnite preyo mando yogaksemad vrnite.

2. Both the excellent and the pleasant approach a human. The wise one, having considered them carefully, discerns. The wise one chooses the excellent instead of the pleasant; but the dull minded chooses the pleasant for his material and physical wellbeing.

Notes: Which is better, the actions which lead to liberation or the ones which lead to earthly joys and pleasures. From a spiritual perspective, it is the former. However, the deluded ones choose the latter as they lack discrimination.

3. sa tvam priyan priyarupams ca kaman abhidhyayan naciketo'tyasraksih; naitam srnkam vittamayim avapto yasyam majjanti bahavo manusyah.

3. *You Naciketas have discarded the desirable things that are pleasant and seemingly delightful, having studied them carefully. You have not resorted to the path of wealth by which people come to grief.*

4. duramete viparite visuci avidya ya ca vidyeti jnata; vidya-bhipsinam naciketasam manye na tva kama bahavo'lolupanta.

4. *These two are widely different and divergent, which are known as ignorance and knowledge. I consider you, O Naciketas, to be desirous of knowledge as you are not tempted by the desire for many pleasures.*

5. avidyayam antare vartamanah svayam dhirah panditam manyamanah; dandramyamanah pariyanti mudha andhenaiva niyamana yathandhah.

5. *Those who dwell in ignorance, considering themselves wise and learned, go round and round along crooked paths, with their minds deluded, like blind men led by the blind.*

6. na samparayah pratibhati balam pramadyantam vitta-mohena mudham; ayam loko nasti para iti mani punah punar vasam apadyate me.

6. *The other world is not revealed to the callow person who is careless and deluded by material wealth. This is the only world, the other does not exist, thinking thus, they fall repeatedly under my control.*

Notes: You will find an echo of the Bhagavadgita in this verse.

7. sravanayapi bahubhir yo na labhyah srnvanto'pi bahavo yam na vidyuh; ascaryo vakta kusalo'sya labdha'scaryo jnata kusalanusistah

7. *Many do not get even to hear about it. Even those who have heard about it, do not get to know it. It is a wonder to find a person who can speak about it proficiently or who can attain it. It is a wonder to know about it from a knower who is proficient in its instruction.*

8. na narenavarena prokta esa suvijneyo bahudha cintyamanah ananya-prokte gatir atra nasty aniyan hyatarkyam anupramanat.

8. *A person without the purity of sattva cannot speak about it. Nor can it be understood since it is contemplated variously and spoken variously. Other than with the help of the one who has reached it, there is no other way (it can be understood), for it is beyond reason and it is subtle than the subtler.*

9. naisa tarkena matir apaneya proktanyenaiva sujnanaya prestha: yam tvam apah satyadhrtir batasi tvadrn no bhuyan naciketah prasta.

9. It is not attained mentally by reasoning. Only when spoken to you, my dear, by a different person (who has attained it without reasoning) you will know it well. By abiding in truth steadfastly you have attained it. May I always find a (truthful and resolute) questioner like you.

10. janamy aham sevadhir ity anityam, na hy adhruvaih prapyate hi dhruvam tat; tato maya naciketas cito'gnir anityair drav-yaih praptavan asmi nityam.

10. I know this treasure (of material wealth) is impermanent. Not through the unstable is the stable is reached. Therefore, with the burnt remains of the Naciketa fire made by me with the impermanent offerings (I have dropped into the sacrifice), I have attained the eternal.

Notes: Naciketas renounced worldly pleasures and worldly treasures, which he deemed impermanent. By offering those impermanent things, that is by renouncing them, in the sacrifice of life, he attained the eternal. According to Shankara, Naciketas did not perform the Naciketa fire sacrifice yet. Therefore these words were spoken by Yama himself, not by Nackietas.

11. kamasyaptim jagatah pratistham krator anantyam abhayasya param stomam mahadurugayam pratistham drstva dhrtya dhiro naciketo'tyasraksih.

11. By ending the desires by which the world is supported and which lead to endless fruit of actions, having seen fearless, praiseworthy, extensive and well established, transcendental (Self), O wise Naciketas, you have firmly renounced (the pleasant).

12. tam durdarsam gudham anupravistam guhahitam gahvarestham puranam adhyatmayogadhigamena devam matva dhiro harsasokau jahati.

12. Concentrating upon the inner Self with his senses withdrawn, and contemplating upon that deity who is hard to see, deeply hidden, inaccessible, lodged in the cave (of the heart), and dwelling in the (body which is the) abyss of misery, the wise one, renounces both joy and sorrow.

13. etac chrutva samparigrhya martyah pravrhya dharmyam anumetam; apya sa modate modaniyam hi labdhva vivrtam sadma naciketasam manye

13. *Having heard this, grasped the knowledge, detached from the body, abiding in duty, and having attained this subtle one, the (enlightened) mortal being rejoices since he has attained that which is worth rejoicing. I think that the house of Brahman is wide open for Naciketas.*

Notes: The stages in the realization of the Self are described here. It begins with hearing the knowledge from a self-realized teacher, then comes the understanding of it through study and contemplation, and then comes the practice of detachment and duties with sacrificial attitude. In the end, comes the happy and blissful union with the Self. The Self is blissful and union with it results in freedom from sorrow and the cycle of births and deaths. Hence the occasion is worth rejoicing. The world of Brahman is open only to those who have realized their true Selves. Naciketas reached this austere goal. Hence he was very much qualified for entering the world of Brahman.

14. anyatra dharmad anyatra dharmad anyatrasmat krtakrtat; anyatra bhutacca bhavyacca yat tat pasyasi tad vada

14. *Other than duty, other than not performing duty, other than what is done, different from what is not done, and other than the past and future, whatever that you see please tell me.*

Notes: Naciketas wanted to know how to realize the Self or Brahman by means other than the traditionally known ones.

15. sarve veda yat padam amananti tapamsi sarvani ca yadvadanti; yad icchanto brahmacaryam caranti tatte padam samgrahena bravimy aum ity etat.

15. *That attainable goal which all the Vedas declare, for that which all the austerities are said to be, desiring which celibacy is practiced, I will speak to you in brief of that goal. Aum, it is.*

16. etad hy evaksaram brahma etadd hy evaksaram param etadd hy evaksaram jnatva yo yad icchati tasya tat.

16. *Indeed this syllable is Brahman only. This syllable is the most supreme. By knowing this syllable, whatever is desired that is fulfilled.*

17 etad alambanam srestham etad alambanam param; etad alambanam jnatva brahmaloke mahiyate.

17. *This support is the best. This support is the highest. Knowing this support one becomes great in the world of Brahman.*

Notes: Aum is the support.

18 na jayate mriyate va vipascin nayam kutascin na babhuva kascit; ajo nityah sasvato'yam purano na hanyate hanyamane sarire.

18. The intelligent one does not take birth and does not die. He does not arise from anything and nothing arises from him. He is unborn, eternal, permanent and ancient. He is not slain even when the body is slain.

19. hanta cen manyate hantum hatas cen manyate hatam; ubhau tau na vijanito nayam hanti na hanyate

19. If the killer thinks he kills, or if the killed thinks that he has been killed, both do not know (the true nature of Self). This one does not kill, nor is it killed.

Notes: This is similar to the verse presented in the Bhagavadgita regarding the nature of the Self.

20. anor aniyan mahato mahiyan atmasya jantor nihito guhayam; tam akratuh pasyati vitasoko dhatuprasadan mahiman amatmanah.

20. Subtler than the subtle, greater than the great, the Self of a living being is deeply hidden in the cave (of the heart). The inactive one watches Him, free from sorrow, with the organs of his body at rest, (beholding) the glory of the Self.

Notes: Akrtah in the context of a householder means he who does not perform desire-ridden actions and in the context of an ascetic who has renounced worldly life, it means he who does not perform any willful actions. In both cases the implication is that actions are free from the fruit of karma.

21. asino duram vrajati sayano yati sarvatah; kastam madamadam devam madanyo jnatum arhati.

21. Seated he goes far. Resting he goes everywhere. Who, except me, is qualified to know that Deity who is both with joy and without joy?

Notes: The Self is seated in the body, but he goes wherever the body goes, and as the enjoyer, wherever the senses go. In a resting person, the Self is active either dreaming or astral travelling. Hence, as this verse states, resting he goes everywhere. Lastly, who can know the Self except oneself? You alone can know your Self. Others may know you physically or mentally but they do not know your true Self, until they find their own true Selves.

22. asariram sariresu anavasthesv avasthitam; mahantam vibhum atmanam matva dhiro na socati;

22. Knowing the Self as the one without a body in the body, seated in the unstable, great, and all pervading, the wise one does not grieve.

Notes: There is sorrow for him who identifies himself with his mind and body. Since both are unstable, perishable and subject to desires and dualities, he is bound to suffer from fear and insecurity. When one realizes that the mind and body are mere vehicles for the Self, and knows the true nature of Self as infinite and eternal, one is instantly freed from all mental modifications.

23. nayam atma pravacanena labhyo na medhaya na bahuna srutena; yamevaisa vrnute tena labhyas tasyaisa atma vivrnute tanum svam.

23. *The Self is not attained by preaching, nor by intellect, nor by listening to the Vedas. He is attained only by him whom the Self chooses. To him, the Self reveals its own nature.*

24. navirato duscaritan nasanto nasamahitah; nasantamanaso vapi prajnanenainam apnuyat

24. *Not by the one who has not turned away from evil conduct, whose senses are not in restful mode, whose mind is not collected, whose mind is not restful, can this be attained even by higher knowledge.*

25. yasya brahma ca ksatram ca ubhe bhavata odanah; mrtyur yasyopasecanam ka ittha veda yatra sah.

25. *How can then one know this mighty Self for whom both the brahmanas and the warriors become food and death itself becomes a side dish?*

Section 3

What Leads to Rebirth and Salvation

1. rtam pibantau sukrtasya loke guham pravistau parame parardhe; chayatapau brahmavido vadanti pancagnayo ye ca trinaciketah

1. *There are two that savor the fruit of their good deeds, having entered into the secret cave, the supreme abode. The knowers of Brahman speak of them as light and shade, so also those who maintain the five fires and perform the triple fire sacrifice of Naciketas.*

Notes: This is a reference to the two selves of an embodied being, the physical and the real. Both are important for the existence of the being, jiva. One participates in life, while the other remains in the background as the support. They are compared here to shade and light respectively. The physical being is compared to shade because it is made up of the tattvas and gunas, which are considered impure. Besides, it also accumulates karma and past life impressions (samskaras). Hence it is described as shade. On the other hand, the true Self is pure and bright. Hence it is described as radiant. Some commentators refer to them as the Individual Self and the Supreme Self respectively, instead of physical self and real Self. According to this verse, self-realization comes not only by knowing Brahman but also by performing sacrifices such as the five sacrifices and the triple fire sacrifice of Naciketas

2. yah setur ijananam aksaram brahma yat param; abhayam titirsatam param naciketam sakemahi.

2. That bridge for those who perform sacrifices, that imperishable Brahman, the highest, fearless for those who wish to cross over to the other shore, may we master that Naciketa fire.

3. atmanam rathinam viddhi sariram rathameva tu; buddhim tu sarathim viddhi manah pragrahameva ca.

3. Know that the Self is the occupant of the chariot and the body is the chariot. Know that the intellect is the charioteer and the mind is verily the bridle.

Notes: Rathinam, the occupant of the chariot does little other than enjoying the ride. He is compared to the Self which is seated in the body and acts as the enjoyer. The body is the chariot. The intellect (buddhi) is the charioteer because it provides discerning wisdom to direct and regulate our lives. The mind is the bridle with which we reign in the senses that act as the horses.

4. indriyani hayanahurvisayamstesu gocaran; atmendriyamanoyuktam bhoktety ahur manisinah.

4. The senses, they say, are the horses, and the sense-objects the paths. The discerning ones say that the Self yoked to the body, the mind and the senses is the enjoyer.

5. yas tv avijnanavan bhavaty ayuktena manasa sada; tasyendriyany avasyani dustasva iva saratheh.

5. He who is without discernment, whose mind is not always yoked, his senses are out of control like the wicked horses of a charioteer.

6. yas tu vijnanavan bhavati yuktena manasa sada; tasyendriyani vasyani sadasva iva saratheh

6. But he who has discernment, whose mind is always yoked, his senses are under his control like the good horses of a charioteer.

7. yas tv avijnanavan bhavaty amanaskah sada'sucih; na sa tat padam apnoti samsaram cadhigacchati.

7. He who has no discernment, whose mind is not under his control and which is impure, does not reach that goal and keeps wandering in the phenomenal world.

8. yastu vijnanavan bhavati samanaskah sada sucih; sa tu tat padam apnoti yasmad bhuyo na jayate.

8. But he who has discernment, whose mind is under control and always clean, he attains the goal from which he is not born again.

9. vijnana sarathir yastu manah pragrahavan narah; so'dhvanah param apnoti tad visnoh paramam padam.

9. That human being who has discerning wisdom as his charioteer, and the reins of whose mind are under control, he reaches the end of the journey, that highest place of Lord Vishnu.

10. indriyebhyah para hy artha arthebhyasca param manah; manasastu para buddhir buddher atma mahan parah.

10. The sense objects are higher than the senses. Higher than the sense objects is the mind. Higher than the mind is the intellect; and higher than the intellect is the great Self.

Notes: Among the tattvas or the component realities of Nature, intelligence (buddhi) is the highest. It is in the intelligence that the light of the Self shines. Intelligence guides and controls our lives and destinies. In the Aitareya Upanishad, God Himself is compared to intelligence (prajnanam brahma). Intelligence is responsible for our discerning wisdom, or the discretion to know the right from the wrong and the real from the unreal. Without it our lives will be out of control. In the practice of yoga, we have to use this sequence to control our minds and bodies. We have to pray to the Self or meditate upon it to purify our intelligence. We have to use our intelligence to restrain our minds, our minds to restrain our senses and withdraw them from the sense-objects.

11. mahatah param avyaktam avyaktat purusah parah; purusan na param kincit sa kastha sa para gatih.

11. Higher than the great one is that which is not manifested and higher than that which is not manifested is Purusha, the Cosmic Being. Nothing else is higher than the Cosmic Being. That is the end. That is the highest goal.

Notes: Different interpretations are available for avyaktam, that which is not manifested. Both Brahman and Nature (Prakriti) have manifested and the unmanifested aspects. In the context of this verse and the sequence mentioned, it means the undifferentiated Nature or the Primal Nature in which the gunas and the tattvas are not differentiated but from which the manifested Nature originates in the beginning of creation. Purusha, the Cosmic Being, another name for the manifested Brahman, is above the primal Nature. He is the highest goal and the culmination of spiritual practices.

12. esa sarvesu bhutesu gudho'tma na prakasate; drsyate tvagryaya buddhya suksmaya suksma darsibhih.

12. The secret Self hidden in all beings does not shine bright (for all to see); but it is seen by the seers of subtle vision with their pointed and subtle intelligence.

13. yacched van manasi prajnastad yacchej jnana atmani; jnanam atmani mahati niyacchet, tad yacchec chanta atmani.

13. The intelligent one should restrain speech by mind, mind by intelligence, intelligence by the great Self, and that (great Self) he should restrain by the peaceful Self.

Notes: The great Self is the individual Self and the peaceful Self (santa atma) is the Supreme Self or the Cosmic Being (Purusha) mentioned before. As implied in this verse, although the unmanifested Nature is higher than the great Self, it has no role in the practice of yoga. One's focus should be on the Supreme Self but not the unmanifested Nature.

14. uttisthata jagrata prapya varan nibodhata; ksurasya dhara nisita duratyaya durgam pathastat kavayo vadanti.

14. Elevate and awaken (your consciousness) by knowing (the Self) with the boons obtained (by you). The sages say that the path (to that state) is as pointed as the razor's edge, difficult to cross and hard to travel.

Notes: Varan also means enlightened or gifted masters. Therefore the first part of the verse may also be translated as elevate and awaken (your consciousness) by knowing (the Self) from the gifted masters.

15. asabdam asparsam arupam avyayam tatha arasam nityam agandhavac ca yat; anady anantam mahatah param dhruvam nicayya tan mrtyumukhat pramucyate

15. One is freed from the face of death by ascertaining clearly that which is without sound, without touch, without form, without decay, and likewise without taste, eternal, without smell, without beginning, without an end, infinite, supreme and fixed.

Notes: You cannot ascertain any of these qualities with your mind or senses. The only way you can comprehend the eternal reality is by knowing the Self within directly.

16. naciketam upakhyanam mrtyu proktam sanatanam; uktva srutva ca medhavi brahmaloke mahiyate.

16. The discourse of Naciketas spoken by Death is eternal. By speaking or hearing it, a wise person attains greatness in the world of Brahman.

17. ya imam paramam guhyam sravayed brahmasamsadi; prayatah sraddhakale va tad anantyaya kalpate; tad anantyaya kalpata iti.

17. He who recites this utmost secret in the company of Brahmanas during the funeral time, that person become infinite, that person does become infinite in this manner.

Chapter 2

Section 1

Knowing the Self, the Eternal Lord

1. paranci khani vyatrnat svayambhu tasmat paran pasyati nantaratman; kas cid dhirah pratyagatmanam aiksadavrtta caksur amrtatvam icchan.

1. The Self-born Lord pierced the senses. Therefore they perceive what is outside but not the inner Self. However, wishing for immortality, with his eyes covered, a wise person sees his indwelling Self.

Notes: The orientation of the senses is outward, not inward. They are meant to grasp the objects but not the subject (the Self) within.

2. paracah kaman anuyanti balaste mrtyor yanti vitatasya pasam; atha dhira amrtatvam viditva dhruvam adhruvesviha na prarthayante.

2. Men of low intelligence go after external pleasures. They become entangled in the snares of widespread death. Therefore the wise, knowing (the truth) do not pray for the permanent among the things that are impermanent.

Notes: There is no point in seeking permanence among things that are impermanent. Worldly pleasures are not going to last forever. Hence the wise ones seek liberation rather than births and deaths and the worldly pleasures that one may enjoy in each birth.

3. yena rupam rasam gandham sabdan sparsams ca maithunan; etenaiva vijanati kimatra parisisyate etadvai tat.

3. Whatever form, taste, smell, sound, touch and intercourse one knows through this (Self) only. What else is there? This verily is that.

Notes: All experiences are possible because you are present in your body. You are the enjoyer, the knower and the perceiver. What else is there in you other than you? That is the question this verse raises and answers too.

4. svapnantam jagaritantam cobhau yenanupasyati; mahantam vibhumatmanam matva dhiro na socati.

4. Having known the great and the omnipotent (Self) by which one perceives until the end in both the dream state and the waking state, a wise person does not grieve.

5. ya imam madhvadam veda atmanam jivamantikat; isanam bhutabhavyasya na tato vijugupsate etadvai tat.

5. *He who knows this enjoyer of the sweet nectar (of works), the supporter of living beings until the end as the lord of the past and the present does not cringe from him. This verily is that.*

6. yah purvam tapaso jatam adbhyah purvam ajayata; guham pravisya tisthantam yo bhutebhir vyapasyata etadvai tat.

6. *He who in the past was born of austerity, who was born prior to water, and who having entered the cave (of heart) and remaining seated therein, watches the elements, this verily is that.*

7. ya pranena sambhavaty aditir devatamayi; guham pravisya tisthantim ya bhutebhir vyajayata etadvai tat.

7. *He who created prana, who is the soul of Aditi and gods, who having entered the cave (of the heart) is seated in all living beings, this verily is that.*

8. aranyor nihito jataveda garbha iva subhrto garbhinibhih; dive diva idyo jagrvadbhir havismadbhir manusyebhir agnih; etadvai tat.

8. *The all-knowing sacrificial fire hidden in the wooden sticks used to kindle fire (arani), like the well protected fetus in the womb of pregnant women, who is worshipped day after day by men who are awakened and who offer oblations, this verily is that.*

Notes: Arani means the two wooden sticks used to kindle sacrificial fire. Arani also means the Sun, and according to Shankara, the fire lodged in the cave of the heart. The fire is safely lodged in the wood like the fetus in the womb, means the fire is never extinguished.

9. yatas codeti suryo'stam yatra ca gacchati; tam devah sarve'rpitastadu natyeti kascana etadvai tat.

9. *From which the sun rises and into which it sets, in which all the gods are established, that (which) none can surpass, this is that.*

10. yadeveha tad amutra yad amutra tad anviha; mrtyoh sa mrtyum apnoti ya iha naneva pasyati.

10. *What indeed is here that is there; what is there, that is also here. He who sees any difference (between the two) here attains death after death.*

Notes: The Self is the same here and everywhere else because He is unchangeable. Those who perceive the individual Self that is hidden within oneself and the Supreme Self pervading the whole universe as different, remain bound to the cycle of births and deaths.

11. manasaivedam aptavyam neha nanasti kim cana; mrtyoh sa mrtyum gacchati ya iha naneva pasyati.

11. Through the mind only one must realize here that even a little difference (between the two) does not exist. He who sees any difference here goes from death to death.

12. angusthamatrah puruso madhya atmani tisthati; isano bhuta bhavyasya na tato vijugupsate etadvai tat.

12. The Person of the size of a thumb is seated firmly in middle of the body. He is the lord of the past and the future by knowing whom one does not shrink from anything. This verily is that.

13. angusthamatrah puruso jyotir ivadhumakah; isano bhuta-bhavyasya sa evadya sa u svah etadvai tat.

13. The Person of the size of the thumb is like a flame without smoke. He is the lord of the past and future. He is now and He will be tomorrow. This verily is that.

Note: Flame without smoke means He is pure light without any impurities and modifications. He is now and He will be tomorrow, means He is eternal and constant.

14. yathodakam durge vrstam parvatesu vidhavati; evam dharman prthak pasyams tan evanuvidhavati.

14. As water fallen on a hard to reach mountain flows down, so also he who sees the duties differently (from his duty) follows the same (downhill) path.

Notes: Our duties are not different from those of God. Our obligatory duties (dharmas) arise from God and abide in God. We must perform them without assuming ownership or doer-ship since the doer of all deeds is God only. We have a role and responsibility in the creation of God and our duties are part of His Duty only. This verse suggests that anyone who sees difference between his duties and those of God would keep on performing desire-ridden actions egoistically and keep on incurring karma; and thereby he would remain bound to the mortal world. The karma arising from performing such actions leads to his downfall just as the water that falls on a mountain top keeps flowing down without benefiting anyone.

15. yathodakam suddhe suddham asiktam tadrg eva bhavati; evam muner vijanata atma bhavati gautama.

15. But as the water that is pure remains the same when poured into pure water, so also the (actions of the) seer, O Gautama, who has become one with the Self.

Note: The seer who has become one and who does not see any difference between his duties and those of the Self is not bound by his actions. Since he performs them for the Self and as the Self, without desiring anything for himself, the Self becomes his doer. Just as pure water joins pure water, he remains pure like the Self even when he performs actions.

Section 2

What Happens to the Self Upon Death

1. puram ekadasadvaram ajasyavakracetasah; anusthaya na socati vimuktas ca vimucyate etadvai tat.

1. In the city of eleven gates is the unborn with a mind that is free from deformities. By establishing firm control (upon the city), one does not grieve; and becoming free (from it) one becomes really free. This, verily, is that.

Notes: Avakra cetasam means a mind that is free from crookedness. For lack of better expression, it is translated here as above. The city of the eleven gates is the body and the openings are the openings in the body, namely the openings in the ears, the eyes, the nostrils, the mouth, the navel, the two lower openings and one in the top of the head through which the soul departs at the time of death. Austhaya na socati mean by having firm control upon the eleven gates of the city one does not grieve.

2. hamsah sucisat vasur antariksasad hota vedisat atithir duronasat; nrsat varasat rtasat vyomasat, abja goja rtaja adrija rtam brhat.

2. He is the swan in the pure heaven, Vasu in the mid region, Hotri priest at the sacrificial altar, a guest in the drinking vessels. He is the dweller in men, in the gifted, in the orderly, and in the space. He is born of water, born of the earth, born of sacrifice, born of the mountains, and all that is perfect and great.

Notes: The swan in the pure world is the sun that hovers in the heavenly region which is pure and bright. Vasu is the air or the breath found in the mid region. Hotri priest is a reference to fire in the sacrificial altar. Athithir duronasat means a guest in the drinking cups, which is usually a reference to Soma or the moon reflected in the soma juice poured into the drinking vessels during the night ceremonies. Rtm or rta means order and regularity of the worlds which determines the orderly progression of time, the movement of planets and the arrangement of different worlds and planes of existence.

3. urdhvam pranam unnayaty apanam pratyag asyati; madhye vamanam asinam visve deva upasate.

3. Who moves the upward breath upwards, the downward breath downwards, the short one seated in the middle (of the heart), him all gods worship.

Notes: Vamana means Vishnu in his incarnation as the dwarf. Here it is a reference to the Self, which is described previously as a flame of the size of a thumb.

4. asya visramsamanasya sarirasthasya dehinah; dehad vimucyamanasya kim atra parisisyate, etadvai tat

4. When the embodied one dwelling in the body is loosened, when he is freed from the body, what else remains? This, verily, is that.

Notes: The Self is the support for the body. The body exists only to house the Self. When the Self departs, the body serves no other purpose. Hence, without the Self, it perishes.

5. na pranena napanena martyo jivati kas cana; itarena tu jivanti yasminn etav upasritau

5. Neither by the upward breath nor by the downward breath does a mortal being live. By something else all these live in which both have their refuge.

6. hanta ta idam pravaksyami guhyam brahma sanatanam; yatha ca maranam prapya atma bhavati gautama.

6. Well, O Gautama, I will explain to you the secret of Brahman who is eternal; so also what happens to the Self upon death.

7. yonim anye prapadyante sariratvaya dehinah; sthanum anye'nusamyanti, yatha karma yatha srutam

7. As per the actions and as per the revelatory knowledge, some embodied souls enter wombs to acquire (new) bodies; while others enter the stationary ones.

Notes: The stationary ones are the trees. The meaning of this verse is upon death some assume human and animal bodies by entering wombs and some enter the stationary ones like plants according to their respective knowledge and the merit of their actions.

8. ya esa suptesu jagarti kamam kamam puruso nirmimanah; tad eva sukram tad brahma tad evamrtam ucyate; tasmin lokah sritah sarve tad u natyeti kascana etadvai tat.

8. That which is awake in those who are asleep, creating desire after desire, that indeed is bright, that is Brahman, that verily is called the immortal. In it reside all the worlds. None can ever go beyond it. This, verily, is that.

Notes: Suptesu jagarti means awake in those who are asleep. The sleep may refer to actual sleep or symbolic sleep characteristic of the people who are ignorant and unmindful of their spiritual nature. In both cases, the Self causes them to experience desire after desire and remain bound to their mortal existence.

9. agnir yathaiko bhuvanam pravisto rupam rupam pratirupo babhuva ekastatha sarva bhutantaratma rupam rupam pratirupo bahisca.

9. *Just as one fire, upon entering the world assumes form after form according to the likeness of the many forms (it burns), the one inner Self of all beings assumes form after form according the likeness of forms (it enters), and yet exists without.*

10. vayur yathaiko bhuvanam pravisto rupam rupam pratirupo babhuva ekastatha sarvabhutantaratma rupam rupam pratirupo bahisca.

10. *Just as one air, upon entering the world, assumes form after form according to the likeness of the many forms (it burns), the one inner Self of all beings assumes form after form according the likeness of forms (it enters), and yet exists without.*

11. suryo yatha sarvalokasya caksurna lipyate caksusair bahyadosaih; ekastatha sarvabhutantaratma na lipyate loka duhkhena bahyah

11. *Just as the sun, the eye of all the worlds, is not tainted by the external impurities that can be seen with the eyes, so is the one within all beings is not tainted by the sorrow of the world, being external.*

Notes: The sun is not tainted by the impurities of the objects when its rays fall upon them. So also the Self is not subject to any modifications or impurities even when it comes into contact with the bodies of all the living beings. Since, even though it resides in them, it is still external to them.

12. eko vasi sarvabhutantaratma ekam rupam bahudha yah karoti; tam atmastham ye'nupasyanti dhirah tesam sukham sasvatam netaresam.

12. *The one controller, the indwelling Self all beings, with one form appears diversely. The wise ones who see him dwelling within themselves, to them is the eternal bliss, but not to others.*

13. nityo'nityanam cetanas cetananam eko bahunam yo vidadhati kaman; tam atmastham ye'nupasyanti dhiras tesam santih sasvati netaresam

13. *The eternal among the transient, the awakened among the unawakened, one who ordains the desires of many, the wise ones perceive Him within themselves. To them is the eternal peace, but not to others.*

14. tad etad iti manyante' nirdesyam paramam sukham; katham nu tad vijaniyam kimu bhati vibhati va.

14. This is that, thus they think about the indeterminate state which is supremely blissful. How may I know whether it shines or reflects the light?

Notes: The Self is said to be self-effulgent. It shines (bhati), but the intellect (buddhi) only reflects (vibhati) the light of the Self. Both are comparable to the sun and the moon respectively. Here the questioner wants to know how he may discern the difference because the Self is spoken in vague terms as "this is that," and its state is said to be indeterminate or indescribable. The problem, therefore, is how to express the inexpressible or compare the incomparable Self to other things.

15. na tatra suryo bhati na candratarakam nema vidyuto bhanti kuto'yamagnih tam eva bhantam anubhati sarvam tasya bhasa sarvam idam vibhati.

15. The sun does not shine there, nor do the moon and the stars. The lightning does not flash there, not to speak of the earthly fire. Only when He shines, everything else shines. By His light only all this shines.

Section 3

Asvattha Tree - The Tree of Creation

1. urdhvamulo'vaksakha eso'svatthah sanatanah; tadeva sukram tad brahma tadevamrtamucyate, tasmin lokah sritah sarve tadu natyeti kascanaetadvai tat.

1. With roots above, branches below, is the Asvattha tree, which is evergreen. That, indeed is, pure, that is Brahman, that is also said to be immortal. All the worlds abide in it. None can ever surpass it. This, verily, is that.

Notes: The Asvattha tree, often compared to the banyan tree, is Manifested Brahman. Whatever that is manifested by Brahman and all beings and planes of existence rest upon it. Being Brahman Himself, it is eternal. None can surpass it because it is infinite and provides the support. Its roots are in heaven because its source is God in heaven. The branches, leaves and aerial roots are the manifested reality, as worked out by Nature.

2. yad idam kin ca jagat sarvam prana ejati nihsrtam, mahad bhayam vajram udyatam ya etad vidur amrtaste bhavanti.

2. Whatever is here in the world, all that breathes, act listening obediently (to the commands of Brahman), out of great fear, as if they heard a rolling thunder. They who know that become immortal.

Notes: Nihsrtam means what is heard through the srutis or the Vedas. All the beings follow the commands voiced to them through such means by Brahman. The fear that is felt while following them is not just fear but fear mixed with awe, which is comparable to the fear people experience when they hear a rolling thunder or see a flash of lightning.

3. bhayad asyagnis tapati bhayat tapati suryah; bhayad indras ca vayus ca mrtyur dhavati pancamah.

3. For fear of him the fire burns, for fear of him the sun blazes, for fear of him Indra, and Vayu, and Death go forth in five different ways.

Notes: 'Panchama' is translated by many, including Shankara, as the fifth. It is translated here as five ways because it is used as an adverb to qualify 'dhavati,' rather than a noun. The conjunction 'ca' is added before vayu and mrtyu but not before panacama. Indra and Vayu act in five different ways as the controllers of the five senses and five breaths. while, Yama, the Lord of Death, metes out five punishments to the sinners for violating the five yamas (restraints) and committing the five evil actions, namely hurting or injuring, lying, stealing, lusting and harboring greed, and for indulging in the five chief evils namely lust, anger, pride, greed and envy.

4. iha ced asakad boddhum prak sarirasya visrasah; tatah sargesu lokesu sariratvaya kalpate.

4. If one is able to know (what has been said above) before the body is cast off, because of that one becomes fit for assuming a body in the ancestral world.

Note: This verse is also translated by many rather erroneously. This verse should be read in conjunction with the previous ones which speak about the eternal Asvattha tree and the fear arising from Brahman which makes the worlds move. Those who know about the Asvattha tree, the nature of creation and the fact that Brahman is the Lord of all manifestation, that knowledge alone ensures that they will have a proper body in the ancestral world where they can prolong their existence even if their descendents do not offer sacrificial food to them, as part of their obligatory duties, to build their bodies.

5. yathadarse tathatmani yatha svapne tatha pitrloke; yathapsu pariva dadrse tatha gandharvaloke chayatapayoriva brahmaloke.

5. As in a mirror so to oneself. As in a dream so in the world of ancestors. As in the water so in the world of gandharvas. Shade and light, indeed, in the world of Brahman.

Notes: How the embodied self or the Self with a body is perceived in different worlds that have been manifested by Brahman (sarga loke) is explained here. In the mortal world, the beings have gross bodies. Hence to the naked eye, they are what they see themselves in their reflections. In the ancestral world the souls have only subtle bodies. Hence they appear very much like in a dream without a real body but only with their astral bodies. The world of gandharvas (beings with exceptional musical skills) is a world of vibrations. Hence, just as one appears in the undulating surface of water, beings appear like waves in that world of sound vibrations. In the world of Brahman, only the purest of the pure reside. They appear as light to those who are pure and knowledgeable themselves and as shade, or simply hidden or non-existent, to those who are impure and ignorant.

6. indriyanam prthagbhavamudayastamayau ca yat; prthagutpadyamananam matva dhiro na socati

6. *Knowing the distinct nature of the senses, their rising and falling, and their distinct origin, a wise person does not grieve.*

Notes: The senses are distinct and different in their nature and origin. They act according to different desires and tastes and originate from different deities and elements. They are also distinct in the way they perceive and grasp the sense-objects and the way they bring them back to the mind.

7. indriyebhyah param mano manasah sattvam uttamam; sattvadadhi mahanatma mahato'vyaktam uttamam.

7. *The mind is higher than the senses, above the mind is the pure and excellent (intelligence), higher than the pure (intelligence) is the great Self and above the great Self is the highest and unmanifested great Mahat.*

Notes: Mahat means the great one. It is the unmanifested primal or the indeterminate Nature (mula-prakriti) whose dynamic aspect (Prakriti) is responsible for all diversity in creation. Intelligence is the highest and purest tattva in the domain of Nature and our own bodies. When it is pure, it reflects the brilliance of the Self. It is superior to the mind, because with sharp intellect we can control our thoughts and desires and guide our actions. In terms of proximity also intelligence is the closest to the Self. If the senses are the boundaries of the field (the body), intelligence is the core and the Self is the center.

8. avyaktat tu parah puruso vyapako'linga eva ca; yam jnatva mucyate jantur amrtatvam ca gacchati.

8. *Higher than the unmanifested is the Cosmic Person who is all pervading and without any distinguishing features, by knowing whom the animal becomes free and attains immortality.*

Notes: Jantu means animal and in the context of this verse a human being. Animal like human being attains immortality by knowing the Cosmic Self. This is the meaning.

9. na samdrse tisthati rupam asya na caksusa pasyati kascanainam; hrda manisa manasabhiklpto ya etad vidur amrtaste bhavanti.

9. *His form does not sit in the vision; nor can he be perceived with the senses such as the eyes. It is reflected in the heart, in intelligence and in the mind. Those who know this become immortal.*

Notes: The Self cannot be seen outwardly with the help of the senses. Even the intelligence and the mind cannot know it if they are impure and disturbed. Only with restrained senses, tranquil mind, and pure intelligence one can find it in the cave of the heart.

10. yada pancavatisthante jnanani manasa saha; buddhis ca na vicestati tam ahuh paramam gatim.

10. Only when the five senses and the knowledge (they bring), together with the mind, come to rest, and the intellect remains unwavering, that they say the highest state is reached.

Notes: What is described here is the state of self-absorption which comes after a prolonged practice of the various limbs of yoga. Stability, concentration and tranquility are vital to experience the transcendental state within oneself. A disturbed mind cannot experience the supreme state of the Self just as the sun cannot be seen in a turbulent sky.

11. tam yogam iti manyante sthiram indriyadharanam; apramattas tada bhavati yogo hi prabhavapyayau.

11. That (state) they consider yoga which is stable with the senses firmly restrained. Then only one becomes mindful, for the (state of) yoga comes and goes.

Notes: This verse defines yoga as a tranquil mental state in which the senses are firmly restrained and drawn into the mind itself. When the mind is stable one is attentive and mindful. Yoga is not an induced sleep. It is a sattvic practice, which leads to inner awakening. Therefore, in the state of yoga, one is not distracted or prone to carelessness (apramattam). These arise only in tamasic states, when one is asleep, tired or intoxicated. However, one cannot take the state of yoga for granted since it comes and goes according to the circumstances and prior practice.

12. naiva vaca na manasa praptum sakyo na caksusa; astiti bruvato'nyatra katham tadupalabhyate

12. Not by the speech, not by the mind, not by the senses such as the eyes can He be grasped. Other than saying, "He is," how can He be understood at all?

Notes: Existence which encompasses everything, both known and unknown, which is infinite and incomparable, cannot be described in relative terms except by suggesting its state, which is existence itself. Hence you can say it is, but cannot explain what it is, or why it is.

13. astity evopalabdhavyas tattvabhavena cobhayoh; astity evopalabdhasya tattvabhavah prasidati.

13. He should be understood in both ways, as "He is," and then as a reality. When He is understood as "He is" then the state of His reality presents itself.

Notes: The nature of Self or Brahman cannot be known empirically or through study or perception. He cannot be known by any means other than by entering into His state with a tranquil mind and becoming one with it. He can be known only when the state of duality between the knower and the known disappears. When one merges into that unified or absorbed state, one becomes what He is. This is the only way one can know the supreme transcendental state of Brahman. With such realization, subsequently one also becomes aware of the reality of Brahman (brahma tattvam) in comparison to the tattvas of Nature (prakriti tattvas) such as mahat, intelligence, mind, ego, senses and so on.

14. yada sarve pramucyante kama ye'sya hrdi sritah; atha martyo'mrto bhavaty atra brahma samasnute.

14. When all desires that have taken refuge in the heart are cast away, then the mortal becomes the immortal here itself.

Notes: The key to achieve the supreme state of yoga or immortality is not having any desires. When all the desires that besiege our hearts are cast away, then one becomes immortal. Atra may mean here in the body itself or here in the world.

15. yada sarve prabhidyante hrdayasyeha granthayah; atha martyo'mrto bhavaty etavad dhyanusasanam

15. When all the knots of the hearts are cut asunder, then the mortal becomes immortal even here. This much is the instruction.

Notes: Desires arise from attachments. So to be free, one must cut asunder all the attachments. When the attachments are gone, the desires will automatically subside. Then one can enter into the state of yoga easily and experience Brahman.

16. satam caika ca hrdayasya nadyastasam murdhanam abhinihsrtaika; tayordhvam ayann amrtatvam eti visvann anya utkramane bhavanti.

16. One hundred and one are the veins of the heart. Of them only one goes up to the tip of the head. Going upwards by that only is immortality. The others serve for going in different directions (according to their desires and actions.)

Notes: The aperture in the top of the head is known as brahmarandhra or the Brahman aperture. It is the doorway to the world of immortality. The souls that depart from the body through other arteries go to the ancestral world and return to take birth again according to their past actions and dominant desires.

17. angusthamatrah puruso'ntaratma sada jananam hrdaye sannivistahtam svac charirat pravrhen munjad ivesikam dhairyenatam vidyac chukram amrtam tam vidyac chukram amrtamiti.

17. The Person, of the size of the thumb, is forever seated in the hearts of people. Him one should patiently separate from the body as one separates a blade of munja grass from its midrib. Him one should know as pure and immortal. Yes, Him one should know as pure and immortal in this manner.

18. mrtyuproktam naciketo'tha labdhva vidyametam yogavidhim cakrtsnam; brahmaprapto virajo'bhud vimrtyur anyopy evam yo vid adhyatmam eva.

18. Having acquired the knowledge taught by Death, and the practice of yoga in its entirety, Naciketas attained Brahman and became free from passion, and free from death. So should anyone else, who becomes a knower of the indwelling Self.

Mundaka Upanishad

The Mundaka Upanishad is part of the Atharvaveda. This is declared in the beginning of the Upanishad itself. It has three chapters, each with two sections. Mundaka Upanishad literally means the secret knowledge of the shaved ones or the liberated ones, meaning it is meant for those who have completely given up worldly life, shaved off their ignorance and attachments and are now in their advanced state of spiritual practice. The Upanishad is clearly marked for those who have decided to renounce worldly life and take up asceticism as a way of life to achieve liberation. The last verse confirms this, suggesting that its knowledge should be taught only to those who have shaved their heads as a mark of renunciation and who are grounded in Brahman. The Upanishad markedly favors renunciation and pursuit of Brahman and shows an emphatic disdain towards those who perform sacrifices and rituals for worldly gains. It draws a clear distinction between higher knowledge and lower knowledge and argues why higher knowledge is superior and desirable. Lower knowledge is the knowledge of the eighteen forms of Vedic rites practiced by those whose minds are unsteady and who wallow in ignorance. Higher knowledge is the knowledge of imperishable Brahman pursued by those who dwell in forests and perform penances, with tranquil hearts and their passions cut off. The former leads to rebirth, while the latter to liberation.

Presented here is a new translation of the Mundaka Upanishad by Jayaram V.

Chapter (Mundaka) 1

Section 1

Two Types of Knowledge

1. brahma devanam prathamah sambabhuva visvasya karta bhuvanasya gopta; sa brahmavidyam sarvavidyapratistham atharvaya jyesthaputraya praha.

1. Brahma, was born as the first among the gods. He was the creator of the universe and the protector of the world. He imparted the knowledge of Brahman, which is the foundation of all knowledge, to Atharvanan, his eldest son.

2. atharvane yam pravadeta brahmatharva tam purovacangire brahmavidyam; sa bharadvajaya satyavahaya praha bharadvajo'ngirase paravaram.

2. That knowledge of Brahman, which Brahma declared to Atharvan, Atharvan of the olden times declared to Angirasa. He (Angirasa) to Satyavaha of the Bharadvaja lineage. He of the Bharadvaja lineage to Angirasa both the higher and the lower.

Notes: Two Angirasas are mentioned here. They belonged to different times. It was a common practice in ancient India to keep certain types of teachings within certain families or lineages.

3. saunako ha vai mahasalo'ngirasam vidhivadupasannah papraccha; kasminnu bhagavo vijnate sarvamidam vijnatam bhavatiti.

3. Saunaka, the great householder, approached Angirasa in a due manner and asked, "Godman, by knowing what all this becomes known?"

Notes: We have to infer that Saunaka completed his life as a householder and took up an ascetic way of life or decided to do so before he approached Angirasa and asked him this question. Angirasa, who is mentioned here was probably head of an ascetic sect or a teacher tradition who lived in the forests and practiced penances to achieve liberation.

4. tasmai sa hovaca, dve vidye veditavye iti ha sma yad brahmavido vadanti para caivapara ca

4. To him, he said, "Two types of knowledge should be known, as the tradition goes, say the knowers of Brahman, namely the higher and the lower.

5. **tatrapara rgvedo yajurvedah samavedo'tharvavedah siksa kalpo vyakaranam niruktam chando jyotisamiti; atha para yaya tadaksaramadhigamyate.**

5. *Of them, the lower is (the knowledge of) Rigveda, Yajurveda, Samaveda, Atharvaveda, Sikhsa, Kalpa, Vyakarna, Nirukta, Chandah and Jyotishya. Now, the higher (knowledge) is that by which the Imperishable is attained.*

Notes: Lower knowledge comes from the study of the Vedas and associated subjects. The most important scriptures are the four Vedas. They are inviolable and eternal. The remaining six subjects that are mentioned here are called the limbs of the Vedas (Vedangas). They help the students to master the Vedas in the right manner and learn their main duties (ashrama dharmas) correctly. The sacrifices are the backbone of Vedic tradition. They are part of God's eternal duty delegated partly to the human beings as their obligatory duties to sustain and uphold order and regularity of the world and society. Their knowledge is better practiced with the help of the six Vedangas. Siksha is the science of pronunciation. Kalpa is the study of rituals. Vyakarna contains the rules of Sanskrit grammar. Nirukta teaches the etymology of Sanskrit words. Chandah deals with meter and Jyotishya. All this knowledge constitutes the lower knowledge or the worldly knowledge. Higher knowledge is the spiritual knowledge of the Self which leads to liberation. It is introduced to the students through the Upanishads, but truly acquired only through practice and self-realization.

6. **yat tadadresyamagrahyamagotramavarnamacaksuhsrotram tadap anipadam; nityam vibhum sarvagatam susuks-mam tadavyayam yad bhutayonim paripasyanti dhirah.**

6. *That which is invisible, ungraspable, without lineage, without color, without eyes or ears, that which is without hands or feet, eternal, all pervading, all knowing, very subtle, inexhaustible, that which is the womb of all beings, the wise see everywhere.*

Notes: Those who are free from ignorance and delusion see the play of Brahman in every aspect of creation. They know His essential nature and they know how He manifests in creation and upholds it both externally and internally.

7. **yathornanabhih srjate grhnate ca yatha prthivyamosadhayah sambhavanti; yatha satah purusatkesalomani tathaksaratsambhavatiha visvam.**

7. *As the spider sends out and draws in (the thread), as the plants grow upon the earth, as the hair grow from the head and the body of a living person, so does the universe comes into existence from the Imperishable.*

Notes: The world is woven by the thoughts of God. The Upanishads do not agree with the notion that creation was an automatic process. The creative power of Brahman spreads out in all directions as from a center like in a web. The diversity of creation is interconnected and also connected to its source, which is Brahman. Hence the description of creation as a web is very appropriate. The spider creates the web for its existence. It feeds upon the insects that are caught in it. In the web of God's creation, the living beings (jivas) are the insects. Brahman as Kala (Time or Death) feeds upon them. Now, we should not consider God as an awful Being who feeds upon His own creation. The truth is Brahman is both the spider and the insects. He feeds upon His own materiality (objects) as Death or Time and as the deities or gods of heaven. The material creation is a huge web. Its creator, controller and enjoyer is Brahman. Each being in it is also a web in itself. Its enjoyer is the individual Self. Through the Self the Self enjoys. Through the Self, the Self makes the offerings to gods. Creation is thus a huge personal sacrifice of God in which the end product is enjoyment. Our scriptures do not agree that creation is the product of blind Nature. It is a self-willed and intelligent process, which is outgoing in its mode and definitive in its results. Hence it is very much like a projection or superimposition spreading from a source of great power and intelligence. It is held together by His Will and programmed to be perishable, mutable, and subject to growth and decay like the spider's web or the hair that grows on the head or the plants that spring from the earth. However, Brahman Himself, who is its source, is imperishable.

8. tapasa ciyate brahma tato'nnamabhijayate; annatprano manah satyam lokah karmasu camrtam.

8. Brahman expands by the heat generated from penance and then from Him food is born; from food life, mind, truth, the worlds, obligatory duties and immortality.

Notes: Brahman is the source of everything, the food we eat, the air we breathe, the mind with which we think, the truth we are expected to practice and even the obligatory duties. Our duties upon earth are part of God's eternal duties. By performing them sincerely and selflessly as an offering to God we participate in the divine act of upholding dharma and thereby the worlds.

9. yah sarvajnah sarvavid yasya jnanamayam tapah; tasmadetad brahma nama rupamannam ca jayate.

9. He who is all discerning, all knowing, whose austerity is filled with pure intelligence, from that Brahman arise name, form and food.

Notes: Tapah means the bodily heat or glow generated from the practice of penances and austerities. Symbolically in many Upanishads, Brahman is compared to the sun. The sun radiates heat in the form of light. That light which illuminates our higher minds (buddhi) is perceived in the subtle planes both as breath (prana) and as intelligence (jnana). From That only names and forms are created and the worlds are sustained.

Section 2

The Inferior Nature of Sacrifices

1. tad etat satyam mantresu karmani kavayo yany apasyams tani tretayam bahudha samtatani; tany acaratha niyatam satyakama esa vah panthah sukrtasya loke.

1. This is the truth. The actions which the sages saw in the sacred hymns are extended in many ways in the three Vedas. Perform them regularly abiding in truth. This is the path to the world of good deeds.

Notes: An alternative interpretation for tretayam, suggested by Sankara, is the Treta age.

2. yada lelayate hy arcih samiddhe havyavahane; tad ajyabhagav antaren ahutih pratipadayec chraddhaya hutam.

2. When the fire is ignited and the flames shoot up, then one should pour the oblation with faith in between the two places where oblations are poured.

3. yasyagnihotram adarsam apaurnam asamacaturmasyam anagrayanam atithivarjitam ca; ahutam avaisvadevam avidhina hutam asaptamams tasya lokan hinasti.

3. He whose Agnihotra sacrifice is not followed by the new-moon sacrifice, the full-moon sacrifice, the four month sacrifice and the Agrayana sacrifice, without inviting guests, without offerings, without invoking the Visvadevas, without due procedure destroys his world up to the seventh.

Notes: Agnihotra sacrifice is the domestic fire sacrifice performed by a Brahmana householder as part of his daily obligatory duty. This sacrifice should be performed in conjunction with the other sacrifices mentioned here. The four month sacrifices are performed at the beginning of each new season. Agrayana rituals are performed during the harvest season with freshly harvested corn. If these sacrifices are not performed in due manner, as per established procedure, without the presence of guests or without offerings, this verse declares that the sacrificer will not be able to join his ancestors up to seven births. Alternatively, it may also mean he will harm the rebirth prospects of his ancestors in the ancestral world up to seven generations.

4. kali karali ca mano java ca sulohita ya ca sudhumravarna; sphulingini visvaruci ca devi lelayamana iti sapta jihvah.

4. Kali, Karali, Manojava, Sulohita, Sudhumravarna, Sphulingini, and Visvaruci, these are the seven flaming tongues of fire.

Notes: Kali means the black one, karali means the very black one, manojava means the one, which is swifter or flickering like the mind, sulohita means, the red one, sudhumravarna means the smoke colored one, sphulingini means the sparkling one, visvaruci means the one who is liked by all or the most common form of flame. These are the seven flaming (lelayamana) tongues of fire that arise from the sacrificial fire. They are also seven forms of energy that manifest in the body during internal sacrifice or tapah.

5. etesu yascarate bhrajamanesu yathakalam cahutayo hyadadayan; tam nayanty etah suryasya rasmayo yatra devanam patireko'dhivasah.

5. *Whoever performs the sacrifices making offerings at the right time into these blazing fires, his offerings as sun rays lead him up to that where the lord of the gods presides above all.*

6. ehy ehiti tam ahutayah suvarcasah suryasya rasmibhir yajamanam vahanti; priyam vacam abhivadantyo'rcayantya esa vah punyah sukrto brahmalokah.

6. *"Come, come," thus saying, these radiant offerings invite the sacrificer and carry him by the rays of the sun, adoring him and honoring him with pleasant words, "This is the world of Brahman attained by good deeds."*

7. plava hy ete adrdha yajnarupa astadasoktam avaram yesu karma; etac chreyo ye'bhinandanti mudha jaramrtyum te punarevapi yanti.

7. *Unsteady boats and perishable are these eighteen forms that participate in the sacrifices, which are declared inferior action (by the scriptures). The deluded ones who rejoice in them thinking that they lead to good return repeatedly to the world of aging and death.*

Notes: Sankara listed eighteen forms that take part in the sacrifices as the sixteen priests, the sacrificer and his wife.

8 avidyayam antare vartamanah svayam dhirah panditam manyamanah; janghanyamanah pariyanti mudha andhenaiva niyamana yathandhah.

8. *Remaining within the confines of ignorance, considering themselves wise and thinking within their minds that they are learned, the deluded ones, afflicted with the troubles (of mortal life), go around like blind men led by the blind.*

9. avidyayam bahudha vartamana vayam krtartha ityabhimanyanti balah; yatkarmino na pravedayanti ragat tenaturah ksinalokas cyavante.

9. *Prevailing in their ignorance in various ways, the purely physical ones think, "We have reached our goal." Thus these men who perform actions do not understand (their consequences) because of attachment. Thereby, afflicted with sorrow, they are deprived of the subtle worlds.*

Notes: Because of their gross physical nature or their reliance upon pure physical actions and their attachment to gross objects, they cannot enter the subtle worlds (ksina lokah).

10. istapurtam manyamana varistham nanyacchreyo vedayante pramudhah; nakasya prsthe te sukrte'nubhutvemam lokam hinataram va visanti.

10. Thinking that the sacrifices and good works are the most important, these deluded ones do not know any other good. Having enjoyed an exulted position in the ancestral world by their good deeds, they enter again this world or a lower one.

Notes: Good deeds do not lead to liberation. This fact is repeatedly affirmed in the Vedas. Good deeds lead to a good life in the ancestral world, but after exhausting the merit, the souls have to return again and take another birth according to their past actions. Liberation alone prevents rebirth. How to achieve it is explained next.

11. tapah sraddhe ye hy upavasanty aranye santa vidvamso bhaiksyacaryam carantah; suryadvarena te virajah prayanti yatramrtah sa puruso hy avyayatma.

11. Those who practice penance with faith, the knowers with tranquil hearts, who dwell in the forests and go around begging for alms, depart with their passions cast off, through the door of the sun, to the (world) where lives the immortal and the imperishable Person.

Notes: Performing good deeds such as the sacrifices as a householder only ensures a place in the ancestral world. However, if one turns to the life of a forest dweller and renunciation in the third and fourth and final phases of life, as per the established norms of ashrama dharma, practicing detachment, meditation and self-control, will attain liberation. Upon his departure from the body, he will travel by the northern path to the Sun and enter the immortal world of Brahman.

12. pariksya lokan karmacitan brahmano nirvedam ayan nastyakrtah krtena; tad vijnanartham sa gurumevabhigacchet sami-tpanih srotriyam brahmanistham.

12. Having examined the burnt remains of sacrificial actions in the world, a Brahmana should become dispassionate and detached thinking that there is nothing here that is not the result of actions. For the sake of knowing That, with fuel in his hand, he should approach a teacher for the recitation of the Vedas and stabilizing his mind in Brahman.

Notes: A Brahmana who is devoted to the pursuit of the Vedas should realize the futility of performing desire-ridden actions since they do not prevent rebirth and his actions lead to both good and bad results. Having seen and understood how karma shapes our world and our lives, he should turn to acquiring the knowledge of Brahman with the help of an enlightened teacher and work for his liberation.

13. tasmai sa vidvan upasannaya samyak prasanta cittaya samanvitaya; yenaksaram purusam veda satyam provaca tam tattvato brahmavidyam.

13. *To him who has approached in a proper manner (with fuel in hand), with a tranquil mind and the organs of his body under firm control, the enlightened one should teach the truths found in the Vedas about the imperishable Being, whereby he knows the essential truths underlying the knowledge of Brahman.*

Chapter (Mundaka) 2

Section 1

Brahman as the Source of All

1. tad etat satyam yatha sudiptat pavakad visphulingah sahasrasah prabhavante sarupah; tathaksarad vividhah somya bhavah prajayante tatra caivapi yanti.

1. *This is the truth: just as thousands of sparks are born from a brightly glowing fire, and glow alike, in the same manner, my dear, manifold existences arise and return into That.*

2. divyo hy amurtah purusah sa bahyabhyantaro hy ajah; aprano hy amanah subhro hy aksarat paratah parah.

2. *Divine and formless is the Person. He is within and without, unborn, with no breath at all, no mind, very pure, imperishable and the highest of the high.*

3. etasmaj jayate prano manah sarvendriyani ca; kham vayur jyotir apah prthivi visvasya dharini.

3. *From Him arise the breath, the mind, all the senses, space, air, fire, water and earth. He is the supporter of all.*

4. agnir murdha caksusi candrasuryau disah srotre vag vivrtas ca vedah; vayuh prano hrdayam visvam asya padbhyam prthivi hyesa sarvabhutantaratma.

4. *Fire is His head, the moon and the sun are the eyes, the quarters are the ears, the Vedas are speech, the air is the breath, the universe is the heart, the earth is born of his feet. Indeed, He is the inner Self of all beings.*

5. tasmad agnih samidho yasya suryah somat parjanya osadhayah prthivyam; puman retah sincati yositayam bahvih prajah purusat samprasutah.

5. *From Him only arise fire, of which the Sun is the fuel, the rain that falls from the moon, and the herbs that grow upon the earth; When a male drops semen into a female manifold beings are born from the Person.*

6. tasmad rcah sama yajumsi diksa yajnas ca sarve kratavo daksinas ca; samvatsaras ca yajamanas ca lokah somo yatra pavate yatra suryah.

6. *From Him are the Riks, the Samans and the Yajus, initiation, all sacrifices, sacrificial gifts, the year, the host of the sacrifice, and the worlds that are purified by the moon and the sun.*

7. tasmac ca deva bahudha samprasutah sadhya manusyah pasavo vayamsi; pranapanau vrihiyavau tapas ca sraddha satyam brahmacaryam vidhis ca.

7. *From Him are born numerously divinities, celestial beings of the mid-region, human beings, animals, birds, the in-breath and the down breath, rice and barley, penance faith, truth, chastity, and fate.*

8. sapta pranah prabhavanti tasmat saptarcisah samidhah sapta homah; sapta ime loka yesu caranti prana guhasaya nihitah sapta sapta.

8. *From Him are born the seven breaths, the seven flames, the seven fuels, the seven oblations, these seven worlds in which move the breath, (and) the seven (arteries each further) divided into seven hidden in the heart.*

9. atah samudra girayas ca sarve asmat syandante sindhavah sarvarupah; atas ca sarva osadhayo rasas ca yenaisa bhutais tisthate hy antaratma

9. *From Him are born the oceans and the mountains, from Him flow all the rivers of various forms; from Him are all the herbs, and juices by which the self remains seated in the elemental body.*

Notes: The Self is the enjoyer. The herbs and the juices extracted from them which serve as food as well as medicine and from which arise semen and other bodily fluids, keep the body active and healthy and enable the Self remain within the body and enjoy the sense-objects.

10. purusa evedam visvam karma tapo brahma paramrtam; etadyo veda nihitam guhayam so'vidyagranthim vikiratiha somya.

10. The Person alone is all this universe, actions, penances, the creator Brahma, who is transcendental and immortal. He who know that which is hidden in the heart, my dear, he destroys the knot of ignorance even here.

Notes: Brahman is the source. He alone is the truth. Everything else is His manifestation, which included the Vedas, the gods and the sacrificial offerings. One should therefore focus upon the source rather than its effects. The teacher is implying this while speaking about the glory and the greatness of Brahman.

Section 2

Knowing the Self

1. avih samnihitam guhacaram nama mahat padam atraitat samarpitam; ejat pranan nimisac ca yade tat janatha sad asad varenyam param vijnanad yad varistham prajanam.

1. Seen most closely abiding in the cave of the heart is the great place. On that is fixed all that moves, breathes and sees. Know that as the gross and subtle, supremely desirable, and distinct from the intelligence considered excellent by human beings.

Notes: The Self can be seen most intimately within one's own heart. It is the support for the entire body and its activities. Life is possible because of that only. It is both immanent and transcendental. Finally, the intelligence of the Self is nothing like any we know, even that which we regard as the most excellent, such as the discerning wisdom and the rationality that leads to our material well being, peace and happiness.

2. yad arcimad yad anubhyo'nu ca yasmin loka nihita lokinas ca; tad etadaksaram brahma sa pranastadu van manah, tad etat satyam tad amrtam tad veddhavyam somya viddhi.

2. What is bright, what is smaller than the smallest, in which are set the worlds and the beings of such worlds, that is the imperishable Brahman, that is breath, that is speech, mind, that is truth, that is immortal, that which should be known, my dear, you should know.

3. dhanur grhitva upanisadam mahastram saram hy upasanisitam samdhay ita; ayamya tad bhavagatena cetasa laksyam tad evaksaram somya viddhi.

3. Take the Upanishads as the bow, the mighty weapon. Place in it the arrow sharpened by meditation. Draw it with the mind absorbed in the Supreme Being. Know that imperishable, my dear, as the target.

Notes: The arrow, saram, that is mentioned here is either the intention or the concentration sharpened by meditation and contemplation.

4. pranavo dhanuh saro hy atma brahma tal laksyam ucyate; apramattena veddhavyam saravat tanmayo bhavet.

4. Pranava (Aum) is the bow. The Self, indeed, is the arrow. Brahman is said to be the target of that (arrow called Self). It must be hit with diligence. Then the arrow (called Self) experiences blissful union (with the target called Brahman).

5. yasmin dyauh prthivi cantariksam otam manah saha pranais ca sarvaih; tam evaikam janatha atmanam anya vaco vimuncatha amrtasyaisa setuh.

5. He in whom are strung together the heaven, the earth and the mid-region, along with the mind and all the breaths, know Him alone as the Self. Leave behind all other utterances. This (Self) is the bridge to immortality.

6. ara iva rathanabhau samhata yatra nadyah sa eso'ntascarate bahudha jayamanah; aumity evam dhyayatha atmanam svasti vah paraya tamasah parastat.

6. Where the arteries of the body are yoked together like spokes to the center of a wheel, in that (heart region) this Lord moves about becoming many forms. Meditate upon Aum with your mind fixed in your Self. May you fare well in crossing over to the other shore beyond darkness

7. yah sarvajnah sarvavid yasyaisa mahima bhuvi; divye brahmapure hy esa vyomny atma pratisthitah.

7. He who is all discerning, all knowing, whose is all the glory and greatness upon earth, in the divine city of Brahman, in the space within the heart, indeed, that Self is established.

8. manomayah pranasariraneta pratisthito'nne hrdayam sannidhaya; tad vijnanena paripasyanti dhira anandarupam amrtam yad vibhati.

8. Controlling the mind and the breath bodies as their ruler, established firmly in the food body, remaining treasured inside the heart, with the discerning wisdom arising from that (effort), the wise see clearly the blissful and immortal form (of the Self) that shines forth.

Notes: The verse refers to the various bodies (kosas) found inside a human being. Control over these bodies is necessary to experience the blissful and immortal Self. These bodies, from outside to inside, are the food body (annamaya), the breath body (pranamaya), the mind body (manomaya), the intelligence body (vijnanamaya) and the bliss body (anandamaya). The outer three bodies are mentioned here clearly. The other two are mentioned rather indirectly. The intelligence body is close to the heart, where the Self is located. When these various bodies are firmly controlled and yoked together, one is able to see the bliss body (ananda rupam), beyond which lies the immortal Self.

9. bhidyate hrdayagranthis chidyante sarvasamsayah; ksiyante casya karmani tasmin drste paravare.

9. The knots of the heart are untied, all doubts are dispelled, the fruits of his action shrivel when one sees him within oneself and outside of oneself.

10. hiranmaye pare kose virajam brahma niskalam; tacchubhram jyotisam jyotih tad yad atmavido viduh.

10. In the ultimate golden sheath shines Brahman, who is without impurities. It is pure, light of the lights. It is That which the knowers of the Self know.

11. na tatra suryo bhati na candratarakam nema vidyuto bhanti kuto'yam agnih; tam eva bhantam anubhati sarvam tasya bhasa sarvam idam vibhati.

11. There the sun does not shine, nor the moon nor the stars, nor these lightnings shine. Then what to say about the earthly fire? Everything shines only after that light. By His light only all this shines.

12. brahmaivedam amrtam purastad brahma pascad brahma daksinatas cottarena; adhascordhvam ca prasrtam brahmaivedam visvam idam varistham.

12. All this is immortal Brahman. Brahman is in the front; Brahman is in the back; to the south and to the north; He is spread below and high above. Brahman only is this universe, the most supreme.

Chapter (Mundaka) 3

Section 1

Truth Alone Triumphs

1. dva suparna sayuja sakhaya samanam vrksam parisasvajate; tayor anyah pippalam svadv atty anasnann anyo abhicakasiti.

1. Two birds, close companions who are related and always together, remain bound to the self-same tree. Of these two, one tastes the sweet fruit of the tree, and the other looks on without eating.

Notes: According to the most common interpretation, the tree is the body and the two birds represent the individual Self and the Supreme Self. The former is the enjoyer who eats the fruit of the works done by the body and its organs, while the Supreme Self, being pure and not subject to delusion and duality, does not participate in any of the activities of the body. Alternatively, we may interpret the two birds as the physical Self (being) who eats the fruit of his actions and the individual Self (atman) who remains in the background as the witness Self untouched by the actions of the physical being.

2. samane vrkse puruso nimagno'nisaya socati muhyamanah; justam yada pasyaty anyam isam asya mahimanam iti vitasokah.

2. On the self-same tree, the individual Self remains absorbed (in sorrow). Because of delusion, he thinks he is helpless and lacks self-mastery. When he sees the other, the Lord and His splendor, he becomes free from sorrow.

Notes: Sorrow prevails as long as a being is deluded. Self-realization brings an end to sorrow. A human being is not actually helpless in controlling his thoughts and emotions. However, he thinks so as long as he is ignorant and deluded.

3. yada pasyah pasyate rukmavarnam kartaram isam purusam brahma yonim; tada vidvan punyapape vidhuya niranjanah paramam samyam upaiti.

3. When a seer sees the Person who is golden hued, the creator, the Lord, the Being, the source of god Brahma, then, he, the knower (of the Self), cleansed of both sin and merit, free from impurities, attains the highest through samyama.

Notes: Samyama is an advanced state of yoga in which concentration, meditation and self-absorption are practiced simultaneously. It is possible only when the mind is free from all modifications and remains in perfect equilibrium

4. prano hy esa yah sarvabhutair vibhati vijanan vidvan bhavate nativadi; atmakrida atmaratih kriyavanesa brahmavidam varisthah.

4. Breath indeed is this one who shines in all beings. The knower who discerns him does not indulge in farfetched discussions. Absorbed in an inner play of his own, delighting within himself, this practitioner of kriya yoga is the greatest among the knowers of Brahman.

Notes: Sankara interpreted kriyavan as performing spiritual activities rather than obligatory duties because the greatest among the knowers of Brahman are not expected to engage in any obligatory duties. However, the word seems to be a direct reference to the practice of kriyayoga, which is defined in the Yogasutras of Patanjali as a spiritual action consisting of penance (tapas), self-study (svadhyaya) and devotion (isvara-paridhana) which leads to the advanced state of samayama discussed before.

5 satyena labhyas tapasa hy esa atma samyagjnanena brahma-caryena nityam; antah sarire jyotirmayo hi subhro yam pasyanti yatayah ksinadosah.

5. This one, verily, is attained by truth, austerity, perfect knowledge, (and) continuous practice of celibacy. Those who strive hard (by these) with their impurities diminished, see him as resplendent and pure inside their bodies.

Notes: To practice austerities (tapas) truth is the foundation. To attain perfect knowledge arising from one pointed intelligence and stabilized mind, austerity is the support. All these come to naught if one does not practice self-control and chastity. Hence they are mentioned in the same degree of importance.

6. satyam eva jayate nanrtam satyena pantha vitato devayanah; yenakramanty rsayo hy aptakama yatra tat satyasya paramam nidhanam.

6. Truth alone wins (the Self), but not untruth. By truth is laid out the path of the immortal gods, by which the sages, who are without any desires, ascend to where that supreme treasure of Truth is.

Notes: The Self is attained only by truth means self-realization is achieved only by knowing truth, by discerning truth, by practicing truth, by abiding in truth and by centering oneself in one's true Self, which is hidden and different from the false self consisting of the body, the mind and the senses. Truth means that which is true forever, independent of conditions, relationships, interpretations, opinions and knowledge. That truth is Brahman, who is eternal, constant and imperishable and that truth can be known only by overcoming ignorance and delusion through detachment and renunciation. Those who attains this truth that is hidden within themselves go by the path known as devayana or the path of the gods, which leads to the immortal world of Brahman, for which the sun is said to be the door. Others go by the path of the ancestors (pitrayana) to the ancestral world in the moon and return to the earth again after exhausting their karmas.

7. brhacca tad divyam acintyarupam suksmac ca tat suksma-taram vibhati; duratsudure tad ihantike ca pasyatsv imha iva nihitam guhayam.

7. It is vast, divine, of unimaginable form, and subtler than the subtle. It shines. It is far, farther than the farthest. Yet It is seen by the seers even here in this (body) seated in the cave (of the heart).

8. na caksusa grhyate napi vaca nanyair devaih tapasa karmana va; jnanaprasadena visuddhasattvas tatas tu tam pasyate niska-lam dhyayamanah.

8. He is not grasped by the eyes, nor by speech, nor by any other deities (organs in the body), not by austerity, nor by obligatory actions. But with the wisdom derived from intelligence, purity arising from (the predominance of) sattva, with a mind absorbed in deep meditation, that (Self) can be seen as having no parts.

9. eso'nuratma cetasa veditavyo yasmin pranah pancadha samvivesa; pranais cittam sarvam otam prajanam yasmin visuddhe vibhavaty esa atma.

9. The subtle Self should be known with pure intelligence (in the heart region) where the five different breaths come and join together. In the beings, the whole mind-body awareness (citta) is pervaded by breath. When that is purified (with sattva), it shines with (the effulgence of) the Self.

10. yam yam lokam manasa samvibhati visuddhasattvah kamayate yams ca kaman; tam tam lokam jayate tams ca kamams tasmad atmajnam hy arcayed bhutikamah.

10. Whatever world the one with pure sattva reflects upon within his mind and whatever desires he desires, that world he attains and the desires. Therefore he who desires material things, should worship the knower of the Self.

Notes: The knower of the Self does not desire anything for himself; but, being one with Brahman, he has the power of manifestation, whereby whatever he thinks or visualizes within his mind or seeks from the universe, he obtains them. Therefore, worldly people are advised to worship the knowers of the Self to fulfill their dreams and desires.

Section 2

The Self is Known By the Self

1. sa vedaitat paramam brahma dhama yatra visvam nihitam bhati subhram; upasate purusam ye hy akamas te sukram etad ativartanti dhirah.

1. He knows the highest abode of Brahman in which all that is placed shines with utmost purity. The wise who worship this person, without desires, transcend the seed (of birth).

Notes: In the last verse of the previous section, we have read that those who worship a self-realized person with desires, obtains them. Now, this verse states that those who worship him without desires are freed from the cycle of births and deaths and attain liberation. Sukram also means demonic or deluded nature. Thus, an alternative translation is, those who worship this person transcend their delusion or demonic nature.

2. kaman yah kamayate manyamanah sa kamabhir jayate tatra tatra; paryaptakamasya krtatmanas tu ihaiva sarve praviliyanti kamah.

2. He who hankers after his desires, his mind thinking of them, he is born again with those desires and goes wherever they lead him. But the one who has satisfied his desires, with his mind stabilized, for him even here in this world all desires become dissolved.

3. nayam atma pravacanena labhyo na medhaya na bahuna srutena; yamevaisa vrnute tena labhyas tasyaisa atma vivrnute tanum svam.

3. The Self is not attained by extensive study, by thinking, nor by hearing many times (about it). That very Self which this one seeks, by that only it is attained. To him the Self reveals its very Self.

Notes: The meaning implied in this verse is that the Self cannot be realized by mere human intention or effort. It has to happen through the Self only as the culmination of a great inner transformation. One may prepare for self-realization but it has to happen on its own. This makes sense because you cannot reach the Self with desires or expectations. Spiritual actions should be performed without desiring the fruit of such actions. One should be completely free from desires to attain the Self. It means, self-realization has to happen spontaneously on its own as and when the Self chooses to reveal itself or when the time comes. It goes without saying that prior preparation has its own value. The Self will reveal itself only when a person is pure and free from desires and delusion.

4. nayam atma balahinena labhyo na ca pramadat tapaso vapy alingat; etair upayair yatate yastu vidvams tasyaisa atma visate brahmadhama.

4. The Self is not attained by any weakness, nor by chance (or negligence) while practicing austerity or living the aimless life of an ascetic. But whoever strives through these means, who is a knower, his Self enters into the abode of Brahman.

Notes: The Self is not attained by any weakness or imperfection. For example self-realization does not happen when a person is asleep, sick or unconscious even though in that state his senses are withdrawn, his mind and body are stable and his desires are silent. It also does not happen due to chance or negligence or error in practicing austerities or living a life of renunciation or asceticism. Creative solutions may arise by chance but not self-realization. Sincere and prolonged effort is required for self-realization. The mind and body need to be completely purified and stabilized, before one can realize the Self.

5. samprapyainam rsayo jnanatrptah krtatmano vitaragah prasantah; te sarvagam sarvatah prapya dhira yuktatmanah sarvam evavisanti.

5. Upon attaining Him, the seers become tranquil, satisfied with their knowledge, abiding in themselves and free from passions. Having attained the omniscient in all places, the wise with their minds yoked to the Self enter into all.

Notes: The seers become satisfied with their knowledge, because they have nothing else to learn. With doubts cleared and ignorance removed they know clearly the essential nature of the Self.

6. vedanta vijnana suniscitarthah samnyasa yogad yatayah suddhasattvah; te brahmalokesu parantakale paramrtah parimucyanti sarve.

6. *Having minutely ascertained the knowledge of the Vedanta by cultivating supreme purity assiduously through the yoga of renunciation, they all attain the immortal world of Brahman in the final moment of their death.*

Notes: The seers who have been mentioned before, whose minds have been yoked to the Self arrive at the end of the knowledge of the Vedas (Vedanta) which is liberation through union with the Self and the Supreme Self. Having reached the end of knowing, they easily enter the world of Brahman at the time of their death.

7. gatah kalah pancadasa pratistha devas ca sarve pratidevatasu; karmani vijnanamayas ca atma pare'vyaye sarva ekibhavanti .

7. *The fifteen parts return to their foundations; and all the gods return to their corresponding deities; the fruit of actions and the Self shining with its own intelligence become one with the supreme imperishable.*

Notes: The fifteen parts are the ten senses and the five breaths. they are the deities, which return to their original source in the macrocosm. Since the seers perform their actions selflessly, without desire for the fruit of such actions and since they offer them to Brahman without claiming ownership and doership, in the end the consequences of such actions go to Brahman only and become dissolved in Him. Since the seers are self-realized, their souls are not enveloped in delusion. Hence at the time of their departure to the world of Brahman, they shine brightly with pure intelligence.

8. yatha nadyah syandamanah samudre'stam gacchanti namarupe vihaya; tatha vidvan namarupad vimuktah paratparam purusam upaiti divyam.

8. *As the rivers flowing towards the ocean become indistinguishable upon reaching it by losing their names and forms, so is a wise person, freed from name and form, reaches the higher than the high divine Person.*

9. sa yo ha vai tat paramam brahma veda brahma iva bhavati nasyabrahmavit kule bhavati; tarati sokam tarati papmanam guhagranthibhyo vimukto'mrto bhavati.

9. *Verily, he who knows that supreme Brahman becomes Brahman Himself. In his family none would be born who would not know Brah-*

man. *He crosses over sorrow, crosses over sin, and freed from the knots of the cave (of his heart), he becomes immortal.*

10. tad etad rcabhyuktam kriyavantah srotriya brahmanisthah svayam juhvata ekarsim sraddhayantah; tesam evaitam brahmavidyam vadeta sirovratam vidhivad yaistu cirnam.

10. This is what is declared in a verse of the Rigveda. Those who are engaged in kriya yoga, who are well versed in the scriptures, who are intent upon Brahman, who offer themselves as an oblation to the one Seer with faith, and who have undergone the rite of holding fire upon their shaven heads as per the prevailing practice, to them only one should declare this knowledge of Brahman.

Note: Sirovratam is Vedic ceremony practiced by the students of Atharvaveda, in which the worshippers put embers upon their shaven heads to symbolize the heat (tapas) generated in the body during austerity.

11. tad etat satyam rsir angirah purovaca naitadacirna-vrato'dhite; namah paramarsibhyo namah paramarsibhyah .

11. This is the truth. The seer Angirasa declared it in the past. He who has not performed the (head) rite should not learn this. Salutation to the great seers! Salutation to the great seers!

Notes: The verse declares that this knowledge should not be taught to those who have not performed tapas or austerity with their heads. Symbolically it means the knowledge should not taught to those who have not ignited the fire of knowledge in their heads or who do not carry the burden of austerity and discipline upon their heads.

Mandukya Upanishad

Editor's Note

The Mandukya Upanishad belongs to the Atharvaveda. It contains only 12 verses. Yet, it occupies an important place in the development of Vedic thought and in many ways forms the basis for the Advaita school of Hindu philosophy or monism. Its importance grew further, following a commentary (karika) upon it by Gaudapada, who is considered one of the earliest proponents of the Advaita. The school believes that Brahman alone is true, one and only, and the rest is one big illusion, which we mistakenly accept as true because of our own delusion and ignorance. His karika, a voluminous work, compared to the Upanishad itself, became the basis for subsequent works on Advaita, including those of Shankara who is believed to be a student of a teacher from the same lineage to which the tradition of Gaudapada belonged. The Upanishad deals with the symbolic significance of the sacred syllable Aum and its correlation with the four states of consciousness, namely the wakeful consciousness, the dream state, the deep sleep or dreamless sleep state and the transcendental state in which all divisions and duality disappears and the Self alone exists in its pure state, all by itself.

Presented here is a revised translation of the Upanishad by Jayaram V.

Invocation

aum bhadram karnebhih srnuyama devah, bhadram pasyemakshabhir yajatrah' sthirair angais tustuvaga sas tanibhih, vyasema deva-hitam yad ayuh, svasti na indro vrddha-sravah, svasti nah pisha visva-vedah, svasti nas tarkshayo arishtanemih, svasti no brhaspatir dadhatu. aum santih santih santih.

Aum! O gods, may we hear with our ears what is auspicious for us. While we perform the sacrifices, may we see what is auspicious. Offering praise with steady limbs and bodies, may we spend our lives for the good of the gods. May Indra, of the ancient glory, be auspicious to us, may the universal god, Pusan, be auspicious to us. May Tarksya of the unhurt wheel bestow blessings upon us. May Brihaspati, the destroyer of evil, be auspiciously inclined towards us.

Translation

The Four States of Consciousness

1. aum ity etad aksaram idam sarvam tasyopa vyakhyanam bhutam bhavad bhavisyad iti sarvam aumkara eva; yaccan yat trikalatitam tad apy aumkara eva.

1. Aum, this syllable, that is all this. Of it, this is the explanation. The past, the present and the future, all this, verily, is of the form of Aum only. And whatever is beyond these three division of time is also of the form of Aum only.

Notes: Brahman manifested the world becoming sound. Hence He is also known as Isvara. He used sacred sounds to perform a great sacrifice from which issued forth worlds and beings. Some of these sacred sounds are available to us in the form of the Vedas with which we too can participate in the creation of God and uphold dharma. Of the sounds, Aum is the seed syllable (bijaksaram). It is hidden in every other sound. Whether we chant it or not, it precedes all the mantras in the Vedas and uplifts them heavenwards when they are uttered during sacrifices. It is imperishable and verily compared to manifested Brahman. Time, one of the earliest of God's manifestation, is also a form of Aum only. What is beyond time, the eternal, that also is Aum. Aum is thus everything, what is here and what is above and what is manifestation and that which is beyond manifestation.

2. sarvam hy etad brahma ayam atma brahma so'yam atma catuspat.

2. All this, verily, is Brahman only. This Self is Brahman. That very Self is four-footed.

Notes: Catuspat, means four-footed. Shankara preferred to translate it as four quarters (of a karsapana coin, ancient currency unit) since the four states of consciousness found in a person merge progressively into one state as the person falls asleep. The four feet refers to the four states or planes of consciousness. In truth, Brahman has no states. He is absolute. These states refer to the four planes of existence found in creation as well in one's own consciousness. They are His reflections in Nature.

3. jagaritasthano bahisprajnah saptanga ekonavimsati mukhah sthula bhug vaisvanarah prathamah padah.

3. The wakeful state, which is outwardly conscious, having seven limbs and nineteen mouths, in which one enjoys the gross objects, is vaisvanarah, the first state.

Notes: The vaisvanarah is the state in which all the senses are fully awake and remain engaged outwardly with the external sense-objects. In this state, the body is subject to hunger and, like fire, acts as a devourer, consuming various objects as food. In this state the mind acts directly upon the perceptions. Based on a verse from the Chandogya Upanishad (5.18.2), Shankara stated the seven limbs as the head, the eye, breath, the middle part, the bladder, the feet and the mouth. He listed the nineteen mouths as the five senses, the five organs of action, the five breaths, the mind, the intellect, the ego and the mind-stuff (citta). In creation, the earthly world symbolizes the vaisvanarah state.

4. svapna sthano'ntahprajnah saptanga ekonavimsati mukhah praviviktabhuk taijaso dvitiyah padah.

4. The dream state, the inwardly conscious, with seven limbs and nineteen mouths, the enjoyer of subtle things, is taijasa, the second state.

Notes: We experience taijasa, the luminous state, in dreams, when our senses are asleep and withdrawn and we are mentally active within ourselves, unmindful of what is happening outside. It is an intermediate state between sleep and wakefulness. In this state the mind acts upon the impressions stored in it rather than the direct perceptions. The seven parts and seventeen mouths which we discussed before are the same as in case of Vaisvanara state. However, in this state, except for the mind and the mind-stuff, they remain largely latent or inactive. In creation, the moon or the ancestral world, symbolizes the dream state.

5. yatra supto na kamcana kamam kamayate na kamcana svapnam pasyati tat susuptam; susupta sthana ekibhutah prajnana-ghana evanandamayo hy anandabhuk cetomukhah prajnastrtiyah padah.

5. That is deep sleep, in which the sleeping one does not desire any desire whatsoever, and does not see any dream whatsoever. The state of deep sleep has only one element, is endowed with pure consciousness, and filled with bliss. It verily is an enjoyer of bliss, with the mind as its face. This is Prajna, the third state.

Next: In deep sleep all physical activities comes to rest. Only the pure mind filled with pure consciousness remain awake. Hence it has mind as its face. It has only one element, the space. Since it is free from desires and dreams, it is the enjoyer of bliss. Symbolically, in creation this state is represented by space or heaven. The one element is space.

6. esa sarvesvarah esa sarvajna eso'ntaryamyesa yonih sarvasyaprabhavapyayau hi bhutanam.

6. This one is the lord of all; this one is omniscient; this one is the womb of all. This one, verily, is the origin and the end of all beings.

Notes: Deep sleep is not tamasic state of withdrawal but a state of complete calm, which is the natural state of an adept yogi who has trained his mind and body and managed to suppress the modifications of his mind. It is filled with pure consciousness (prajna), devoid of any modifications and latent impressions. As the state of Brahman it is the origin for all beings and as the state of liberation it is also the end for them.

7. nantahprajnam na bahisprajnam nobhayatahprajnam na prajnanaghanam; na prajnam na prajnam; adrstam avyavaharyam agrahyam alaksanam acintyam avyapadesyam ekatma pratyayasaram prapancopasamam santam sivam advaitam caturtham manyante sa atma; sa vijneyah.

7. It is considered the fourth state, which is not conscious of the inside, not conscious of the outside, not conscious of both, not a mass of awareness, not consciousness, not unconsciousness, invisible, not into worldly ways, ungraspable, without qualities, unthinkable, indescribable, in essence the one soul, the ultimate relief from the phenomenal world, peaceful, auspicious, without duality.

Notes: This is turiya, the indeterminate, indefinable, indescribable, transcendental fourth state descriptive of the very nature of Self and Brahman. It is not consciousness. It is not aware of anything other than itself, since it is not subject to duality. Hence it has no awareness of what is inside the body or outside and anything else whatsoever. You cannot describe it as consciousness or unconsciousness. It is not of this world. Hence it is not conversant with worldly ways. You cannot reach it with your thoughts. Hence it is ungraspable and unthinkable. The remaining qualities described in this verse also point to the transcendental nature of the Self.

8. so'yamatmadhyaksaram aumkaro'dhimatram pada matra matrasca pada akara ukaro makara iti.

8. This is the Self. Viewed from the standpoint of syllables, it is of the form of Aum. Viewed from the standpoint of letters, the quarters are its letters, and the letters are its quarters, in the form of A, in the form of U and in the form of M.

9. jagaritasthano vaisvanaro'karah prathamamatrapter adimattvadvapnoti ha vai sarvankam anadis ca bhavati ya evam veda.

9. *The letter A represents the wakeful state vaisvanara, the all pervasive first letter having the precedence. He who knows this realizes all desires and becomes the foremost.*

Notes: The letter A is the first in all alphabets. The sound is also universal and hidden in every other sound. Hence it is described as all pervasive, like Brahman Himself.

10. svapnasthanah taijasa ukaro dvitiya matrotkarsat ubhayatvadvotkarsati ha vai jnana samtatim samanas ca bhavati nasyabrahmavit kule bhavati ya evam veda.

10. The letter U represents the dream state taijasa, the second letter of excellent form having the qualities of both. He who knows thus acquires knowledge and sameness and none in his family who would be born without the knowledge of Brahman.

Notes: Since in the dream state one is partially awake, it has some aspects of wakeful state and some aspects of sleep state. Hence, it is rightly described here as having the qualities of both the wakeful and sleep states. U is also the uprising and outward going sound in contrast to either A or E. Therefore, it is considered the most excellent like prana itself.

11. susuptasthanah prajno makarastrtiya matra miterapiterva minoti ha va idam sarvamapitisca bhavati ya evam veda

11. The letter M represents the deep sleep state prajna, the third letter, that limits as a measure and dissolves (the other two). He who knows this, measures all this and experiences self-absorption.

Notes: The third letter M serves as a measure by limiting the extent of both wakeful and the dream states. Since both end up being dissolved into deep sleep, it is also a state of resolution or dissolution of all phenomena, parts and forms. Hence the letter M serves as the limit as well as the end of all.

12. amatrascaturtho'vyavaharyah prapancopasamah sivo'dvaita evam aumkara atmaiva samvisatyatmanatmanam ya evam veda.

12. The fourth is that without forms, without this worldliness, in which the world finds peace. It is auspicious, without duality. Thus the form of Aum is the Self itself. He who knows thus enters into the Self by himself.

Notes: At the end of Aum what you reach is silence, the end of all sounds. That is the silenc of the Self. It is the state of the ascetic yogis (munis), who reach the end of desires. This state, which is beyond the deep sleep and beyond all sounds, is the inexhaustible, imperishable deep calm, the eternal transcendental state that is indefinable and inexpressible. It is a state in which both the knower and the knowing are absent. Hence nothing can be said about it.

Free Translation

Notes: The following is a free translation of the Mundaka Upanishad done by Jayaram V several years ago. It published originally on Hinduwebsite.com. We included it in this collection since it captures the essence of the Upanishad with brevit and simplicity.

1. This syllable AUM is verily all this
This is the explanation about AUM:
The past, the present and the future are AUM,
And That beyond these three is also AUM.

2. Brahman is indeed all this.
This self in us is also Brahman.
And this self has four planes.

3. Vaisvanara is the first stage.
Wakeful, outwardly conscious,
With seven limbs and nineteen mouths,
He is the enjoyer of the gross objects.

4..Taijasa is the second stage.
Dreaming, inwardly conscious,
With seven limbs and nineteen mouths,
He is the enjoyer of the subtle objects.

5. In deep sleep, seeking no desires,
Dreaming no dreams, unified into
The mass of greater consciousness,
Full of bliss, enjoying bliss only,
Face turned towards Chetasa,
Is Prajna the third stage.

6. This is the Master of All, the Omniscient,
The Inmost Dweller and source of
Creation and destruction of all beings.

7. Conscious neither internally nor externally,
Nor either ways, neither ordinary consciousness,
Nor the greater and the deeper consciousness,
Invisible, otherworldly, incomprehensible,
Without qualities, beyond all thoughts,

Indescribable, the unified soul in essence,
Peaceful, auspicious, without duality,
Is the fourth stage, that self, that is to be known.

8. *The same Atman is AUM among the syllables,*
Each syllable in the word AUM is a stage. They
Are the letter A, the letter U and the letter M.

9 *The wakeful Vaishwanara is the*
First letter "A", being the first letter and
All pervasive. He who knows thus realizes
All his desires and becomes foremost too.

10. *The dreaming Taizasa is the second*
Letter "U", being superior and situated in
The middle. He who knows thus attains
Knowledge and children equally and none
In his family would be ignorant of Brahman.

11. *In the world of deep sleep, Prajna, is the*
Third letter "M", being the limit and the end of
All diversity. He who knows thus is free from
All diversity and becomes one with the Self.

12. *The fourth state is without parts and entanglements*
Not bound to this world, It is auspicious and non-dual
Thus the form of AUM is verily the Self itself
He who knows thus enters into his own Self by himself.

Prasna Upanishad

Editor's Note

It is believed that the Prasna Upanishad might have been originally an independent text, but was later included in the Atharvaveda due to the association of Pippalada, the teacher of the Upanishad, with the Atharvaveda. As the name suggests, it is an Upanishad of six main questions, asked by six seekers of truth and answered by sage Pippalapada. The questions cover a wide range of subjects concerning the origin of creation, superiority of breath, the supporting and illuminating powers of manifest creation, the source of life for the physical body, the paths of breath in the body, the nature of dream and deep sleep states, the benefits of chanting the sacred mantra Aum and the significance of the sixteen tattvas or realities of Nature. From the Upanishad, we learn that an enlightened master would not reveal the secrets of higher knowledge unless he was satisfied that the recipients were qualified and disciplined. Pippalapada, the son of Dadhichi, was a historic person, considered a teacher of the Atharvaveda and founder of an ancient school of thought. He probably lived a few centuries or decades before the Buddha and some of his disciples might be contemporaries of the Buddha. His name suggests that he had some connection with the Pipal tree, or with its fruit which he was said to be fond of, or with a branch of ascetics who meditated traditionally under the tree because of its miraculous powers. It is a known fact that even the Buddha got enlightenment under a pipal tree. Pippalapada used to insist that his disciples stayed with him for a year before he would answer them any questions they asked.

Presented here is a new translation of the Prasna Upanishad by Jayaram V. Previously, a partial translation of it by Jayaram V was published on Hinduwebsite.com.

Invocation

aum bhadram karnebhih srnuyama deva bhadram pasyemaksabhir yajatrah; sthirair angais tustuvamsas tanubhir vyasema devahitam yad ayuh.

1. Aum, O gods, may we hear with our ears what is auspicious. O those who are qualified for worship, may we see with our eyes what is auspicious. May we enjoy the life given to us by gods, with bodies of strong limb, living for the sake of gods.

svasti na indro vrddhasravah svasti nah pusa visvavedah; svasti nastarksyo aristanemih svasti no brhaspatir dadhatu; aum santih santih santih.

2. May Indra, of ever increasing vigor, bestow upon us prosperity. May Pusan, the knower of all, bring to us prosperity. May Tarksya, the obstructer of misfortune, grant us prosperity. May Brihaspati, give us prosperity. Aum, peace, peace, peace.

Question 1
Manifestations of Prajapati

1. Aum, sukesa ca bharadvajah saibyasca satyakamah sauryayani ca gargyah kausalyas casvalayano bhargavo vaida-rbhih kabandhi katyayanaste haite brahmapara brahman-isthah param brahmanvesamana esa ha vai tat sarvam vaks-yatiti te ha samitpanayo bhagavantam pippaladam upasannah.

1. Once Sukesa, son of Bharadvaja, Satyakama son of Sibi, Gargya grandson of Surya, Kausalya son of Asvala, Bhargava of the Vidarbha country, Kabandhi son of Katya, these, devoted to Brahman, their minds fixed in Brahman, and searching for the highest Brahman, approached the godman, Pippalada, with sacrificial fuel in their hands, thinking that he would explain to them all about That.

Notes: Six students approached sage Pippalada with fuel in their hands hoping that he would teach them about Brahman. We do not know how these six students approached him all at once, whether they just happened to meet him by chance or whether they came as a group because they belonged to a particular school or tradition. What we know is that they had doubts and curiosity about Brahman and they were eager to learn about Him by asking questions, which became the starting point of discussion for each of the six chapters. Of these six, Kabandhi Katyayana or one of his immediate descendents was said to be a contemporary of the Buddha.

2. tan ha sa risir uvaca bhuya eva tapasa brahmacaryena sraddhaya samvatsaram samvatsyatha yathakamam prasnan pricchata yadi vijnasyamah sarvam ha vo vaksyama iti.

2. The seer said to them, "Stay for a year, practicing austerity, chastity and faith. Then ask me whatever you desire to ask and if we know, we shall, indeed, tell you all about it."

Notes: It is said that it was customary for the students of Pippalada to stay with him for a year before he gave them initiation.

3. atha kabandhi katyayana upetya papraccha; bhagavan kuto ha va imah prajah prajayanta iti

3. Then, Kabandhi, son of Katya approached him and asked, "Godman, from what, indeed, all these creatures arise?"

Notes: Kabandhi wanted to know the source of creation or the deity who was responsible for manifesting life forms. Creation is a mystery. Even now, in this age, we are not sure how life originated upon earth and how so much diversity manifested. Even if science manages to find out the truth concerning our creation, it would not be able to fathom the reasons for it. No scientist can tell you why the world came into existence or why beings manifested upon earth. They may tell you how, but not why. Only philosophical enquiry can throw some light upon it, though vaguely. Hence we have speculative philosophies that try to fill in the gaps in our understanding of life and creation, which science or empirical studies fail to explain.

4. tasmai sa hovaca prajakamo vai prajapatih sa tapo'tapyata sa tapastaptva sa mithunamutpadayate; rayim ca pranam ca ityetau me bahudha prajah karisyata iti.

4. To him he said, "Prajapati, the Lord of all creatures, desirous of offspring, performed penance, and by practicing that penance produced the pair, matter and life, thinking that they would produce manifold beings for him in diverse ways.

Notes: Rayi, stone, represents gross matter or the physical body. Prana, (life), which keeps the body breathing, represents the subtle energy or the subtle body. Thoughts, feelings, emotions arise and exist in us because of prana. Without prana, beings would be lifeless. The component realities of Nature (tattvas) arise from both. Therefore, beings are made of both. Each being has a gross body and a subtle body, one visible and the other invisible, one sustained by food (rayi) and the other by subtle energy (prana) that circulates in the body through various channels led by the breath (prana). Both these constitute the beingness. They are different and distinct from the inner Self, but depend upon it entirely, while the Self is completely independent and self-existing.

5. adityo ha vai prano rayir eva candrama rayir va etat sarvam yan murtam camurtam ca tasman murtir eva rayih.

5. *Aditya, the sun, indeed, is life, the moon the matter. Matter indeed is all this, whatever that has a definite form and has no form. Therefore body (of a being), indeed is matter only.*

Notes: Matter exists either in recognizable forms, as objects, or in its primal and formless state as the basic raw material, such as energy or clay. Whether it has a form or not, clay is still matter only. We may distinguish an object from a lump of clay for our understanding, but they are essentially made of the same substance, the earth. The body has a form; but when it is reduced to its elemental state, it has no recognizable form. Yet all states of corporeality and embodiment represent different states of matter only.

6. athaditya udayan yat pracim disam pravisati tena pracyan pranan rasmisu sannidhatte; yad daksinam yat praticim yad udicim yad adho yad urdhvam yad antara diso yat sarvam prakasayati, tena sarvan pranan rasmisu sannidhatte.

6. *Now, after the sun arises, he enters (this world) from the eastern side. There, he bathes with his effulgent rays all that lives in the east. Then he shines brightly upon whatever is in the south, whatever is in the west, whatever is in the north, all that is below, above and in between. Thereby, he bathes with his effulgent rays all living beings (in all quarters and directions).*

Notes: The sun is prana. He is the life giver. He is the source of all energy. This is a verifiable fact. The sun shines equally in all directions and upon all beings. We are able to exist because the Sun is unconditional in giving light and radiates in all directions.

7. sa esa vaisvanaro visvarupah prano'gnir udayate; tad etad rica'bhyuktam.

7. *This is he, the Vaisvanara fire of innumerable forms, (verily), who rises as life and fire. Of this there is this verse from the Rigveda*

Notes: The sun exists in the body as Vaisvanara, the indwelling fire. He circulates in the body as five breaths that move in their respective channels and keep the bodily temperature (tapah) intact so that the organs (deities) carry out their respective functions.

8. visvarupam harinam jatavedasam parayanam jyotir ekam tapantam; sahasrarasmih satadha vartamanah pranah prajanam udayaty esa suryah.

8. *Of innumerable forms, golden colored, the knower of all, the object of study, the one light, the result of austerity, with a thousand rays, who exists in a hundred forms, the life in all beings, thus rises the Sun.*

Notes: The Vedas are considered the verbal testimony to establish spiritual truths. Hence, Pipplalada quoted a verse from the Rigveda in support of his teaching that the sun indeed exists in the body as the Vaisvanara fire and responsible for its life as well as its warmth.

9. samvatsaro vai prajapatih tasyayane daksinam cottaram ca; tadye ha vai tad istapurte kritam ity upasate te candramasam eva lokam abhijayante; ta eva punaravartante tasmad eta risayah prajakama daksinam pratipadyante; esa ha vai rayiryah pitriyanah.

9. *The year, indeed, is Prajapati, the Lord of beings. He has two paths, the southern and the northern. Now as to those, who perform sacrificial actions out of desires and worship thus, conquer the world in the moon. They return again. Therefore, the sages, who desire offspring, attain the southern path. This one, which is called the path of ancestors, is verily matter.*

Notes: There are two paths, the southern path by which the departing souls go to the world of ancestors that exists in the moon and return from there to take another birth again. In the ancestral world they become food to the deities. Hence it is called the food or matter (rayi). The other one is the northern path, which leads to the world of immortals. It is described in the next.

10. athottarena tapasa brahmacaryena sraddhaya vidyaya atmanam anvisyadityam abhijayante; etadvai prananam ayatanam etad amritam abhayam etat parayanam etasmanna punar avartante ity esa nirodhah, tadesa slokah.

10. *Now, by the northern path conquer the sun, those who search for their true Selves through austerity, celibacy, faith and knowledge. This, indeed, is the container of life breath; this is immortal, the fearless; this is the highest goal. From this none ever returns. This one prevents (rebirth). Of this there is the verse.*

Notes: These two paths are mentioned in other Upanishads also. The northern path leads to the world of immortals believed to exist in the sun. Those who go there would never return. It is attained only by the practice of yoga and renunciation. Thus, the mortal beings have two options. By seeking material things, or indulging in desires and selfish actions, they revolve in the cycle of death and rebirth. However, by ascetic practices and generating bodily heat (tapa) through penances (tapas), they can transform their physical and subtle bodies and attain immortality.

11. pancapadam pitaram dvadasa kritim diva ahuh pare ardhe purisinam; atheme anya u pare vicaksanam saptacakre sadara ahurarpitamiti.

11. *They say this deity is the father of five seasons and twelve forms, seated high in the heaven, amidst waters. Now, others say (he is) wise, who is endowed with (a chariot of) seven wheels, (each having) six spokes.*

Notes: The symbolism in this verse refer to the divisions of time. The deity, Kala or Time, often equated with Prajapati, is the father of five seasons and twelve months.

He is also endowed with the seven days of a week and the six divisions of four hours each in each day. Time has great significance in Hindu cosmology. It is one of the earliest manifestations of Brahman, which is responsible for diversity, the world order, the fructification of karma, rebirth, recurring phenomena such as day and night, weeks, months, years and the seasons, and death.

12. maso vai prajapatih tasya krisnapaksa eva rayih suklah pranah tasmad ete risayah sukla istim kurvanti itara itarasmin.

12 The month, verily, is Prajapati, the Lord of the creatures. Of this the dark half is matter and the bright half is life. That is why, the seers perform sacrifices in the bright half; while others perform them in the other half.

13. ahoratro vai prajapatih tasyahar eva prano ratrir eva rayih pranam va ete praskandanti ye diva ratya samyujyan te brahmacaryam eva tad yad ratrau ratya samyujyante.

13. Day and night are, indeed, Prajapati, the Lord of the creatures. Of this, day is life and the night is matter. Those who unite in sexual acts during the day waste their life-energy; while those who unite in sexual acts during the night remain (pure as the) chaste.

Notes: There is a time for everything. According to this nighttime intercourse is not sinful, but daytime one is. According to this verse, daytime intercourse will result in the wastage of bodily heat (tapa).

14. annam vai prajapatih tato ha vai tad retah tasmad imah prajah prajayanta iti.

14. Food, indeed, is Prajapati, the Lord of creatures. From that only is semen. From that are born these beings.

15. tadye ha vai tat prajapativratam caranti te mithunam utpadayante; tesam evaisa brahma loko yesam tapo brahmacaryam yesu satyam pratistitam.

15. Thus, those who practice the vow of Prajapati, the lord of creatures, produce both (sons and daughters). For them only is meant this world created by Brahma, in whom austerity, chastity and truth are established.

Notes: Isa brahman loka means this world of Brahma. It refers to our world or the earthly world.

16. tesam asau virajo brahma loko na yesu jihmam anritam na maya ceti.

16. To them belongs the bright and spotless world of Brahman, in whom there is no crookedness, falsehood or delusion.

Question 2

Deities in the Body and Breath

1. atha hainam bhargavo vaidarbhih papraccha; bhagavan katyeva devah prajam vidharayante katara etat prakasayante kah punaresam varistha iti.

1. Then Bhargava of Vidarbha asked, "Godman, how many deities support a being? Which of them illumine it? Who is superior among them?"

Notes: The question is essentially about the organs that support the body or the gods who uphold the material body of creation.

2. tasmai sa hovaca, akasa ha va esa devo vayur agnir apah prithivi van manas caksuh srotram ca; te prakasyabhivadanti vayam etad banam avastabhya vidharayamah.

2. He said, "Space, verily, is this deity; so also air, fire, water, earth, speech, the mind, eyes, and ear. Having illumined the body, they declare, "We support this aggregate of the body by holding it together."

Notes: Each organ in the body is a deity performing certain functions to help the body survive. The body is a creation in itself. It represents the entire cosmos in a minute form. It has its own dharma, derived from the highest Supreme Self Himself. The organs uphold it and share the burdens of the body. They do it not only to support the body, but also to serve the soul that is hidden in it. The body is a vehicle for the soul, its Lord, and every organ in it is meant to play its dutiful role to provide enjoyment to the soul and allow it to continue its existence in a mortal form until its liberation. Feeding the body is an act of sacrifice. The food is the sacrificial offering. The body is the kshetra, the sacrificial pit. The offering is accepted by the digestive fire vaisvanara on behalf of all other organs, just as the sacrificial fire accepts the sacrificial offerings poured into a sacrifice and apportions them among the gods according to their appointed share.

3. tan varisthah prana uvaca; ma moham apadyatha aham evaitat pancadhatmanam pravibhajya etad banam avastabhya vidharayami iti.

3. Breath, the foremost among them, said to them, "Do not fall into delusion. I am the one who supports and sustains this body by dividing myself into fivefold."

Notes: In simple terms, prana means breath. in broader terms, it is the life sustaining energy arising from the sun externally and the subtle energy sustained internally in the body by the five different breaths which will be discussed later. Although, loosely speaking, prana means breath, it does not convey the true meaning of prana, which is not only the breath we inhale and exhale but also the life energy derived from the sun which flows in our veins (nadis) along particular channels and keeps us alive.

4. te asraddadhana babhuvuh so'bhirmanad urdhvam utkrmata iva, tasminn utkramaty yathetare sarva evotkra-mante, tasmims ca pratisthamane sarva eva pratisthante, tad yatha maksika madhukararajanam tukramantam sarva evotkramante tasmims ca pratisthamane sarva eva pratisthante evam van manat caksuh srotram ca, te pritah pranam stunvanti.

4. *They did not believe. Out of pride, he seemed to go up. As he went up, then all others also went up. When he settled down, they also settled down. Just as all the bees fly out, when the queen bee flies out and all settle down when she settles down, so did speech, mind, eye, ear. Having been satisfied, they praised prana.*

Notes: Creation has a structure and hierarchy. The deities have to settle that among themselves so that they can be functionally effective and keep their chain of command flowing. The organs in the body, which are supposed to function as a team, went through this storming and norming process by challenging each other and eventually accepted prana as superior among them. Prana is superior to the bodily organs because it sustains life in the body. The bodily organs depend upon it, since it facilitates the flow of the Vaisvanara fire in the body and the distribution of food among them. We know that the body cannot survive, if breath departs from it. So is the case with all the bodily parts. They cannot survive if breath departs from the body. Without prana, they will be reduced into the five basic elements (mahabhutas). The same is emphasized here. Madhukara-rajanam means the ruler among the bees. It is translated here as the queen bee since there is no king-bee.

5. eso'gnistapatyesa surya esa parjanyo maghavan esa vayuh; esa prithivi rayirdevah sada asac camritam ca yat.

5. *This one burns like fire; this one is the sun; this one is the rain; this one is the air; this one is the earth, matter, deity; he is what is and what is not and what is immortal.*

6. ara iva rathanabhau prane sarvam pratisthitam; rico yajumsi samani yagyah ksatram brahma ca.

6. *As spokes (are fixed) in the hub of a wheel, breath is established in all (organs), in the hymns of the Rigveda, Yajurveda, Samaveda, in sacrifices, warriors and the brahmanas.*

Notes: Breath is hidden in the hymns of the Vedas because to chant them you need breath in the mouth. So also, it flows equally in people of all castes.

7. prajapatis-carasi garbhe tvameva pratijayase; tubhyam prana prajastvima balim haranti yah pranaih pratitisthasi.

7. *You verily wander in the wombs like the lord of creation, and you are then born again (in children). O Breath, for you alone, who dwells in the organs, all these creatures bring their sacrifices.*

8. devanamasi vahnitamah pitrinam prathama svadha; risinam caritam satyam atharvangirasam asi.

8. You are the best carrier for the gods, first offering to the ancestors; you are the truth in the conduct of the seers such as the Atharvas and the Angirasas.

Notes: Shankara translated risinam as the bodily organs and atharvangirasam as the essence of atharva present in the organs.

9. indras tvam prana tejasa rudro'si pariraksita; tvam-antarikse carasi suryastvam jyotisam patih.

9. O Breath, you are Indra, in vigor you are Rudra, who protects from all sides; you wander in the mid-region (as air), you are the sun (in the heaven), the lord of the lights.

10. yada tvam abhivarsasy athemah prana te prajah; anandarupas tisthanti kamayannam bhavisyati iti.

10. When you pour down then, O breath, these beings of yours appear happy (thinking) that there will be as much food as they desire.

11. vratyas tvam prana ekarsiratta visvasya satpatih; vayam adyasya datarah pita tvam matarisva, nah.

11. You are very pure, O Matarisva, the one seer, the eater, and the universal lord of all that exists. We are the offerers of the food (you eat).

Notes: Matarisva, an epithet of vayu, used here to invoke Breath.

12. ya te tanurvaci pratisthita yasrotre yaca caksusi; yaca manasi santatasivam tam kuru motkramih.

12. Make pure and auspicious, settling firmly, the speech, the ears, the eyes, and the whole mind. Do not rise up and go away.

13. pranasyedam vase sarvam tridive yat pratisthitam; mateva putran raksasva sris ca pragyam ca vidhehi na iti.

13. All this here is under the control of breath. It is firmly established in the three worlds. Protect us as a mother (protects) her son, give us wisdom and destine for us prosperity and wisdom.

Question 3

The Origin and Manifestations of Breath

1. atha hainam kausalyas casvalayanah papraccha; bhagavan kuta esa prano jayate katham ayaty asmim charire atmanam va

pravibhajya katham pratisthate kenotkramate katham bahyam abhidhate katham adhyatmam iti.

1. The Kausalya Asvalayanah asked him, "Godman, from where does this breath born? How does it enter into this body? And having established, how does it divide itself in the body? How does it leave? How does it support what is outside and what is within oneself?"

2. tasmai sa hovaca atiprasnan pricchasi brahmistho'siti tasmat te'ham bravimi.

2. To him, he said, "Very difficult questions you ask. You are interested in Brahman. Therefore, I will tell you."

3. atmana esa prano jayate; yathaisa puruse chayaitasminn etad atatam manokritenayaty asmin sarire.

3. From the self this breath is born. Like this shadow of a person, the breath spreads in this body (from the Self) by the actions of the mind.

4. yatha samradevadhikritan viniyunkte; etan graman etan graman adhitistasvety evam evaisa prana itaran pranan prithak prithag eva sannidhatte.

4. Just as an emperor appoints officers, saying, "Preside over this and this village," so does Breath allots separate duties to the other pranas (in the body).

Notes: The other pranas are the five pranas that circulate in the body, which are described in the next verse.

5. payupasthe'panam caksuh srotre mukhanasikabhyam pranah svayam pratistate madhye tu samanah; esa hy etadd hutam annam samam nayati tasmad etah saptarciso bhavanti.

5. He established apana in the two lower apertures, breath itself in the eye, in the ears and in the mouth, and samana in the middle. It distributes the food that has been offered equally. Therefore seven flames arise from this.

Notes: Apana is the breath that goes down and out through the lower apertures. Prana is that which goes upward through the throat, nostrils, the eyes and the ears. The samana is equalizing breath that circulates in the middle region. It is responsible for digestion.

6. hridi hyesa atma; atraitad ekasatam nadinam tasam satam satam ekaikasyam dvasaptatir dvasaptatih pratisakha nadisahasrani bhavanty asu vyanas carati.

6. The Self, indeed, is in the heart. In that (heart) are one hundred and one arteries. Each of them again has a hundred and each of these branches into seventy two thousand sub-branches. Vyana moves in them.

Notes: Vyana is the diffused breath. It circulates in the entire bodies through these fine arteries issuing from the heart and its main arteries. It is important to remember that these arteries of prana are not blood vessels, but subtle channels through which pranic energy flows in the body. If these channels are blocked for one reason or the other, a person may develop physical and mental ailments.

7. athaikayordhva udanah punyena punyam lokam nayati papena papam ubhabhyam eva manusya lokam.

7. Now rising up through one of these udana leads by means of merit to the world of merit and by means of sin to the world of sin and by means of both to the world of mortals.

Notes: Udana is the breath that goes upwards through the artery susumna

8. adityo ha vai bahyah prana udayaty esa hy enam caksusam pranam anugrihnanah; prithivyam ya devata saisa purusasya apanam avastabhyantara yad akasah sa samano vayur vyanah.

8. The sun indeed is the external breath. It rises up empowering the breath in the eye. The earth is that very deity which draws a person's apana towards itself. The mid-region in between is samana. Air is vyana.

9. tejo ha va udanah tasmad upasantatejah; punar bhavam indriyair manasi sampadhyamanaih.

9. Light indeed is udana. Therefore, he whose light has departed, attains another existence together with his senses drawn into his mind.

Notes: At the time of death, udana, the upward breath, travels through one of the veins leading from the heart and escapes the body through an aperture in the head.

10. yat cittas tenaisa pranam ayati; pranas tejasa yuktah sahatmana yatha sankalpitam lokam nayati.

10. Whatever thought he had (at the time of death), with that he enters into breath. Yoked to the light (udana) and along with the Self, breath leads him to the world as intended by him.

11. ya evam vidvan pranam veda na hasya praja hiyate'mrito bhavati tadesah slokah.

11. He who knows breath thus, has no shortage of progeny. He becomes immortal. Of this, there is this verse.

12. utpattim ayatim sthanam vibhutvam caiva pancadha; adhyatmam caiva pranasya vijnayamritam asnute vijnayamritam asnuta iti.

12. *Knowing the origin, the entry, the placement, and the fivefold manifestation of breath within oneself, one attains immortality. Knowing one does indeed attain immortality.*

Question 4

Who Remains Awake in Sleep

1. atha hainam sauryayani gargyah papraccha; bhagavan etasmin puruse kani svapanti kany asmijn jagrati katara esa devah svapnan pasyati kasyaitat sukham bhavati kasmin nu sarve sampratistita bhavantiti.

1. *Then Sauryayani Garya asked him, "Godman, which organs remain asleep and which organs remain awake in this person? Who is the deity who watches the dreams? Who happens to be happy and in whom they become fully resolved?*

2. tasmai sa hovaca; yatha gargya maricayo'r arkasyastam gacchatah sarva etasmis tejomandala ekibhavanti; tah punah punar udayatah pracaranty evam ha vai tat sarvam pare deve manasy ekibhavati tena tarhy esa puruso na srinoti na pasyati na jighrati na rasayate na sprisate nabhivadate nadatte nanandayate na visrijate neyayate svapitity acaksate.

2. *To him he said, "Just as, O Gargya, the rays of the sun become one in the sphere of the sun and spread out as he dawns again and again, so do all these organs become one in the highest deity, the mind. Therefore, during that time the person does not hear, does not see, does not smell, does not taste, does not touch, does not speak, does not grasp, does not rejoice, does not expel, and does not move. He is sleep, they say.*

3. pranagnaya evaitasmin pure jagrati; garhapatyo ha va esopanah vyano'nvaharyapacanah yad'garhapatyat praniyate pranayanad ahavaniyah pranah.

3. *In this city(the body) it is the fires of prana that remain awake. This apana is indeed the garhapatya fire. Vyana is the anvaharyapacana fire. Since the ahavaniya fire is extracted from the garhyapatya fire, which is the source of extraction, Prana is the Ahavainya fire.*

Notes: Garhapatya, anvaharyapacana and ahvaniya fires are the domestic fires expected to be kept by the householders, especially those belonging to the Brahmana caste, for the purpose of performing daily sacrifices. The three fires have to be maintained at three different locations in the house. They are compared here to the three types of breath mentioned before.

4. yad ucchvasa nihsvasav etav ahuti samam nayatiti sa samanah; mano ha va va yajamanah; istaphalam evodanah; sa enam yajamanam ahar ahar brahma gamayati.

4. Since it equalizes these (two) oblations, the inhalation and exhalation, therefore it is (called) samana. The mind is indeed the host of the sacrifice. The desired fruit of the sacrifice is udana. Day after day it leads the host of the sacrifice to Brahman.

Notes: Samana is the presiding prana of the mid-region (atmosphere). It equalizes both the inhalation and exhalation. These are likened in this verse to the oblations offered in the fire (Agnihotra) sacrifice. Udana travels upwards into the head region. Since it accompanies the beings to sleep, it is described here as the one which takes the host of the sacrifice to Brahman day after day.

5. atraisa devah svapne mahimanam anubhavati; yad dristam dristam anupasyati srutam srutam evartham anusrinoti desadigantarais ca pratyanubhutam punah punah pratyanubhavati dristam cadristam ca srutam casrutam canubhutam cananubhutam ca sac casac ca sarvam pasyati sarvah pasyati.

5. There, in the dream state, that deity experiences greatness. Whatever he has seen, he sees again, heard, he hears again; whatever he experiences in places and regions, he experiences them again and again; whatever he has seen and not seen, whatever he has heard and not heard, whatever was felt and not felt, whatever exists and not exists, he sees all becoming all.

Notes: A dream is a rehash of existing memories, sensations, feelings, perceptions and experiences with imagination intermixed. In a dream, the mind, which is the deity described here, becomes the creator (sarvah) as well as creation (sarvam). He attains greatness (mahiman) by transcending the physical barriers that exist in the physical world. In short, in dream state, you have no limits to what you can experience or go.

6. sa yada tejasa'bhibhuto bhavati; atraisa devah svapnanna pasyaty atha tad etasmin sarire etat sukham bhavati.

6. When he is overwhelmed by light, then that deity does not see the dreams. Then peace and happiness arise in this body.

7. sa yatha sobhya vayamsi vasovriksam sampratisthante; evam ha vai tat sarvam para atmani sampratisthante.

7. *Just as the birds, O radiant one, fly towards the tree that shelters them, so does everything, so also all this proceeds towards the supreme Self to rest there.*

8. **prithivi ca prithivimatraca apas capomatra ca tejas ca tejomatra ca vayus ca vayumatra ca akasas cakasamatra ca caksus ca drastavyam ca srotram ca srotavyam ca granam ca ghratavyam ca, rasas ca rasayitavyam ca tvak ca sparsayitavyam ca vak ca vaktavyam ca hastau cadatavyam ca upasthas canandayitavyam ca payusc ca visarjayitavyam ca yadau ca gantavyam ca manas ca mantavyam ca buddhis ca boddhivyam ca ahankaras ca ahankartavyam ca cittam ca cetayitavyam ca tejas ca vidyotayitavyam ca pranas ca vidyarayitavyam ca.**

8. *The earth and the earth element, water and the water element, light and the light element, air and the air element, space and the space element, eyes and the object of seeing, ears and the object of hearing, nose and the object of smelling, tongue and the object of tasting, skin and the object of touching, speech and what can be spoken, hands and what can be handled, the sex organ and the pleasure it can produce, the mind and what can be thought of, the intellect and what can be discerned, the ego and its egoism, consciousness and what can be consciously experienced, light and what can be illumined with lightning, the breath and all that it can hold together.*

Notes: The tattvas or the component realities of Nature are listed here, the five elements, the senses and their objects, the mind, the intellect, the ego, the internal organ or citta and what can be experienced through it, light and breath. Matra means measure, number, quality or element.

9. **esa hi drasta sprastasrota ghrata rasayita manta boddha karta vijnanatma purusah; sa pare'ksara atmani sampratisthate.**

9. *And this one, indeed, is the seer, the touching one, the hearing one, the smelling one, the tasting one, the thinking one, the discerning one, the doer, the person who is the knower himself. He remains established in the supreme imperishable Self.*

10. **param evaksaram pratipadyate sa yo ha vai tad acchayam asariram alohitam subhram aksaram vedayate yastu saumya; sa sarvagyah sarvo bhavati; tadesa slokah.**

11. *He who knows that one who is without shadow, without body, without color, and who is pure and imperishable, O dear, attains the*

supreme and the imperishable. He becomes all and all-knowing. Regarding this there is this verse.

11. vigyanatma saha devais ca sarvaih prana bhutani sampratisthanti yatra; tad aksaram vedayate yas tu saumya sa sarvagyah sarvam evavivesa iti.

11. He who knows that imperishable one, in whom are established the all-knowing Self, along with all the deities, breaths and elements, that one, O dear, becomes all-knowing and enters into all.

Question 5

Significance of Aum Meditation

1. atha hainam saibyah satyakamah papraccha; sa yo ha vai tab bhagavan manusyesu prayanantam aumkaram abhidhyayita; katamam va va sa tena lokam jayatiti.

1. Then Satyakama Saibhya asked him, "Godman, he who among men mentally fixes his mind upon Aum until the end of his life, which world he wins by that?

2. tasmai sa hovaca, etadvai satyakama param caparam ca brahma yad aumkarah; tasmad vidvan etena iva yatanenaikataram anveti.

To him he said, "Satyakama, this very transcendental and immanent Brahman, indeed, is that Aum only. Therefore, the knowledgeable one arrives at one or the other through this means only."

3. sa yadhy ekamatram abhidhyayita sa tenaiva samveditas turnam eva jagaty abhisampadhyate; tam rico manusyalokam upanayante sa tatra tapasa brahmacaryena sraddhaya sampanno mahimanam anubhavati.

3. If he meditates upon the one letter (A), having attained equanimity quickly by that alone, he attains the physical world. The Rics lead him to the world of humans, and there through austerities, the practice of celibacy, endowed with faith, he experiences greatness.

Notes: The first letter of Aum is A. When one meditates upon even that single letter, one attains a good birth in the earthly world. The hymns of the Rigveda, which he learns by virtue of his previous birth in a good family, enables him to attain greatness

4. atha yadi dvimatrena manasi sampadhyate so'ntariksam yajurbhir unniyate saumalokam; sa saumaloke vibhutim anubhuya punar avartate.

4. Now, if (he meditates) upon the two letters (AU) the attains the subtle world. Led by the Yajus through the mid-region, he is lifted to the world of the moon. Having experienced supernatural existence, he returns again.

Notes: The Yajus are the hymns of the Yajurveda containing sacrificial formulas. The world of the moon is the ancestral world. Those who go there return to the earth again once they exhaust their karmas

5. yah punar etam trimatren aum ity etenaivaksarena param purusam abhidhyayita sa tejasi surye sampannah; yatha padodaras tvaca vinirmucyata evam ha vai sa papmana vinirmuktah sa samabhir unniyate brahmalokam sa etasmaj jivaghanat paratparam purusayam purusam iksate; tad etau slokau bhavatah.

5. Again, he who meditates upon the Supreme Self with the three letters of Aum, he becomes endowed with the light of the sun. Just as a snake is freed from its slough, in the same manner he becomes free from sin. Led by the Samans, he is lifted to the world of Brahman. In the congregation of living entities, he sees the highest of the high and the Person hidden in the persons.

6. tisro matra mrityumatyah prayukta anyonya saktah anaviprayuktah; kriyasu bahyabhyantara madhyamasu samyak prayuktasu na kampate jnah.

6. The three letters are within the confines of death. They should be yoked and applied together. By applying (the unified Aum) in kriya yoga, the awakened one does not waver in the external, internal, intermediate and self-absorbed states.

Notes: This verse explains the significance of Aum in the practice of kriya yoga, which is also mentioned in the Yogasutras of Patanjali (2.1). He described kriya yoga as having three important elements, austerity (tapas), self-study (svadhyaya) and devotion (isvara paridhana). This verse explains the benefit of using Aum in the practice of kriya yoga so that the awakened yogi (jina) would remain in the state of samyak cetana all the time and in all states.

7. rigbhir etam yajurbhir antariksam samabhir yat tat kavayo vedayante; tam aumkarena ivayatanenanveti vidvan yat tac chantam ajaram amritam abhayam param ceti.

7. *The knowledgeable one knows this world by the Riks, the mid-region by the Yajus, and That (Brahman world) by the Samans. However, with the help of Aum, the learned one attains that which is the highest, calm, free from old age and death, harmonious, without fear and supreme.*

Notes: The chanting of Aum is superior to the study and chanting of the triple Vedas. The study of the Vedas gives us the knowledge of the immanent, the three worlds; but the chanting of Aum takes us to the immortal world of Brahman.

Question 6
The Being with Sixteen Parts

1. atha hainam sukesa bharadvajah papraccha; bhagavan hiranyanabhah kausalyo rajaputro mam upetyaitam prasnam apricchata; sodasa kalam bharadvaja purusam vettha; tam aham kumaram abruvam naham imam veda; yadhy aham imama vedisam katham te navaksyam iti; samulo va esa parisusyati yo'nritam abhivadati tasman narhamy anritam vaktum; sa tusnim ratham aruhya pravavraja; tam tva pricchami kvasau purusa iti.

1. *Then Sukesa Bharadvaja asked him, "Godman, Hiranyanabha, the prince of Kosala, approached me and asked this question,'O Bharadvaja, do you know the person of sixteen parts?'I said to that prince, 'I do not know him. If I know him, why would I not tell you? Truly, up to the roots withers he who speaks untruth. Therefore, I cannot speak to you untruth.' Silently, (having heard this), he mounted his chariot and went away. Regarding that person now I ask, 'Where is that person?'"*

2. tasmai sa hovaca; ihaivantah sarire saumya sa puruso yasminn etah sodasa kalah prabhavanti iti.

2. *To him he said, "Here, inside this body only, my dear, is that person, in whom the sixteen parts manifest."*

Notes: Pipplalada was said be a proponent of the theistic Samkhya philosophy. In this verse he referred to the tattvas that constituted the subtle body (linga sarira) inside the gross body. The sixteen parts that went into its making are listed in the verse 4 below.

3. sa iksacakre; kasminn aham utkranta utkranto bhavisyami kasmin va pratistite pratistasyam iti.

3. *That one reflected, "By whose going up, I too happen to go up, and by whose staying, I stay firmly established?"*

4. sa pranam asrjata pranac chraddham kham vayur jyotir apah prithivindriyam manah annam annad viryam tapo mantrah karma loka lokesu ca nama ca.

4. *He created prana; from prana faith, space, air, light, water, earth, senses, mind, and food; from food sperm, heat, sacred chants, action, worlds and in the worlds name.*

5. sa yathema nadhyah syandamanah samudrayanah samudram prapyastam gacchanti bhidhyete tasam namarupe samudra ity evam procyate; evam evasya paridrastur imah sodasa kalah purusayanah purusam prapyastam gacchanti bhidhyete casam namarupe purusa ity evam procyate sa eso'kalo'mrito bhavati tadesa slokah.

5. *Just as these flowing rivers go towards the ocean and having reached the ocean end up completely dissolved in it, and with their names and forms completely lost are simply spoken as the ocean, so does the sixteen parts of this all seeing one, moving towards the person and on reaching the person, disappear, and with their names and forms lost, they are spoken as the person only. He (who reaches that person and unites with him like the rivers unite with the ocean) becomes without parts, immortal. Regarding this there is this verse.*

Notes: Name and form, distinction and diversity exists only so long as the beings remain distinct and separate from the inner Self. Duality and division disappear, as in case of deep sleep, when a person enters into union with the inner Self. The tattvas are part of the body. The individual Self is free from them, even when it is embodied.

6. ara iva rathanabhau kala yasmin pratistitah; tam vedhyam purusam veda yatha ma vo mrityuh parivyatha iti.

6. *In whom the parts are established like the spokes in the nave of a wheel, know that person who should be known so that death will not cause you suffering from any side.*

7. tan hovaca etavad evaham etat param brahma veda; natah paramast iti.

7. *To them, he said, "I know this much only about this supreme Brahman. Nothing is higher than that."*

8. te tam arcayantah tvam hi nah pita yo'smakam avidhyayah param param tarayasi iti; namah param arisibhyo namah parama-risibhyah.

8. Worshipping him with ritual offerings, they said, "You, indeed, are our father who has taken us across to the other side of ignorance. Salutations to the supreme seers, salutations to the supreme seers."

Notes: A guru is responsible for the spiritual birth of a student. By imparting them the knowledge of liberation, he is also responsible for their birth in the world of Brahman. He is therefore worthy of worship as one's very father.

Svetasvatara Upanishad

Editor's Note

The Svetasvatara Upanishad derives its name from the sage, Svetasvatara, who composed it. Svetasvatara also means a star named the white horse. It belongs to the Taittiriya school of the Yajurveda. From a historical perspective, it points to the rise of Saivism as a major Hindu religious sect and the popularity of Lord Siva, who was once feared and revered alike by the Rigvedic people as Rudra. The Upanishad is divided into six chapters and contains in all 113 verses. The significance of the Svetasvatara Upanishad lies in the fact that in it we come across almost all the basic teachings and concepts of the Bhagavadgita including their emphasis upon Samkhya yoga. The difference is basically in their presentation. In the Bhagavadgita, Lord Krishna is the Bhagavan, the Supreme Lord of the universe, whereas here it is Lord Siva, who is described as the Lord of all, and the master of the immanent and transcendent reality, by knowing whom one can attain Brahman. Lord Siva is invoked as Isvara, the awakened Brahman, the Supreme Being, the Universal Self who initiates the process of creation, having manifested Himself in pure sattva.

We find the basic concepts of Saivism in these teachings, namely pasu, pasa and pati. Pasu, meaning the animal, is the individual being with an embodied soul. Pasa, meaning the bond, is the attachment that keeps the beings chained to the world of illusion and mortality, and pati, meaning the husband, is Lord Siva Himself, the controller of the universe, who ultimately liberates his dear devotees from bondage. We also come across the elements of bhakti or devotion in the verses. The Upanishad suggests that Brahman can be realized through the mind as well through ones heart. The heart signifies the importance of feelings in the form of devotion or love as the means to self-realization. Isvara, Prakriti and the individual soul are the triad in which Isvara is above all, while the latter two engage themselves in enacting their respective roles. Freedom from the hold of Prakriti is possible for the individual souls only through the grace of God. We also come across a reference to the wheel of creation, in which the hub and the circumference are described as Brahman, while the middle part as the manifestation of prakriti with all its diversity. The law of karma is also dealt with in some detail in the Upanishad. The individual soul having come into this world wanders about according to the nature of its deeds assuming various forms in various conditions. (5.7-11). He is bound to the world because he becomes the enjoyer and assumes responsibility for his actions without recognizing the invisible hand of God in his life. We are also introduced to the concept of breath control and some techniques of yogic meditation. There are verses extolling the significance of syllable AUM and the greatness of Savitr, the sun god, as an acknowledgement that the science of self-realization was pioneered by him among the mortals.

Presented here is a revised translation of the Svertasvatara Upanishad by Jayaram V published originally on Hinduwebsite.com.

Invocation

aum purnamadah purnamidam purnat purnam udachyate; purnasya purnam adaya purnam eva vasisyate. aum santih santih santih.

Aum! That is full. This also is full. From that full arises this full. Taking the full from the full, the full remains full. Aum, peace, peace, peace.

Notes: There is an indeterminate factor hidden in all determinate things and that is Zero. Zero stands for the unmanifested (avyakta) Brahman, the complete number (purnam), from which even if you take its fullness, it still remains full. Multiply zero with a thousand and the result is zero. Multiply one with zero and the result is again zero. Hence, mathematicians prefer to avoid bringing zero into an equation. For the ascetics zero is the goal. For the worldly people, anything but zero. Zero is the mystery and zero is the Aum of numbers. The fullness is also a reference to the Sun, who is always full even when he sheds light and heat day after day. Unlike the moon, he never waxes and wanes.

aum saha navavatu; saha nau bhunaktu; saha veeryam karavavahai; tejasvi navadheetamastu, ma vidvisavahai. aum santih santih santih.

May He protect us both; may He nourish us both together; May we both become energetic by working together; may our study illumine (our minds); may there be no hatred between us. Aum, peace, peace, peace.

Chapter 1

Brahman Perceived as a Wheel with Parts

1. brahmavadino vadanti kim karanam brahma kutah sma jata jivamah kena kva ca sampratisthah adhisthitah kena sukhetaresu vartamahe brahmavido vyavastham

1. Those who debate about Brahman say, "What is the cause? Was it Brahman? From where are we born and established on what we thrive here? O knowers of Brahman, please tell us under whose lordship we live here variously, experiencing various states of pleasure and pain?"

Notes: Enquiry is the first step in the exploration of truth. The Svetasvatara Upanishad starts with a few fundamental questions regarding our existence and then tries to find answers to these questions. This has been the case with most of the Upanishads. They do not start with assumptions, but with a certain degree of sincerity to explore truth and understand the mysteries of our existence and our relationship with the Creator. The approach is mostly neither dogmatic nor didactic, but open minded, inquisitive, exploratory and analytical. The overall approach of the Upanishad is brought out in the first verse stating that we are one but live variously.

2. kalah svabhavo niyatir yadrccha bhutani yonih puruseti cintyam; samyoga esam na tv atmabhavad atma hy anisah sukhaduhkhahetoh

2. What should we consider as the cause? Is it time, inherent nature, necessity, accident, the elements, the womb or the person? A combination of these could not have caused it, because the soul exists independent of them. Even the self seems to be powerless before the cause of pain and pleasure.

3. te dhyanayoganugata apasyan devatmasaktim svagunair nigudha; yah karanani nikhilani tani kalatmayuktany adhitisthaty ekah.

3. Those who practiced dhyana yoga, saw the power of the divine Self hidden deeply in its own qualities. And he presides over all other causes starting from time to the Self.

Notes: The qualities are sattva, rajas and tamas. Dhayana means meditation or contemplation. Dhyana yoga is a yoga practice in which the mind is stabilized through concentration, meditation and mindful observation.

4. tam ekanemim trivrtam sodasantam satardharam vimsati pratyarabhih; astakaih sadbhir visvarupaika pasam trimargabhedam dvinimittaikamoham.

4. We see Him as a wheel with one axis, three tiers, sixteen ends, fifty spokes (or supports), twenty counter spokes, the six sets of eight, whose one rope has universal form, which has three different paths of salvation and whose delusion arises out of two sets of actions.

Notes: There is a lot of symbolism in this verse. The wheel symbolizes the revolving and cyclical nature of creation, characterized by diversity, duality, change and instability. The one axis is Isvara. The three tiers are the three qualities. The sixteen ends are the five elements, five sense organs, five organs of action and the mind. The fifty spokes are the various states of delusion and ignorance. The twenty counter spokes are the ten senses and their objects. The six sets are Prakriti, matter, abundance, emotions, gods and nature of soul each having eight different modes. The one rope is illusion. The three different paths of salvation are the path of righteousness, the path of unrighteousness and the path of knowledge. They are also the path to the immortal world, the path to the ancestral world and the path to the underworld. The two sets of action are actions done out of attachment and actions done with detachment. The wheel mentioned here is the wheel of existence that comes into shape at the time of creation and revolves continuously until the end. Isvara is a not only a part of this wheel, but also its center.

5. pancasroto'mbum pancayonyugravaktram pancapranormim pancabuddhyadimulam; pancavartam pancaduhkhaughavegam pancasadbhedam pancaparvam adhimah.

5. *We meditate upon him as a river of five streams, having five fierce and crooked sources, whose waves are the five breaths, whose root cause is the five types of intelligence, with five whirlpools, and five fast flowing pains divided into five branches and fifty kinds of suffering.*

Notes: The river is the mind. The five fierce and crooked streams are the senses. The five whirlpools are the five types of delusion namely kama (desire), krodha (anger), lobha (greed), mada (pride) and matsarya (envy). They may also refer to the five modifications of the mind (cittavrittis) described in the Yogasutras. The five pains are said to be the difficulties arising out of ignorance, curiosity, feelings etc.

6. sarvajive sarvasamsthe brhante tasmin hamso bhramyate brahmacakre; prthag atmanam preritaram ca matva justas tatas tenamrtatvam eti

6. *In this vast Brahma wheel, in which revolve all beings and things, the Self (jivatma) revolves under the delusion that the Self hidden inside is different from the mover (the Supreme Self). But in the end by the grace of the Supreme, he attains immortality.*

Notes: The power of illusion is not easy to overcome. The soul is caught in it helplessly and wanders about afflicted with the suffering natural to mortal life. It is only by the grace of God can there be freedom from such a miserable existence.

7. udgitam etat paramam tu brahma tasmims trayam svapratisthaksaram ca; atrantaram brahmavido viditva lina brahmani tatpara yonimuktah

7. *This is sung with the highest praise as the Supreme Brahman. In That are the three. It is the self-established imperishable. By knowing what is in it the knowers of Brahman become merged into Brahman and thereby freed from Nature's womb.*

Notes: The great three are the individual self, the world (virat) and the world soul Hiranyagarbha.

8. samyuktam etat ksaram aksaram ca vyaktavyaktam bharate visvam isah; anisas catma badhyate bhoktrbhavaj jnatva devam mucyate sarvapasaih.

8. *The Lord of the universe supports all this together, both the perishable and the imperishable, the manifested and the unmanifested. And the Self not being the lord becomes bound to the world as he considers himself the enjoyer. Knowing the deity (isa), he becomes freed from all bonds.*

Notes: This verse contains the three basic concepts of Saivism namely pati, the lord, pasu, the deluded individual self and pasa the bonds that keep the latter chained to this world. Isvara is the Isa, the lord, the pati, in control of everything and unbound. The individual soul is anisa, the one without lordship, the pasu, controlled by the forces of Prakriti and bound to the world by its actions. These bonds, pasas, can be cut asunder only through the knowledge of pati.

9. jnajnau dvav ajav isanisav aja hy eka bhoktrbhogarthayukta; anantas catma visvarupo hy akarta trayam yada vindate brahmam etat.

9. Knowledge and ignorance are the two unborn ones. One is the ruler and the other, the ruled. Indeed, there is another, unborn, who is yoked to the enjoyer and his enjoyment. The infinite Self, of universal form, verily, is the non-doer. When this triad is known, that is Brahman

Notes: The two unborn ones are Purusha and Prakriti or Isvara and Maya. The third unborn one is the Atman, the individual Self, who is the hidden witness, and does not engage himself directly in any activity. The enjoyer is the being (jiva), the embodied self who is born again and again in the womb of Nature. Enjoyment is attachment with sense objects. It happens through the activity of the senses. Thus, here we have a complete picture of the constituent elements of the human personality, namely the soul, beingness, duality, and various states of existence namely creation, delusion, attachment, suffering, and liberation.

10. ksaram pradhanam amrtaksaram harah ksaratmanav isate deva ekah; tasyabhidhyanad yojanat tattvabhavad bhuyas cante visvamayanivrttih.

10. The perishable is the primordial matter. The immortal and the imperishable is Hara. This one God rules over both the perishable matter and the imperishable Self. By meditating upon Him, uniting with Him, through the constant practice of reflecting upon His essential nature, one can overcome the delusions of this world.

Notes: Of the triad, the ruler is clearly Isvara. Lord Siva is the Isvara here. Prakriti and the individual soul, which are His instruments, are engaged in a kind of power struggle. As long as the soul is held in control by Prakriti, the former is bound to this world. And to attain freedom from Prakriti, beings have to meditate upon Isvara, and overcome their delusions. This process has been explained further in the next verse.

11. jnatva devam sarvapasapahanih ksinaih klesair janmamrtyuprahanih; tasyabhidhyanat trtiyam dehabhede visvaisvaryam kevala aptakamah.

11. By knowing the deity all bonds are destroyed. When the afflictions are dissolved, there is freedom from the cycle of births and deaths. Meditating upon Him one reaches the third stage; and with the separation from the body, lordship of universal abundance, aloneness and satisfaction of all desires.

Notes: The verse refers to the stages in liberation, beginning with the practice of detachment and renunciation whereby all bonds are destroyed. In the second stage, one is freed from afflictions (klesas) and rebirth. Meditation leads to the third state, which is samadhi or self-absorption. Liberation is freedom from the body, universal lordship, aloneness and complete cessation of all desires.

12. etaj jneyam nityam evatmasamstham natah param veditavyam hi kimcit; bhokta bhogyam preritaram ca matva sarvam proktam trividham brahmam etat.

12. *That which is eternal and rests within the body (or oneself) should be known. Truly, there is nothing else to be known. The enjoyer, the enjoyed and the mover of all - is all that can be said. Threefold is this Brahman.*

Notes: The (real) enjoyer is the inner self. The (false) enjoyer is the being, jiva. The enjoyed is Prakriti or the manifest material world and the cause of all is Isvara. This is the threefold manifestation.

13. vahner yatha yonigatasya murtir na drsyate naiva ca linganasah; sa bhuya evendhanayonigrhyas tadvobhayam vai pranavena dehe.

13. *Just as fire remains hidden in its source, with its form unseen and its subtle body undestroyed, but can still be seized repeatedly from its source by means of fuel, so it is in both cases. It is grasped in the body with Aum.*

Notes: The Self remains hidden in the body like fire in the wood. Just as wood can be rekindled and fire can be brought out, so also with the help of Aum one can grasp the Self that remains hidden in the body.

14. svadeham aranim krtva pranavam cottararanim; dhyananirmathanabhyasad devam pasyen nigudhavat.

14. *Using the body as the lower piece of the wood and the syllable AUM as the upper friction rod, and practicing meditation as the act of friction, one can see the deity who is hidden within oneself.*

15. tilesu tailam dadhaniva sarpir apah srotahsv aranisu cagnih; evam atma atmani grhyate 'sau satyenainam tapasa yo 'nupasyati.

15. *Like the oil in sesame seeds or butter in cream, or water in the river beds or fire in the wooden sticks, so is the Self hidden within oneself, which can be grasped through truthfulness and austerity.*

16. sarvavyapinam atmanam ksire sarpir ivarpitam; atmavidyatapomulam tad brahmopanisatparam tad brahmopanisatparam

16. The Self, is all pervading like butter in milk. The source of self-knowledge and austerity, that is the supreme teaching of Brahman. It indeed is the supreme teaching of Brahman.

Chapter 2

An Ancient Prayer to Savitr

1. yunjanah prathamam manas tattvaya savita dhiyah; agner jyotir nicayya prthivya adhy abharat.

1. In the very beginning, controlling his mind and expanding his thoughts for the sake of truth, Savitr discerned light and brought forth Agni upon earth.

Notes: Savitr is the sun who first performed penance and produced light. He then brought that light in the form of fire to the earth.

2. yuktena manasa vayam devasya savituh save; suvargeyaya saktya

2. When our minds are under our control, we are under the command of divine Savitr. May he give us sufficient strength to attain heaven.

3. yuktvaya manasa devan suvar yato dhiya divam; brhaj jyotih karisyatah savita prasuvati tan.

3. May Savitr, who is capable of controlling the heaven bound gods, through his thoughts inspire them to shed a bright light.

4. yunjate mana uta yunjate dhiyo vipra viprasya brhato vipascitah; vi hotra dadhe vayunavid eka in mahi devasya savituh paristutih.

4. The greatest of the great sages control their minds and thoughts. He who knows the scriptures well has ordered the performance of the sacrificial ceremonies. The divine Savitr is profusely praised.

5. yuje vam brahma purvyam namobhir vi sloka etu pathyeva sureh;srnvanti visve amrtasya putra a ye dhamani diviyani tasthuh.

5. With great veneration and devotion, I join others in your ancient prayer. May my verse follow the path of the Sun. May all the immortal sons of (God) as well as those who have ascended to the heavenly worlds listen to this prayer of mine.

6. agnir yatrabhimathyate vayur yatradhirudhyate; somo yatratiricyate tatra samjayate manah.

6. Where the fire is kindled, where the air is controlled and directed, and where the soma juice flows over, there the mind is born.

Notes: The fire is the individual soul, the air is breath, the soma juice is bliss and the mind is self-realization. The fire is spiritual fervor. Control of air is control of breath. Soma juice is devotion. Mind is knowledge of God or self.

7. savitra prasavena juseta brahma purvyam; tatra yonim krnavase nahi te purtam aksipat.

7. With Savitr as the inspirer, one should take delight in the ancient prayer. Make that your source (of rebirth). Your works will not affect you.

8. trirunnatam sthapya samam sariram hrdindriyani manasa samnivesya; brahmodupena pratareta vidvan srotamsi sarvani bhayavahani.

8. Holding the three parts of the body (the upper chest, neck and head) steady and erect, having established the mind and the senses in his heart, a wise person should cross, by the boat of Brahman, the streams of fear.

Notes: The boat of Brahman is the syllable AUM. The streams of fear is the fear of death, and suffering.

9. pranan prapidyeha sa yuktacestah ksine prane nasikayocchvasita; dustasvayuktam iva vaham enam vidvan mano dharayetapramattah.

9. Holding the breath in his body, controlling his movements to the barest minimum, let him breathe through his nostrils with diminishing breath, restraining his mind with utmost vigilance, the way wild horses are yoked to a chariot.

10. same sucau sarkaravahnivaluka- vivarjite sabdajalasrayadibhih; mano'nukule na tu caksupidane guhanivatasrayane prayojayet.

10. Choosing a place that is plain and clean, free from pebbles, fire and gravel, with soothing sounds of flowing water coming from nearby, and with features that are pleasing to the mind and the eyes, in a secret cave, protected from the disturbances of the wind, let him practice his meditation.

11. niharadhumarkanalanilanam khadyotavidyutsphatikasasinam; etani rupani purahsarani brahmany abhivya-ktikarani yoge.

11. Fog, smoke, the sun, wind, fireflies, lightning, crystal moon, these are the images that appear as manifestations of Brahman in the beginning stages of the Yoga.

12. prthvyaptejo'nilakhe samutthite pancatmake yogagune pravrtte; na tasya rogo na jara na mrtyuh praptasya yogagnimayam sariram.

12. When the modifications arising in the fivefold body made up of the earth, the water, the air, the fire, and the space are stabilized through the fire of yoga, then there is no place for sickness, old age and death.

Notes: These are the immediate benefits of the yoga manifesting in the body as vigor and health.

13. laghutvam arogyam alolupatvam varnaprasadah svarasausthavam ca; gandhah subho mutrapurisam alpam yogapravrttim prathamam vadanti.

13. Lightness, good health, steadiness, improvement in the skin color, smoothness in voice, pleasant body odor, slight excretions are said to be the first modifications arising from the practice of yoga.

14. yathaiva bimbam mrdayopaliptam tejomayam bhrajate tat sudhantam; tad vatmatattvam prasamiksya dehi ekah krtartho bhavate vitasokah.

14. Just as a mirror covered by dust shines brightly after it has been cleaned, so does the one who has experienced oneness with the true nature of the Self within himself, contended and free from sorrow.

15. yad atmatattvena tu brahmatattvam dipopameneha yuktah prapasyet; ajam dhruvam sarvatattvair visuddham jnatva devam mucyate sarvapasaih.

15. Through the true nature of his own Self when he sees, as if by a lamp, the true nature of Brahman, his own real nature as one who is unborn and completely pure, He is freed from all the fetters at once.

16. esa ha devah pradiso 'nu sarvah purvo ha jatah sa u garbhe antah; sa eva jatah sa janisyamanah pratyan janas tisthati sarvatomukhah.

16. He, indeed, is the deity, who pervades all the regions, and verily the first born. He is hidden in the womb. He is born and will be reborn. He is opposite all beings with faces in all directions.

Notes: The being who is referenced here is the Sun, the symbol of manifested Brahman. He is Isvara, the witness (sakshi) to all that goes on here. He is omnipresent and sees everything in all directions simultaneously. The expression "born and will be born again" is a reference to the sun who appears, disappears and reappears day after day. High above the sky, he stands opposite all and spreads his rays in all directions.

17. yo devo agnau yo apsu yo visvam bhuvanam avivesa; ya osadhisu yo vanaspatisu tasmai devaya namo namah.

17. *The deity who is in the fire, in the water, who has pervaded the entire world, who is in the plants, in the trees, to that deity, I offer my salutations, I offer my salutations.*

Chapter 3
Rudra, the Lord of the Universe

1. ya eko jalavan isata isanibhih sarvaml lokan isata isanibhih; ya evaika udbhave sambhave ca ya etad vidur amrtas te bhavanti

1. *The one caster of net, who rules all with his divine powers, who rules all the worlds with His divine powers, who alone creates and makes existence possible, those who know this become immortal.*

Notes: Isvara, the lord of the universe, casts the net of delusion upon the worlds and subjects the beings to delusion and ignorance. Hence, he is known as the holder of net (jalavan) and the caster of maya (mayavi).

2. eko hi rudro na dvitiyaya tasthe ya imaml lokan isata isanibhih; pratyan janas tisthati samcukocantakale samsrjya visva bhuvanani gopah.

2. *One only, indeed, Rudra, without a second, who rules all these worlds with his divine powers. He stands opposite of all creatures. Having created the worlds and protecting them all, in the end he withdraws them.*

Notes: Rudra is another name of Siva. He is equated here with the supreme Brahman.

3. visvataścaksur uta visvatomukho visvatobahur uta visvataspat; sam bahubhyam dhamati sam patatrair dyavabhumi janayan deva ekah.

3. *With eyes everywhere, with faces in every direction, with hands and feet spread everywhere, with His mighty arms and wings, He forges the earth and heaven together and all the men and gods.*

4. **yo devanam prabhavas codbhavas ca visvadhipo rudro maharsih; hiranyagarbham janayamasa purvam sa no buddhya subhaya samyunaktu.**

4. *He who is responsible for the existence and origin of all gods, that lord of the universe and great seer, Rudra, who in the past was responsible for the origin of Hiranyagarbha, may He endow us with pure intelligence.*

Notes: Hiranyagarbha is the cosmic germ, the world soul, the third in the hierarchy, who is identified as Brahma.

5. **ya te rudra siva tanur aghorapapakasini; taya nas tanuva samtamaya girisantabhicakasihi.**

5. *O Rudra, your auspicious body, which is without terror or evil, with that most peaceful form, dweller of the mountains, show your most benign form to us.*

Notes: The word "sivam" means most auspicious. Lord Siva is white in color in contrast to Lord Vishnu who is blue. The blue color is because of his identification with the day's sky. Because of his association with snowy mountains, Siva is also called Girisa, meaning the lord of the mountains. Siva is also the lord of tamas, the dark quality. Hence he has both pleasant and fierce forms.

6. **yam isum girisanta haste bibharsy astave; sivam giritra tam kuru ma himsih purusam jagat.**

6. *O dweller of the mountains, make auspicious the arrow, which you hold in your hands to shoot. O protector of the mountains, injure neither man nor beast.*

7. **tatah param brahma param brhantam yathanikayam sarvabhutesu gudham; visvasyaikam parivestitaram isam tam jnatvamrta bhavanti.**

7. *Higher than this (Self) is the Supreme Brahman, supreme and hidden as the same in the bodies of all creatures, the one who envelops the whole universe, the Lord, by knowing whom one attains immortality.*

8. **vedaham etam purusam mahantam adityavarnam tamasah parastat; tam eva viditvati mrtyum eti nanyah pantha vidyate 'yanaya.**

8. *I know the Highest Supreme Purusha, who is of the color of the sun, beyond darkness. By knowing him one goes beyond death. There is no other way by which one can go there.*

9. yasmat param naparam asti kimcid yasman naniyo na jyayo 'sti kimcit; vrksa iva stabdho divi tisthaty ekas tenedam purnam purusena sarvam.

9. There is nothing that is above Him, nothing that is smaller than Him and nothing that is greater than Him. Like a tree rooted in the heavens, He stands. The whole universe is filled with this one Purusha.

10. tato yad uttarataram tadarupam anamayam; ya etad vidur amrtas te bhavanti athetare duhkham evapiyanti.

10. That which is beyond this world, that is without form and without suffering. Those who know this become immortal. But others experience suffering only.

11. sarvananasirogrivah sarvabhutaguhasayah; sarvavyapi sa bhagavams tasmat sarvagatah sivah.

11. He who is in the faces, heads and necks of all, who is hidden in the cave (heart) of all beings, who is everywhere, He is the divine Lord, the omnipresent Siva.

Notes: Lord Siva is described here as Bhagavan, the lord of the universe having six distinct qualities namely righteousness, fame, prosperity, wisdom and detachment.

12. mahan prabhur vai purusah sattvasyaisa pravartakah; sunirmalam imam praptim isano jyotir avyayah.

12. That Purusha indeed is the greatest ruler, whose actions are induced by the power of sattva. By making this (body) completely pure (with sattva), one attains the Lord who is inexhaustible light.

13. angusthamatrah puruso 'ntaratma sada jananam hrdaye samnivistah; hrda manisa manasabhiklpto ya etad vidur amrtas te bhavanti.

13. The indwelling Self is Purusha, of the measure of a thumb, situated always in the hearts of beings. He is the Lord who is conceived in the hearts and minds. Those who know that become immortal.

14. sahasrasirsa purusah sahasraksah sahasrapat; sa bhumim visvato vrtva atyatisthad dasangulam.

14. *The Purusha with thousands of heads, thousands of eyes and thousands of feet, enveloping the earth from all directions, is also situated beyond by ten fingers' width.*

Notes: The Purusha that is described here is the indwelling spirit, the witness, whose aura spreads beyond the body (referred here as the earth) by some distance.

15. purusa evedam sarvam yad bhutam yac ca bhavyam; utamrtatvasyesano yad annenatirohati.

15. That Purusha is indeed all this, whatever that has been and whatever that will be. He is the Lord of immortality and whatever that grows by food.

16. sarvatahpanipadam tat sarvato'ksisiromukham; sarvatah- srutimal loke sarvam avrtya tisthati.

16. He has hands and feet everywhere, an eye, a head and face he has in every direction and a ear in every place. It stands enveloping all.

16. sarvendriyagunabhasam sarvendriyavivarjitam; sarvasya prabhum isanam sarvasya saranam suhrt

17. The light of all the senses and gunas, yet devoid of all the senses, the over lord and ruler of all, it is the supreme refuge for all.

18. navadvare pure dehi hamso lelayate bahih; vasi sarvasya lokasya sthavarasya carasya ca.

18. The embodied one in the city of nine gates, the bird who moves in and out, the Lord of the whole world, he is both non-moving and moving.

Notes: The city of the nine gates is the body. The soul moves in and out of it as and when it discards an old body and assumes a new one.

19. apanipado javano grahita pasyaty acaksuh sa srnoty akarnah; sa vetti vedyam na ca tasyasti vetta tam ahur agryam purusam mahantam.

19. Without a hand or a foot, yet swiftly moving and grasping, He sees without eyes and hears without ears. He knows all that is to be known, yet none knows Him. They call him the first, and the highest Person.

20. anor aniyan mahato mahiyan atma guhayam nihito 'sya jantoh; tam akratum pasyati vitasoko dhatuprasadan mahimanam isam.

20. Subtler than the subtle, greater than the great is the Self hidden in the cave of the heart of the creatures. By the grace of the Lord, the inactive ones perceive Him as majestic and become free from sorrow.

21. vedaham etam ajaram puranam sarvatmanam sarvagatam vibhutvat; janmanirodham pravadanti yasya brahmavadino hi pravadanti nityam.

21. I know this undecaying, primeval Self, the Self of all, moving everywhere because of His infinity. Speaking of Him thus one can prevent one's rebirth. Those who are well versed in the knowledge of Brahman declare Him as eternal.

Chapter 4
Two Birds on the Tree of Life

1. ya eko 'varno bahudha saktiyogad varnan anekan nihitartho dadhati, vicaiti cante visvam adau sa devah sa no buddhya subhaya samyunaktu.

1. He, who is one without color, using His power, creates many colors for a hidden cause, and into whom the world comes together in the beginning and withdrawn in the end. May he endow us with pure intelligence.

2. tad evagnis tad adityas tad vayus tad u candramah; tad eva sukram tad brahma tad apas tat prajapatih.

2. That, verily, is Agni, that is Aditya, that is Vayu, and that is the moon. That is pure. That is Brahma. That is waters and that is Prajapati.

Notes: The various divinities mentioned here are forms of the same God. They are the many colors (varnas) of the One who is without color.

3. tvam stri tvam puman asi tvam kumara uta va kumari; tvam jirno dandena vancasi tvam jato bhavasi visvatomukhah.

3. You are the woman. You are the man. You are the son and the daughter also. You only, as an old man walk with a a stick, drooping. You are born with faces in all directions.

Notes: Isvara, the manifested Brahman, is a reflection of the unmanifested in the triple qualities. He creates the macrocosm with rich diversity. He is both Purusha and Prakriti united within Himself.

4. nilah patango harito lohitaksas tadidgarbha rtavah samudrah; anadimams tvam vibhutvena vartase yato jatani bhuvanani visva

4. *You are the dark blue bird. You are the green parrot with red eyes. You are the cloud with lightning in your womb. You are the seasons and the oceans. Without a beginning, you move everywhere by your powers, from whom are born all the worlds in the universe.*

5. ajam ekam lohitasuklakrsnam bahvih prajah srjamanam sarupah; ajo hy eko jusamano 'nusete jahaty enam bhuktabhogam ajo "nyah.

5. *Unborn, one, red, white and black, you create many offspring similar to you in form. One unborn lies there enjoying and the other unborn having enjoyed, gives her up.*

Notes: The one unborn is Prakriti, Nature. Red, white and black are the triple gunas. The offspring are the individual souls, who are similar to Brahman in essence and as embodied souls similar to Nature having the same tattvas. Some of them are caught in the cycle of births and deaths, and remain bound while some having overcome their attachments attain liberation. The unborn one who is enjoying is the bound Self and the one who has given up the body is the liberated Self.

6. dva suparna sayuja sakhaya samanam vrksam parisasvajate; tayor anyah pippalam svadv atty anasnann anyo abhicakasiti.

6. *Two birds, ever united in the company of each other, cling to the same tree. Of them, one eats the sweet fruit, while the other just looks on without eating.*

Notes: The Supreme Self and the individual Self, who is caught in the flux of births and deaths, are the two companions who live on the same tree of creation (Asvattha). One enjoys the fruit of his actions and remains bound, while the other watches without being involved.

7. samane vrkse puruso nimagno anisaya socati muhyamanah; justam yada pasyaty anyam isam asya mahimanam iti vitasokah.

7. *On the same tree, the person who is involved with the sorrows of the world remains deluded and depressed feeling helpless. But when he sees the Lord, who is worshipped and His greatness, he becomes freed from sorrow.*

8. rco aksare parame vyoman yasmin deva adhi visve nisedhuh; yas tan na veda kim rca karisyati ya it tad vidus ta ime samasate.

8. *He who does not know that highest and imperishable being of the Rigveda, in whom all the gods of high heaven rest, of what use is the Rigveda to Him? Those who know it thus, all else is fulfilled.*

Notes: A sacrificer who relies upon the chants of the Rigveda to invoke various gods ought to know the ultimate cause of creation and the ultimate recipient of all offerings. Knowledge of Brahman is more important than relying upon mere rituals.

9. chandamsi yajnah kratavo vratani bhutam bhavyam yac ca veda vadanti; asman mayi srjate visvam etat tasmims canyo mayaya samniruddhah.

9. *The Vedas or the Vedic meters (chandas), rituals, sacrifices, the past and the future and whatever the Vedas declare, all this the maker of maya manifests and in this the other is held by maya.*

Notes: Brahman is described here as mayi, the creator of maya or illusion. The outward forms of worship and all that the Vedas declare is also considered as part of maya or illusion, because whatever that is within the field of human awareness can only be a part of the illusion. The other one is the individual soul, mentioned before as the bird perched on the tree, who enjoys the sweet fruit of his actions.

10. mayam tu prakrtim vidyan mayinam tu mahesvaram; tasyavayavabhutais tu vyaptam sarvam idam jagat.

10. *Know that Prakriti (Nature) is maya and Mahesvara is the wielder of maya. All that is here in this world is pervaded by elements that are part of Him.*

Notes: Prakriti (Nature) is the dynamic power of Isvara, consisting of the maya-tattva or the power to delude the worlds and beings. Prakriti is depicted here as a dependent entity, powerless by itself and Mahesvara, the great Lord, as the wielder of that power. Everything that is manifested here is part of Him, including the elements, which are within the domain of Prakriti. Bhuta means both beings (jivas) and the five elements (mahabhutas). The five elements are part of Isvara; and they are present in every aspect of the manifested world (jagat).

11. yo yonim-yonim adhitisthaty eko yasminn idam sam ca vi caiti sarvam; tam isanam varadam devam idyam nicayyemam santim atyantam eti.

11. *He who rules over as the source of all sources, in whom all this dissolves and rises again, who is the overlord, the giver of boons, the deity, by discerning Him one attains supreme peace.*

Notes: Isvara, the Lord of the universe, is the cause of causes. In this regard, the Upanishad differs fundamentally from the traditional Samkhya, which does not recognize the universal Being as the lord of creation.

12. yo devanam prabhavas codbhavas ca visvadhiko rudro maharsih; hiranyagarbham pasyata jayamanam sa no buddhya subhaya samyunaktu.

12. He who is the effulgence and the source of gods, ruler of the universe, Rudra, the red one, and the great seer, who witnesses the birth of Hiranyagarbha at the time of his birth, may He endow us with pure intelligence.

Notes: Prabhava means greatness, the power to rule or effulgence. The light of the gods and their powers arise from Isvara, the Lord (prabhu) of the universe. Hiranyagarbha is the Cosmic Self, who manifests as a reflection of Brahman in the quality of Rajas. Isvara is prior to Him. Therefore, He watches the birth of Hiranyagarbha. Isvara is the reflection in sattva. Hence, he is also the source of purity (sattva) for the intelligence in the body, without which the mind cannot experience equanimity or the supreme peace mentioned before.

13. yo devanam adhipo yasmiml loka adhisritah; ya ise asya dvipadas catuspadah kasmai devaya havisa vidhema.

13. He who is the ruler of gods, in whom worlds are supported, who is the Lord of the two footed and four footed beings, to what other God can we make our offerings?

14. suksmatisuksmam kalilasya madhye visvasya srastaram anekarupam; visvasyaikam parivestitaram jnatva sivam santim atyantam eti.

14. Subtler than the subtlest, in the midst of great confusion, who creates throughout the universe beings of diverse forms, who envelops the whole universe as one in His embrace, knowing Him as the pure and auspicious, one attains exceeding peace.

Notes: Confusion or chaos denotes the impermanent and ever-changing phenomenal world, the body, and Nature which are subject to innumerable modifications. Isvara is described here as the creator, supporter, protector and liberator of the whole creation.

15. sa eva kale bhuvanasya gopta visvadhipah sarvabhutesu gudhah; yasmin yukta brahmarsayo devatas ca tam evam jnatva mrtyupasams chinatti.

15. He, indeed, is the protector of the world in all times, the lord of the universe, hidden in all beings, in whom are united gods and the knowers of Brahman. By knowing Him one breaks apart the chains of death.

16. ghrtat param mandam ivatisuksmam jnatva sivam sarvabhutesu gudham; visvasyaikam parivestitaram jnatva devam mucyate sarvapasaih.

16. By knowing Him who is pure and auspicious (sivam), who is hidden in all beings in a very subtle manner like a very thin layer of clarified butter, who envelops the whole universe as one in his embrace, knowing the deity thus one is released from all bonds.

17. esa devo visvakarma mahatma sada jananam hrdaye samnivistah; hrda manisa manasabhiklpto ya etad vidur amrtas te bhavanti.

17. That God, the architect of all, the great soul, always seated in the heart of beings, he who knows thus in the heart, the intelligence and the mind becomes immortal.

Notes: Feeling, intelligence and knowledge are the three important means suggested here to achieve liberation. The heart is where one experiences devotion. With intelligence, which is the lord of the mind (manisa), one can stabilize the mind and discern the truth. Finally with the practice of concentration and meditation (dharana and dhyana) with a stable mind, one can experience self-absorption. Thus, bhakti-yoga, buddhi-yoga and jnana-yoga are the methods implied here for God-realization.

18. yadatamas tan na diva na ratrir na san na casac chiva eva kevalah; tad aksaram tat savitur varenyam prajna ca tasmat prasrta purani.

18. When there is no darkness of tamas, then neither day nor light, neither beingness nor non-beingness, but only aloneness or oneness. That is imperishable, that is the adorable light of Savitr (the sun). From that spread the ancient wisdom.

Notes: Ignorance is caused by the presence of tamas. When it is replaced with pure and effulgent sattva, then all dualities and pairs of opposites disappear and one alone remains without duality and without a second. That oneness is comparable to the effulgent light of the imperishable sun, which shines alone in the sky. From that state of aloneness spreads the wisdom of truth whereby one is never deluded by the dualities of life.

19. nainam urdhvam na tiryancam na madhye parijagrabhat; na tasya pratima asti yasya nama mahad yasah.

19. Neither above, nor across, nor in the middle one can grasp Him. There is no image of Him which exists. His name is the great glory.

Notes: The senses cannot perceive Him. The mind cannot comprehend Him. No symbol can truly represent him. He has no name but only fame.

20. na samdrse tisthati rupam asya na caksusa pasyati kascanainam; hrda hrdistham manasa ya enam evam vidur amrtas te bhavanti.

20. His form cannot be established by seeing. None can see Him with eyes. But those, who know Him, with their hearts and minds, as abiding in the heart become immortal.

21. ajata ity evam kascid bhiruh prapadyate; rudra yat daksinam mukham tena mam pahi nityam.

21. "You are unborn," thus thinking people approach you with fear filled hearts. O Rudra, may your benign face protect me always.

22. ma nas toke tanaye ma na ayusi ma no gosu ma no asvesu ririsah; viran ma no rudra bhamito vadhir havismantah sadam it tva havamahe.

22. Rudra, please do not cause any hurt in my child or grandchild, nor in my span of life. Please do not cause any harm to our cattle or horses. In your anger please do not slay our warriors. We always pray to you with oblations and mantha sacrifices.

Notes: Rudra has always been worshipped with fear and reverence, because He is perceived as the god of destruction and is known for His destructive outbursts of anger. This has always been a great puzzle to many. How can one who is called Isvara, who is regarded as the most auspicious being and who is so well known for His love and compassion can be destructive at times in his attitude towards others? How can we term Him as controller of the universe, if He cannot control His own anger? The fact is that both creation and destruction are two sides of the same process. Creation involves destruction, and destruction involves creation. There cannot be renewal of life without death and destruction and there cannot be death unless mortal life manifests itself in the form of a being. This is a universal fact, a fact very much inherent in the creation of this universe as well in our very existence. It is the operation of these two which makes possible the evolution life on earth. The great calamities on earth, the loss of life that follows them are part of this divine wrath, a wrath that is pure and benign in its nature, without any malice and evil, without any vehemence, but purely a divine expression born out of love and detachment and compulsions of managing the creative process. Sometimes for the sake of duty you have to perform unpleasant tasks and God's anger is part of that unpleasant duty which He performs without attachment or expectation. For the mortals like us, destruction and death appear as negative consequences of our actions, but in the divine scheme of things it is not so. What appears to us as destruction may in reality be a way of improving things, of making progress possible, sometimes against our wishes and expectations. Suffering is a reality in our world, but it does not exist in the world of Isvara. Suffering exists in our world because there is a purpose behind it. And the purpose is to purify our minds and bodies and prepare us for liberation.

Chapter 5

The Supreme Self and the Individual Self

1. dve askare brahmapare tv anante, vidya'vidye nihite yatra gudhe, ksaram tv avidya hy amrtam tu vidya vidyavidye isate yas tu so'nyah.

1. Hidden in the imperishable, supreme and infinite Brahman are the two, knowledge and ignorance. Ignorance is perishable, but knowledge, verily, is everlasting. There is another who controls both knowledge and ignorance.

Notes: Vidya means not any knowledge but knowledge of Brahman and the individual Self, which leads to liberation. The rest is ignorance, especially whatever contributes to delusion, duality and bondage. The controller of these two is Isvara, who is distinct from both.

2. yo yonim yonim adhitisthaty eko visvani rupani yonis ca sarvah rsim prasutam kapilam yas tam agre jnanair bibharti jayamanam ca pasyet.

2. He who is established in all the wombs as their source, one in all forms and all wombs, He who in the beginning bears the red seer (in His own womb) with knowledge as his body, and beholds as he is born.

3. ekaikam jalam bahudha vikurvann asmin ksetre samharaty esa devah; bhuyah srstva patayas tathesah sarvadhipatyam kurute mahatma.

3. One net, He the Lord of the gods casts variously for each at the time of creation into the field of Prakriti and then withdraws them again. Having created the lords and the great Self, He wields His lordship over all.

Notes: Ksehtra, the field is another name for the body or Nature. It is subject to modifications arising from ignorance and delusion. At the end of creation, all the beings are withdrawn.

4. sarva disa urdhvam adhas ca tiryak prakasayan bhrajate yad vanadvan; evam sa devo bhagavan varenyo yonisvabhavan adhitisthaty ekah.

4. Just as the sun spreads his brilliance above, below and across, so does that one God, glorious, adorable, rules over whatever creatures that are born from the wombs.

5. yac ca svabhavam pacati visvayonih pacyams ca sarvan parinamayed yah; sarvam etad visvam adhitisthaty eko gunams ca sarvan viniyojayed yah.

5. He who acting according to His own Nature, as the source of all, enables all sources to ripen according to their own. One Lord, who mixing the qualities in all, rules over all that exists in the world.

6. tad vedaguhyopanisatsu gudham tad brahma vedate brahmayonim; ye purvam deva rsayas ca tad vidus te tanmaya amrta vai babhuvuh.

6. That which is hidden in the Vedas and the Upanishads, that Brahma knows that as the origin of the Vedas. In the past the gods and the seers who knew It attained Its nature and became immortal.

Notes: Brahman is the source of the Vedas and Brahman is also known as the Vedas.

7. gunanvayo yah phalakarmakarta krtasya tasyaiva sa copabhokta; sa visvarupas trigunas trivartma pranadhipah samcarati svakarmabhih.

7. He who is endowed with gunas and the doer of actions that bear fruit, he is surely the enjoyer of the result of whatever actions He performs. He with numerous forms, triple qualities, treading the triple paths, the ruler of the breaths, wanders about according to his deeds.

Notes: This is the description of the embodied Self, who indulges in desire-ridden actions and suffers from their consequences. The triple qualities are sattva, rajas and tamas. The three paths on which he treads are the cycle of births and deaths, the path of ancestors and the path of gods.

8. angusthamatro ravitulyarupah samkalpahamkarasamanvito yah; buddher gunenatmagunena caiva aragramatro hy avaro 'pi drstah.

8. Of the size of the thumb, in appearance equal to the sun, endowed with will and ego-sense. However, with the qualities of intelligence and the Self, he appears as if of the size of the point of a needle.

Notes: The idea implied in this verse is that the Self is very subtle and small hidden within the body having the light similar to that of the sun. However, when he is mixed up with intelligence, his appearance changes.

9. valagra-satabhagasya satadha kalpitasya ca, bhago jivah sa vijneyah sa canantyaya kalpate.

9. The Self in the living being (jiva) should be known as one hundredth part of the one hundredth part of the point of a hair. Yet it is capable of infinity.

10. naiva stri na puman esa na caivayam napumsakah; yad yac chariram adatte tena tena sa yujyate.

10. It is neither female nor male, nor asexual. Whatever body it takes up, in that form it appears.

11. samkalpanasparsanadrstimohair grasambuvrstya catmavi-vrddhijanma; karmanugany anukramena dehi sthanesu rupany abhisamprapadyate.

11. By will, touch, sight and passions, and with the intake of food and drink there are birth and growth for the (living) Self. According to the nature of its deeds, the embodied Self assumes various forms in various places.

12. sthulani suksmani bahuni caiva rupani dehi svagunair vrnoti; kriyagunair atmagunais ca tesam samyogahetur aparo 'pi drstah.

12. Gross and subtle forms of numerous kinds the embodied Self assumes according to his own qualities. Having become united with them and the qualities of his actions and the qualities of his body, he is seen as another.

13. anadyanantam kalilasya madhye visvasya srastaram anekarupam; visvasyaikam parivestitaram jnatva devam mucyate sarvapasaih.

13. Without a beginning and without an end, in the middle of chaos, creator of all, with innumerable forms, who envelops the whole universe as one in His embrace, he who knows the deity thus is freed from all fetters.

14. bhavagrahyam anidakhyam bhavabhavakaram sivam; kalasargakaram devam ye vidus te jahus tanum.

14. He who is attainable by devotion, who is known as incorporeal, who is the cause of existence and non-existence, who is pure and auspicious, the cause of creation and its parts, he who knows the deity thus leaves the body behind.

Notes: Bhava has many meanings. It means feelings, emotions, state of mind and also devotion. Sarga also has many meanings. It means creation, birth and death, succession of events and so on. Kala may mean arts, parts or even aspects of Nature.

Chapter 6
The One God Who Liberates

1. svabhavam eke kavayo vadanti kalam tathanye parimuhyamanah; devasyaisa mahima tu loke yenedam bhramyate brahmacakram.

1. *One's own nature alone say some wise men, time say others who are deluded. But it is the power of God in the world, by which rotates here the wheel of Brahman.*

Notes: The Upanishadic seers always referred to creation as cyclical, both in structure and process. The very existence of creation, manifested through the creative act of God, is symbolized as a wheel, the hub as well as the circumference, standing for the unity and the upholding aspect of God, while the spokes represent the multiplicity or the diversity as well as the illusory nature of creation. The Brahma Wheel (Brahma Chakra) described here has some affinity with the Dharma Wheel (Dharma Chakra) of Buddhism.

2. yenavrtam nityam idam hi sarvam jnah kalakalo guni sarva-vidyah; tenesitam karma vivartate ha prthivyaptejo'nilakhani cintyam.

2. He by whom verily all this is continuously enveloped, the knower, the creator of time, virtuous, knower of all types of knowledge, it is by His commands actions unfold as what we call the earth, water, fire, air and space.

3. tat karma krtva vinivartya bhuyas tattvasya tattvena sametya yogam; ekena dvabhyam tribhir astabhir va kalena caivatma-gunais ca suksmaih.

3. Having done His work, and rested again, uniting the tattvas together in the (atma) tattva, from the one, two, three or eight, even time and the subtle qualities of the self.

Notes: The one is Purusha, the two are both Purusha and Prakriti, the three are the sattva, rajas and tamas, the eight are the five great elements, (earth, water, fire, air and ether), the mind, buddhi or intelligence and the ego-sense. The subtle qualities of the self are the subtle parts of the living-self, the jiva.

4. arabhya karmani gunanvitani bhavams ca sarvan viniyo-jayed yah; tesam abhave krtakarmanasah karmaksaye yati sa tattvato'nyah.

4. Starting the works arising from the association of the triple qualities He brings forth all the states of existence. When they become non-existent, the (results of the) works that have been performed are destroyed. When works become extinct, he remains as the other Tattva.

Notes: The other tattva is Atmatattvah or Siva tattva.

5. adih sa samyoganimittahetuh paras trikalad akalo 'pi drstah; tam visvarupam bhavabhutam idyam devam svacittastham upasya purvam.

5. *The beginning, the instrumental cause of the union, He is seen as beyond the three times and without parts, having first worshipped that adorable deity, who has numerous forms, the cause for the existence of all beings, and established first in one's own thoughts.*

Notes: Nimittha means instrumental cause and the union is a reference to the union between Purusha and Prakriti. The three times are past, present and future.

6. sa vrksakalakrtibhih paro 'nyo yasmat prapancah parivartate'yam; dharmavaham papanudam bhagesam jnatvatmastham amrtam visvadhama.

6. *He is higher and other than the various forms of the tree (of creation), and time. From Him revolves the world and it is He who establishes selfless duty (dharma) and removes evil. The Lord of creation, by knowing Him as one's own Self, the immortal and the upholder of all, one attains Brahman.*

7. tam isvaranam paramam mahesvaram tam devatanam paramam ca daivatam; patim patinam paramam parastad vidama devam bhuvanesam idyam.

7. *He is the Lord of creation (Isvara), the highest and the greatest Lord. He is the highest God among the gods, and very divine. He is who is the husband among the husbands, and transcendental, let us know that God as the most adorable Lord of the world.*

8. na tasya karyam karanam ca vidyate na tatsamas cabhyadhikas ca drsyate; parasya saktir vividhaiva sruyate svabhaviki jnanabalakriya ca.

8. *Neither His actions nor His organs of action are known. There is nothing that can be seen, which is better than Him or equal to Him. His supreme powers are heard to be numerous. By their own inherent nature, His knowledge and strength work.*

9. na tasya kascit patir asti loke na cesita naiva ca tasya lingam; sa karanam karanadhipadhipo na casya kascij janita na cadhipah.

9. *He has no master in this world, no ruler, nor is there any symbol of Him. He is the cause of all the causes and the ruler of all the rulers. He has no father and no controller above Him.*

10. yas tantunabha iva tantubhih pradhanajaih svabhavatah; deva ekah svam avrnoti sa no dadhad brahmapyayam.

10. *The one God, who spreads around Himself, like a spider, propelled by His own nature, with the threads of the primordial matter (pradhana). May He grant us an entrance into Brahman.*

Notes: The sensory reality, like the virtual reality of the internet, is also a giant web, created by God using the primordial matter (mula prakriti) as His resource. Everything else is caught in this gigantic net, but He moves freely in it, like a giant spider without getting caught in its own net. Creation is envisaged here as an outgoing process, a super imposition upon the space, with Time (kala or death) as its center. The individual souls are the insects who become caught in the web of delusion, births and deaths and consumed by Time.

11. eko devah sarvabhutesu gudhah sarvavyapi sarvabhutantaratma; karmadhyaksah sarvabhutadhivasah saksi ceta kevalo nirgunas ca.

11. One God is hidden in all beings. He is all pervading, the inner Self of all, who presides over all actions, who dwells in all beings, the witness, the sentient, the one and only, and without any qualities.

12. eko vasi niskriyanam bahunam ekam bijam bahudha yah karoti; tam atmastham ye 'nupasyanti dhiras tesam sukham sasvatam netaresam.

12. The one controller who is passive among many (active), who makes the one seed into many. The wise, who perceive Him as situated within themselves, for them is eternal happiness, but not for others.

13. nityo nityanam cetanas cetananam eko bahunam yo vidadhati kaman; tat karanam samkhyayogadhigamyam jnatva devam mucyate sarvapasaih.

13. Eternal among the eternals, intelligent among the intelligences, one in many, the fulfiller of desires, that cause can be known only through Samkhya-yoga. By knowing the deity one is freed from all bonds.

Notes: The Supreme Self is the eternal among the individual souls, who are also eternals. He is the highest intelligence among the many intelligences He creates. He is the One in the diversity of creation. He is the cause of all and known only through Samkhya meaning knowledge and Yoga meaning union. By knowing him in this manner one becomes free from all bonds (pasas)

14. na tatra suryo bhati na candratarakam nema vidyuto bhanti kuto'yam agnih; tam eva bhantam anubhati sarvam tasya bhasa sarvam idam vibhati.

14. There shines neither the sun nor the moon, nor the stars, nor the lightning. Then what to say about fire? Only after He shines, all else shines. All this is illuminated by His radiance.

Notes: The world of Brahman is above all manifestation. Hence, in that sphere there is no sun, no moon, no lightning, no clouds, no stars and no duality whatsoever. He is independent, while everything else depends upon Him for support and nourishment.

15. eko hamso bhuvanasyasya madhye sa evagnih salile samnivistah; tam eva viditvati mrtyum eti nanyah pantha vidyate' yanaya.

15. He, the one bird in the middle of the world, indeed is the fire that has entered into the ocean. By knowing Him alone one can overcome death. No other path is known to achieve it.

16. sa visvakrd visvavid atmayonir jnah kalakalo guni sarvavidyah; pradhanaksetrajnapatir gunesah samsaramoksasthitibandhahetuh.

16. He is the creator of all, knower of all, self-existing, the knower, the author of time, possessor of qualities, knower of all types of knowledge, the chief among the knowers of the field (ksetrajna), the lord of the triple qualities (gunas), the cause of births and deaths (samsara), of liberation (moksha), of continuation and bondage.

Notes: Ksetra means the field or body. Ksetrajna is the knower of the field, or the individual Self. The Supreme Self is the Knower among the knowers of the fields. Samasara means the phenomenal world characterized by the cycle of births and deaths. The cause of this is Isvara, who is also responsible for the creation (sristi), preservation (sthiti) and dissolution (laya) of the worlds. He is also the liberator who grants liberation (moksha) to the beings who are caught in the cycle of births and deaths.

17. sa tanmayo hy amrta isasamstho jnah sarvago bhuvanasyasya gopta; sa ise asya jagato nityam eva nanyo hetur vidyata isanaya.

17. He who is deluded in the body, indeed, is the immortal, established as the lord, the knower, the omnipresent, the protector of the world, he who rules this world forever. No other cause is known for the ruling.

Notes: The individual Self in body, who is deluded (tanmaya), is also the immortal Lord, for there is no difference between the two, except perhaps notionally. He is one and only, who manifests differently in different fields and the only ruler known to the knowers of Brahman.

18. yo brahmanam vidadhati purvam yo vai vedams ca prahinoti tasmai; tam ha devam atmabuddhiprakasam mumuksur vai saranam aham prapadye.

18. To Him who in the past created Brahma, and who verily imparts to Him the knowledge of the Vedas, to that God who illuminates Himself by His own intelligence, for the sake of liberation, I surrender seeking refuge.

19. niskalam niskriyam santam niravadyam niranjanam; amrtasya param setum dagdhendhanam ivanalam.

19. Without parts, without actions, peaceful, without blame, without impurities, the supreme bridge to immortality, like a fire that burns without fuel, is He.

20. yada carmavad akasam vestayisyanti manavah; tada devam avijnaya duhkhasyanto bhavisyati.

20. When humans roll up space (if at all) as if it were a piece of leather, only then perhaps, without knowing Brahman, there may be an end to sorrow.

Notes: The only way to end sorrow is to realize God. This is the only way to transcend the miseries of life, most importantly the sorrow of birth and death. Trying to accomplish this goal, without knowing Brahman, is as impossible as rolling the heaven like a piece of leather. The verse is a rejoinder to those atheistic schools who do not believe in God but speak about liberation.

21. tapahprabhavad devaprasadat brahma ha svetasvataro 'tha vidvan; atyasramibhyah paramam pavitram provaca samyag rsisanghajustam.

21. By the power of austerity, and the grace of God, the learned Svetasvatara has spoken about Brahman to the ascetics of the highest order, that which is transcendental, pure and pleasing to the company of seers.

22. vedante paramam guhyam purakalpe pracoditam; naprasantaya datavyam naputrayasisyaya va punah.

22. The Vedanta which has been declared in the past as the most hidden (esoteric), should not be imparted to those who have not pacified their passions, nor again to the one who is not a son or a pupil.

Notes: Knowledge should be imparted to the qualified. This has been the tradition of Hinduism in the past. Knowledge may be imparted to one's son to preserve the family tradition or to carry forward the traditional duties of the family. It may also be imparted to a pupil who is qualified, who has been chosen by his teacher after careful observation and testing to ascertain his character and readiness to receive it

23. yasya deve para bhaktir yatha tatha gurau; tasyaite kahita hy arthah prakasante mahatmanah, prakasante mahatmanah.

23. These subjects, which have been declared so far, illuminate the great souls, who have the highest devotion to God as well as to the teacher who is as venerable as God is. Yes they do illuminate the great souls.

Paingala Upanishad

Editor's Note

Paingala Upanishad belongs to the White Yajurveda. It is included in some classifications as a minor Upanishad. It is available to us in the form of a conversation between Yajnavalkya and his disciple Paingala, from whom the name of the Upanishad is derived. Paingala Upanishad explains the various manifestations of Brahman, the process of creation and dissolution, and mentions many concepts of the Vedanta such as pancikarana (the fivefold division of the great elements), adhyaropa and apavada (a traditional method to arrive at truth), and the state of a liberated living being (jivanmukta). The Upanishad has few similarities with the Bhagavadgita and qualifies as a Vaisnava Upanishad.

The following is a translation of the Paingala Upanishad by Jayaram V.

Invocation

aum purnamadah purnamidam purnat purnam udacyate; purnasya purnam adaya purnam eva vasisyate. aum santih santih santih.

Aum! That is full. This also is full. From that full arises this full. Taking the full from the full, the full remains full. Aum, peace, peace, peace.

Chapter 1
The Process of Creation

1. atha ha paingalo yagnavalkyam upasam etya dvadasa varsa susrusa purvakam paramarahasyam kaivalyam anubruhiti papraccha.

1. After serving Yajnavalkya for twelve years Paingala approached him and asked, "Please teach me the supreme secret of aloneness."

Notes: Kaivalyam means aloneness or oneness, beyond duality and diversity. It is the state of liberation

2. sa hovaca yagynavalkyah sad eva saumyedam agra asit, tan nitya muktam avikriyam satyagnana anandam paripurnam, sanatanam ekam eva dvitiyam brahma.

2. To him Yajnavalkya said, "In the very beginning, my dear, all this was Undifferentiated Beingness only. It was Brahman, who is eternally free, without modifications, complete in all respects with truth, knowledge and bliss, everlasting, one without a second."

Notes: Sad means truth, or existence in its original state prior to creation, diversity and duality.

3. tasmin marusuktika sthanu-sphatikadau jala-raupya-purusa-rekhadival lohita-sukla-krisna-gunamayi gunasamyanirvacya mulaprakritir asit, tat pratibimbitam yat tat saksi-caitanyamasit.

3. Just as water in a mirage, silver in the pearl of an oyster, a person in a stump of wood, and light and color in a crystal, so also in that (Being) appears the balanced and inexpressible Primordial Nature consisting of the qualities of red, white and black. When its reflection appears, That becomes the witness consciousness.

Notes: The one and only Brahman enters into a state of duality by becoming a witness to His own beingness in the aspects of Nature. The One and alone, now enters into a subject and object relationship. The subject is real, changeless and eternal. The object is unreal, unstable and a mere reflection of the balanced and inexpressible primordial Nature created like an illusion (mirage) by the interplay of the gunas, namely rajas, sattva and tamas, which are represented by red, white and black colors respectively. Thus, this Upanishads emphatically states that manifestation is very much like an illusion that arises in the Beingness of Brahman to create the experience of duality and objectivity.

4. sa punar vikritim prapya sattvo-drikta'avyaktakhyavarana-saktir asit, tat pratibimbitam yat tad isvara-caitanyam asit. sa svadhinamayah sarvagyah sristi-sthiti-layanam-adikarta jagadankura-rupo bhavati. svasmin vilinam sakalam jagad avirbhavayati. prani-karma-vasad esa pato yadvat prasaritah prani-karma-ksayat punas tirobhavayati. tasminn evakhilam visvam sankocita-patavadvartate.

5. When that undergoes modifications, with the preponderance of Sattva, it becomes the unmanifested with the power to veil (or conceal). What is reflected in it becomes the Isvara Consciousness. He controls Maya (delusion). He is all knowing. He is the prime cause of creation, preservation and dissolution. He has the form of the germ of the world. He causes all this that is latent inside to become manifest. Due to the desire-ridden actions of beings, this spreads out like a cloth and when the desire-ridden actions of the beings are exhausted, it becomes withdrawn. In that alone remains the whole universe like a shrunken cloth.

Notes: The refection of Sattva in the Beingness of Brahman manifests as the divine aspect or Isvara Caintanyam. It is the purest, the highest and the most resplendent manifestation of Brahman in His own Being. Everything that partakes that purity becomes divine. In some traditions, this is called Isvara Tattva. Creation is compared to a clothe and Brahman as the weaver. The cloth is however an illusion because it is just a reflection, created by the modifications of Nature and the actions of beings. This Brahman has the power to conceal, whereby He subjects the beings to the delusion of duality and of forgetfulness.

5. isadhisthitavarana-saktito rajo-drikta-mahad-akhya viksepa-saktirasit. tat pratibimbitam yat tad hiranyagarbha-caitanyam asit, sa mahattattvabhimani spastaspasta-vapur bhavati.

5. From the power of veiling, embodied in Isvara, comes into being the power of expansion (or projection) called Mahat because of the predominanc of rajas. What is reflected in it becomes the Hiranyagarbha Consciousness. He, presiding over the Mahat Tattva (reality of Nature) becomes both distinct and indistinct.

6. hiranyagarbhadhisthita-viksepa-saktitas-tamo- driktahanka-rabhidha sthula-saktir asit. tat-pratibimbitam yat tad virat acaitanyam asit. sa tad-abhimani spasta-vapuh sarva-sthula-palako visnuh pradhana-puruso bhavati. tasmad atmana akasah sambhutah. akasad vayuh. vayor agnih, agner apah. adbhyah prithivi. tani panca tanmatrani trigunani bhavanti.

6. From the expanding power of Hiranyagarbha, comes into being, due to the predominance of tamas, the gross power called the ego-sense. What is reflected in it becomes the Virat Consciousness. He, presiding over it as his own, with distinct form, becomes Vishnu, the chief person and the ruler of all gross manifestation. From that arises ether; from ether, air; from air, fire; from fire, water; and from that the earth. These five subtle elements arise from the gunas only.

Notes: The tanmatras are the subtle elements, namely the sound, touch, form, taste and odor. The three qualities from which they arise are sattva, rajas and tamas. Virat is the gross material manifestation, having self-sense or ego-sense, from which arises duality and distinction.

7. srastu-kamo jagad-yonis tamo-gunam adhisthaya suksma-tanmatrani bhutani sthulikartum so'akamayata. sristeh parimitani bhutany ekam ekam dvidha vidhaya punas' caturdha kritva svasvetaradvitiyamsaih pancadha samyojya pancikrita-bhutair-ananta-koti-brahmandani tat-tad-andocita-golaka-sthula-sarirany asrijat.

7. Desiring to create, controlling the quality of tamas, the creator of the universe, wished to change the subtle elements into gross form. He divided each of these limited elements in creation into two. One part (out of the two), he divided again into four equal parts. He mixed each of the four subdivided equal parts with the (undivided) first part and with each of the other four equal subdivided parts, and thus formed a fivefold mixture, each part having one measure of its own element and one fourth measure of the other four elements. From these, he created endless crores of macrocosms, fourteen worlds specific to (each of these macrocosms) and globular gross bodies fit for each (of these worlds).

Notes: Since the wording in the sloka is confusing, I have take some liberates to state the process of pancikarna. The process is explained in some ancient texts like Atmabodha and Tattvabodha. Pancikarana explains how the five subtle elements (tanmatras) were combined to produce their gross forms through a fivefold mixture. According to it, first each of the tanmatras was divided into two. One part out of the two was kept intact while the other was divided into four parts again. Now each of these four parts were combined with the original first half which was left undivided and with one of the four subdivided parts from each element. Thus each element will have 50% of itself and 12.5% of each of the other four elements. As per Shankara, the five gross elements thus formed are subjected to six modifications: existence, birth, growth, change, decay, and death. To those who are not familiar with Indian denominations, a crore is equal to ten millions.

8. sa panca-bhutanam rajomsam caturdha kritva bhagatrayat pancavrittyatmakam pranam asrijat. sa tesam turya-bhagena karmendriyany asrijat.

8. He divided the rajas portion of the five elements into four equal parts. Out of three parts of each of them, he created the (fivefold) breath (prana, apana, vyana etc.). From the (remaining) fourth part, he created the organs of actions.

9. sa tesam sattvamsam caturdha kritva bhaga-traya-samastitah panca-kriya-vrittyatmakam antah-karanam asrijat. sa tesam sattva turiya bhagena jnanendriyany asrijat.

9. He divided the sattva portion of the five elements into four equal parts, Out of the three parts of each of them, he created the internal organ. From the (remaining) fourth part, he created the organs of perception.

10. sattvasamastita indriyapalakan asrijat. tani sristany ande praciksipat. tad-ajnaya samastyandam vyapya tany atisthan. tad ajnayahankara samanvito virad sthulany araksat. hiranyagarbhas tad-ajnaya suksmany apalayat.

10. Out of the entire portion of the sattva, he created the rulers of the sense-organs. Those he created, he cast them into (their respective) spheres. By his orders, they pervaded the entire macrocosm (the whole body). By his order, Virat, who is endowed with self-sense, protected gross elements. By his orders, Hiranyagarbha ruled over the subtle elements.

11. andasthani tani tena vina spanditum cestitum va na sekuh. tani cetanikartum so'akamayata brahmanda brahmarandhrani samasta-vyasti-mastakan vidarya tad evan upravisat. tada jadany api tani cetanavat svakarmani cakrire.

11. Within their spheres, without him, they were incapable of acting or reacting. He desired to make them active. Piercing into the macrocosm through the apertures located in the heads of the individual beings, he entered into them. Then, although they were inert by nature, they were able to function on their own as if they had consciousness.

12. sarvajneso maya-lesa-samanvito vyasti-deham pravisya taya mohito jivatvam agamat. sarira-traya-tadatmyat kartritva-bhoktritvatam agamat; jagrat-svapna-susupti-murccha-marana-dharmayukto ghati-yantravad udvigno jato mrita iva kulala cakra-nyayena paribhramatiti.

12. *The all knowing one, taking hold of Maya, entered into several bodies, and deluded by Maya, attained the beingness of the living entities. Identifying himself with the three bodies (gross, subtle and casual), he attained the state of doer and enjoyer. United with the states of waking, dreaming, sleep, deep sleep, and death, bound like a bucket chained to the water wheel, mentally troubled and dead even while alive, he keeps revolving in the manner of a potter's wheel.*

Chapter 2
Creation of the Body and Beingness

1. atha paingalo yajnavalkyam uvaca sarvalokanam sristi-sthity-anta-krid vibhur isah katham jivatvam agamad iti.

2. *Then Pangala asked Yajnavalkya, "How does the Lord who is the creator, preserver, destroyer and the sovereign in all the worlds attain beingness?"*

Notes: Jivatvam means the quality of a jiva or living being. It is beingness. Brahman has to two aspects, the Manifested and the Unmanifested. The Manifested Brahman has beingness or jivatvam.

2. sa hovaca yajnavalkyah, sthula-suksma-karana-dehodbhava-purvakam jivesvara-svarupam vivicya kathayamiti savadhane-naikagrataya sruyatam. isah pancikrita-maha-bhuta-lesan ada-ya vyasti-samastyatmaka-sthula-sarirani yathakramam akarot. kapalacarmantrasthi-mamsa-nakhani prithivy-amsah, rakta-mutra-lalasvedadikam avamsah. ksut-trisnosna-moha-maithu-nadya agnyamsah, pracaranottarana-svasadika vayv-amsah. kama-krodhadayo vyomamsah. etat sanghatam karmani sanci-tam tvagadi-yuktam balyady avasthabhimanaspadam bahu-dopasrayam sthula-sariram bhavati.

2. *To him Yajnavalkya replied, "I shall explain now, the state of the lord of the beings prior to the origin of the gross, subtle and casual bodies. Listen with full attention and single-minded concentration what you hear. The Lord, taking up small portions of the five elements thus divided into five through pancikarna, created successively gross bodies*

in their individual and aggregate forms. The skull, the skin, the intestines, the bones, the flesh and the nails constitute the earth part. The blood, the urine, saliva, sweat and the like constitute the water part. Hunger, thirst, heat, infatuation, sexual desire and the like constitute the fire part. Walking, lifting, breathing and the like constitute the air part. Lust, anger and the like constitute the space part. All these aggregations assembled under the skin, arising from the accumulated past karmas (sanctia karma), subject to the states of childhood and the like, filled with the wealth of egoism, and inhabited by many sins, becomes the gross body.

Notes: Some translate Jivesvara as Jiva (the beings) and Isvara (the Lord), instead of the Lord of Beings, referring to the embodied Self, which I have followed. Sancitakarma means the karmas that have been bagged (sanci) or accumulated in the past lives which have not yet born fruit at the time of the birth of an individual. It is what you inherit from your past ever since you have been on earth, or since the first time you were born upon earth. Some of it will bear fruit in the present life and the balance will be carried forward to the next life along with the karmas accumulated and not fructified in this life.

3. athapancikrita maha-bhuta-rajomsa-bhaga-traya-samastitah pranam asrijat; pranapana-vyanodana-samanah pranavrittayah. naga-kurma-krikara-devadatta-dhananjaya- upapranah, hridasana-nabhi-kantha-sarvangani sthanani. akasadi-rajoguna-turiya-bhagena karmendriyam asrijat. vak-pani-pada-payupasthas tad vrittayah. vacanadana-gamana-visarganandas tad-visayah.

3. Then, he created breath (prana) from the three parts of rajas quality present in the great elements formed from the fivefold mixture. Prana, apana, vyona, udana and samana are the five modifications of the prana. Naga, kurma, krikara, devadatta and dhananjaya are the auxiliary breaths. The heart, the anus, the navel, the throat and all the limbs in the body are their resting places. Then from the fourth part of the rajas quality present in the elements such as the space, he created the organ of action (karmendriyam). The organ of speech (mouth), the hands, the feet, the excretory and the reproductive organs are its modifications. Speaking, grasping, moving, excreting and enjoying are their functions.

3. athapancikrita maha-bhuta-rajomsa-bhaga-traya-samastitah pranam asrijat; pranapana-vyanodana-samanah pranavrittayah. naga-kurma-krikara-devadatta-dhananjaya- upapranah, hridasana-nabhi-kantha-sarvangani sthanani. akasadi-rajoguna-turiya-bhagena karmendriyam asrijat. vak-pani-pada-

payupasthas tad vrittayah. vacanadana-gamana-visarganandas tad-visayah.

3. *Then, he created breath (prana) from the three parts of rajas quality present in the great elements formed from the fivefold mixture. Prana, apana, vyona, udana and samana are the five modifications of the prana. Naga, kurma, krikara, devadatta and dhananjaya are the auxiliary breaths. The heart, the anus, the navel, the throat and all the limbs in the body are their resting places. Then from the fourth part of the rajas quality present in the elements such as the space, he created the organ of action (karmendriyam). The organ of speech (mouth), the hands, the feet, the excretory and the reproductive organs are its modifications. Speaking, grasping, moving, excreting and enjoying are their functions.*

4. evam bhuta-sattvamsa-bhaga-traya-samastito'antah-karanam asrijat; antah-karana-mano-buddhi-cittahankaras tad-vrittayah. sankalpa-niscaya-smaranabhimananusandhanas tad-visayah. gala-vadana-nabhi-hridaya-bhru-madhyam sthanam. bhuta-satva-turiya-bhagena jnanendriyam asrijat. srotra-tvak-caksur-jivha-ghranas tad vrittayah. sabda-sparsa-rupa-rasa-gandhas tadvisayah; dig-vatarka-praceto'asvi-vahnindropendra-mrityukah; candro-visnus-caturvaktrah sambhus ca karanadhipah.

4. *In the same manner, from the three parts of the sattva quality present in the great elements, he created the aggregates of the internal organ. The internal organ, the mind, intelligence, awareness (citta) and the ego-sense are its modifications. Will, determination, memory, egoism and inquiry are its functions. The throat, face, navel, heart, the place between the eye-brows are its locations. From the remaining fourth part the of sattva quality present in the great elements, he created the organ of perception. The ears, the skin, the eyes, the tongue and the nose are its modifications. Sound, touch, form, taste and smell are its functions. Dik (the directions), Vayu (air), Arka (the sun), Praceta (Varuna), Asvins (gods of medicines), Indra, Upendra, Mritryu (Death), the Moon (Candra), Vishnu (solar deity), Brahma (the four-faced) and Sambhu (Siva) are the presiding deities of the sense-organs.*

5. athannamaya prana-maya-mano-maya-vijnamay-ananda-mayah panca kosah. annarasenaiva bhutvannarasena-bhivriddhim prapyanna-rasa-maya-prithivyam yad viliyate so'anna-maya-kosah. tad eva sthula sariram. karmendriyaih saha pranadi-pancakam prana-maya-kosah; jnanendriyaih saha

mano mano-mayah-kosah. Jnanedriya saha buddhir vijnana-maya-kosah, etat kosa-trayam linga-sariram; svarupa-jnanam-ananda-mayakosah tat karana-sariram.

5. Now, the food body, the breath body, the mind body, the intelligence body and the bliss body, are the five bodies (or sheaths). What consists of the essence of food only, what grows by the essence of food, which dissolves (finally) in the earth filled with the essence of food, that is the food body. It is gross body only. The organs of actions, along with the fivefold breath constitute the breath body. The sense organs along with the mind constitute the mind body. The sense organs along with the intelligence constitute the intelligence body. The three bodies constitute the subtle body. The knowledge of one's own form (Self) constitute the bliss body. It is the casual body.

Notes: Kosa means sheath. There are said to be five sheaths in the body organized into gross, subtle and casual bodies. They are not physical layers, but the gross and subtle aspects of the human personality formed out of the various parts of the body arising from the aggregation of the five elements (maha bhutas) mixed with the qualities (gunas). At the time of death, they return to their elements, while the Self with the casual body formed from the actions (karmas) goes to the higher world. While, the scriptures say that these bodies are formed equally in all beings, it is my conviction that they are not the same in every individual. Just as people differ with the regard to the qualities of their bodies, such as strength, shape, size, color, vigor etc., they also differ with regard to the composition of their inner bodies. In some people the subtle bodies like the mind body or the intelligence body do not grow sufficiently. Hence, they lack the necessary knowledge or intelligence to pursue spiritual aims.

6. atha jnanendriya-pancakam karmendriya-pancakam pran-adi-pancakam viyadadi-pancakam antah-karana-catustayam kama-karma-tamamsy astapuram.

6. Now, the five organs of perception, the five organs of action, prana and the rest of the five breaths, air and the rest of the five elements, and the four fold internal organ constitute the eightfold city (astapuram) of desire, action and darkness (tamas).

Notes: The body has eight aggregates, namely the sense-organs, organs of action, the breaths, the elements, the four aspects of internal organ, namely, the mind, the intelligence, awareness, and the ego-sense. They are subject to the triple influences of desires, actions and darkness.

7. isajnaya virajo vyastideham pravisya buddhim adhisthaya visvatvam agamat. vijnanatma cidabhaso visvo vyavahariko jagrat sthula-dehabhimani karmabhuriti ca visvasya nama bhavati. isajnaya sutratma vyasti-suksma-sariram pravisya mana adhisthaya taijasatvam agamat. taijasah pratibhasikah

svapnakalpita iti taijasasya nama bhavati. isajnaya mayopadhir avyakta-samanvito vyasti-karana-sariram pravisya prajnatvam agamat. prajnovicchinnah paramarthikah susupty abhimaniti prajnasya nama bhavati. avyakta-lesajnanacchadita paramarthika-jivasya tattvamasyadi vakyani brahmanaikatam jaguh netarayor vyavaharika-pratibhasikayoh. antah-karana-pratibimbita caitanyam yat tad evavasthatrayabhag bhavati. sa jagrat-svapna-susupty-avasthah prapya ghati-yantravad udvigno jato mrita iva sthito bhavati. atha jagrat-svapna-susupti-murccha-maranadyavasthah panca bhavanti.

7. Under the command of Isvara, Virat enters the gross body. Presiding over the intelligence, he attains the awareness of the surrounding world (visvatvam) and becomes known by the names of the self of worldly knowledge (vijnanatma), ever effulgent (cicabhasa), universal (visva), empirical (vyavaharika), wakeful (jagrat), identified with gross body (sthula-dehabhimani), made up of karma (karmabhurity) and definitive (visvasva). Under the command of Isvara, the subtle Self (sutratma) enters into the subtle body. Presiding over the mind, he reaches the state of dreams (taijasa). Dream state, illusory reality, product of dreams, these are the names of taijasa. Under the command of Isvara, the bearer of Maya, endowed with the Unmanifested, enters the microcosmic casual body (vasti-karana-sariram) and attains the state of prajna. Superior intelligence (prajna), indivisible (avicchinnah), transcendental (paramardhika),and identified with the sleeping state, these are the names of prajna. Statements such as "You are That," refer to the identify or oneness of Brahman with the particle of unmanifested self held by ignorance ridden metaphysical body (parimardhika jivasyam), but not the empirical (vyavaharika) or the illusory (pratibhasika) selves. It is only that consciousness which is reflected in the internal organ which manifests as the three states. Attaining the wakeful, dream and sleep states, he suffers bound to the states of birth and death like the bucket bound to the water-wheel. Now, the wakeful, dream, sleep, deep-sleep, death, these are the five states (of a jiva).

Notes: Under the command of Isvara, who is the reflection of Brahman in the sattva, His other manifested forms become associated with the elements, resulting in the formation of a living being consisting of empirical, reflective and transcendental selves. They are the aspect of Jiva, the living entity who has five states, the waking, dreaming, sleep, deep sleep and death. The first four are modifications of his beingness caused by the activity or inactivity of his various bodily organs which are listed in this verse and prior verses and which are formed out of the mixing of the five elements with the triple qualities. These are parts of the Jiva and not to be confused with the eternal Self which is not subject to any modifications or impurities and which remains enclosed in the metaphysical body (parimardhika sariram).

8. tat-tad-devatagrahanvitaih srotradi-jnanendriyaih sabdyady-artha-visaya-grahana-jnanam jagrad avastha bhavati. tatra bhru-madhyam gato jiva a-pada-mastakam vyapya krisi-sravanady akhila-kriya-karta bhavati. tat-tat-phalabhuk ca bhavati. lokantaragatah karmarjita-phalam sa eva bhunkte. sa sarvabhaumavad vyavaharacchranta antar-bhavanam pravestum margam asritya tisthati. karanoparame jagrat-samskarottha-prabodhavad grahya-grahaka-rupa-sphuranam svapnavastha bhavati. tatra visva eva jagrad vyavaharalopan nadi-madhyam carams taijasatvam avapya vasana-rupakam jagad-vaicitryam svabhasa bhasayan yathepsitam svayam bhunkte.

8. The perceptual knowledge of sound and such other objects, obtained through ears and such other sense-organs aided by the respective presiding deities of the sense-organs this is the wakeful state (jagrat avasta). In it, the being (jiva), who is located within the middle of the eye-brows and spread throughout the body from head to toe, becomes the doer of all actions, such as toiling, hearing and the like. He becomes the enjoyer of whatever actions he performs; and enjoys in the next world the karmic fruit (karma-phalam) he earns from such actions. Like an emperor who is tired (and want to rest) after taking care of his worldly affairs, he strives to enter into his inner abode by a path that leads to it. When the senses are at rest, the memory of the objects and their perceptions arising from the latent impressions of the wakeful state constitute the dream state. There, the empirical being (visva) alone, with his actions in the wakeful state having ceased, travelling in the middle of the nerve channels, attains the state of Taijasa. A wondrous world of forms shaped by his desires, he illuminates with his own light and himself enjoys them according to his will.

Notes: The jiva, enters the heart during sleep. That is the inner abode (antarbhavanam) mentioned here. From there he travels through the one thousand arthritis that leads to the various parts of the body from the heart and enjoys the residue of his wakeful state left in the form of impressions and latent memories. There he illuminates his own worlds, like the sun in the wakeful state and enjoys the worlds he creates from himself.

9. cittaikakarana susupty-avastha bhavati. bhrama-visranta-sakunih paksau samhritya nidabhimukham yatha gacchati tatha jivo'api jagrat-svapna-prapance vyavahritya sranto'ajnanam pravisya svanandam bhunkte.

10. *The source of sleep state (susupti) is citta (awareness) only. Just as a bird tired of its flying returns to its nest and folding its wings (rests), so does the being tired of his actions in the wakeful and dream states, enters into a state of ignorance and enjoys his own bliss.*

10. akasman mudgaradandadyais taditavad bhayajnanabhyam indriya-sanghataih kampanniva mritatulya murccha bhavati.

11. *The deep sleep state is like death, where the sense organs experience a collective shaking due to fear and ignorance, as if one were struck suddenly by a hammer or club.*

Notes: Ajnanabhayam is the fear arising from not knowing what is going on. It is situation when a person experiencing panic does not know what is happening.

11. jagrat-svapna-susupti-murcchavasthanam anya brahmadi-stamba-paryantam sarva-jiva-bhaya-prada sthula-dehavisarjani maranavastha bhavati. karmendriyani jnanendriyani tat-tad-visayan pranan samhritya kama-karmanvita avidya-bhutavestito jivo dehantaram prapya lokantaram gacchati. prak karma-phala-pakenavartantara-kitavad visrantim naiva gacchati. satkarmaparipakato bahunam janmanam ante nrinam mokseccha jayate.

11. *Other than the wakeful, dream, sleep and deep sleep states is the state of death, which produces fear in all beings from Brahma down to a clump of grass, and which leads to the discarding of the gross body,. After withdrawing the organs of action and the organs of perception from their respective objects, along with the breaths, the being made up of the fruit of their actions, of ignorance and elements, assumes another body and goes to the other world. With the ripening of the fruit of his actions, like an insect caught in a whirlpool, he does not find any rest. Due to the merit of good actions, at the end of many births only, does the desire for liberation arises in a person*

12. tada sad-gurum asritya cira-kala-sevaya bandham moksam kascit prayati. avicarakrito bandho vicaran mokso bhavati. tasmat sada vicarayet. adhyaropapavadatah svarupam niscayikartum sakyate. tasmat sada vicarayej jagaj-jiva-paramatmano jiva-bhava-jagad-bhava-badhe pratyag abhinnam brahmaivavasisyata iti.

12. *Then, resorting to a good teacher, by serving him for a long time, one seeks to attain freedom from bondage. The bondage, which arises from lack of enquiry, becomes liberation through enquiry. Therefore,*

one should always enquire. One should ascertain the nature of the Self using adhyaropa and apavada. Therefore, one should always enquire about the nature of the world, the being and the transcendental Self. When the state of the world and the state of the being are transcended, the state of self undifferentiated from Brahman (pratyagatma) alone remains.

Notes: Adhyaropa and Apavada are the two means of enquiring into the nature of reality used extensively in the study of the Advaita Vedanta. In the Adhyaropa you superimpose upon reality what is not real and in the Apavada, you deny the unreal to arrive at the reality. Thus, in understanding Brahman, first He is superimposed with false attributes and later they are negated. According to Shankara to understand truth that which is inexpressible should be expressed through false attribution and then negated to know the truth. Pratyagatma is the state in which the Self is perceived as universal or indistinct from Brahman. It is the state of seeing oneself in all and all in oneself. In that state there is no beingness, no duality and no distinction. It is a unified vision encompassing all.

Chapter 3
Mahavakyas, the Great Sayings

1. atha hainam paingalah prapaccha yajnavalkyam mahavakya-vivaranam anubruhiti.

1. Then Paingala asked Yajnavalkya, "Please explain in detail the great sayings."

Notes: Mahavakyas are the great sayings found in the Vedas having great philosophical and spiritual significance. Paingala wanted to know about them.

2. sa hovaca yajnavalkyas tat tvam asi tvam tad asi tvam brahmasyaham brahmasmity anusandhanam kuryat. tatra paroksya-sabalah sarvajnatvadi-laksano mayopadhih sac-cid-ananda-laksano jagad-yonis tatpada vacyo bhavati. sa evantah-karana-sambhinnabodho'asmat pratyayavalambanas tvam-pada-vacyo bhavati. parajivopadhimayavidye vihaya tat-tvam-padalaksyam pratyagabhinnam brahma; tattvamasity aham brahmasmiti vakyartha-vicarah sravanam bhavati. ekantena sravanarthanusandhanam mananam bhavati. sravana-manana-nirvicikitse'arthe vastuny ekatanavattaya cetah sthapanam nididhyasanam bhavati; dhyatridhyane vihaya nivatasthita dipavad dhyeyaikagocaram cittam samadhir bhavati. tadanim atmagocara vrittayah samutthita ajnata bhavanti. tah smaranad anumiyante; ihanadisamsare sancitah karmakotayo'anenaiva vilayam yanti. tatobhyasapatavat sahasrasah sada amritadhara varsati. tato yoga-vittamah samadhim dharmamegham prahuh.

vasana-jale nihsesam amuna pravilapite karmasancaye punyapape samulonmulite prak paroksam api karatalamalakavad vakyam apratibaddhaparoksa-saksat-karam prasuyate. tada jivan-mukto bhavati.

2. Yajnavalkya said, "That you are (tat tvam asi), you are that (tvam tad asi), you are Brahman (tvam Brahmasi), Brahman I am (aham Brahmasma), one should engage the mind upon these. That which is the other in the diversified reality (the objective world), the source of the universe (jagat-yoni), who has the quality of all-knowing awareness (sarvajnatavadi), who is the lord of Maya (mayopadhi), who has the quality of truth, consciousness and bliss (sat-cid-ananda), becomes known with the expression Tat (That). That alone, using the internal organ as its support, having a different awareness of self-sense, is known as Tvam. That is the undifferentiated Brahman, who is the object of the words "Tat" and "Tvam," and who has been free from Maya and ignorance, which overtake the transcendental self and the embodied self. Enquiry into the meaning of "Tat Tvam Asi" and "Aham Brahmasmi" constitute Sravana (hearing). Reflecting in solitude upon the meaning of what is being heard is called Mananam (reflection). Fixing the thought with single-minded concentration upon the object of what is being heard or reflected upon is Nidhidhyasana (meditation). Without the distinction of the mediator and the meditation, like a lamp (without flickering) in a windless place, such is the state of Samadhi (self-absorption). In that state, although the modifications arise within oneself, they remain unknown. They are inferred from memory only. Through them only all the accumulated karmas, since the beginning of the cycle of births and deaths, become dissolved. Then, through practice, a thousand streams of nectar flows downs constantly. Therefore, the adepts in Yoga calls this self-absorption with a cloud of virtue raining down (Dharmamegha Samadhi). When the past impressions are dissolved without any residue whatsoever, when the bag of good and bad karmas are fully destroyed to the end, these statements, like the Amalaka fruit in the palm of the hand, bring about the direct and immediate vision of the ultimate reality, though it was imperceptible before. The he becomes a living being who is liberated (Jivanmukta).

Notes: Here we have the definitions and explanations of some very important and fundamental concepts of yoga all brought together in one place. Dharma Megha Samadhi, which results in bliss is so called because virtue is its basis. One does not become an adept in yoga, without practicing virtue. Samadhi is the undisturbed state of self-absorption in which there is no awareness of any modifications and in which the distinction between the knower and the known are absent. What leads to it, hearing, remembering and concentrated meditation.

3. isah panci-krita-bhutanam apanci-karanam kartum so'akamayata. brahmanda tadgata-lokan karyarupams ca karanatvam prapayitva tatah suksmangam karmendriyani pranams ca jnanendriyanyantah-karana-catustayam caikikritya sarvani bhautikani karane bhuta-pancake samyojya bhumim jale jalam vahnau vahnim vayau vayum akase cakasam ahankare cahankaram mahati mahad avyakte'vyaktam puruse kramena viliyate. viradddhiranyagarbhesvara upadhi-vilayat paramatmani liyante. panci-krita-maha-bhuta-sambhava-karmasancita-sthula-dehah karmaksayat sat-karma-paripaka-to'apanci-karanam prapya suksmenaikibhutva karana-rupat-vam asadya tat-karanam kutasthe pratyagatmani viliyate. visva-taijasa-prajnah svasvopadhi-layat pratyaga-tmani liya-nte. andam jnanagnina dagdham karanaih saha paramatmani linam bhavati. tato brahmanah samahito bhutva tat-tvam-padaikyam eva sada kuryat; tato meghapaye-m'asuman ivatm-avirbhavati; dhyatva madhya-stham atmanam kalasantara-dipavat; angustha-matram-atmanam adhuma-jyoti-rupa-kam.

3. *Isvara desired to undo the fivefold division of the five great elements. After causing the universal egg, and the worlds formed in it as its effects to withdraw into their causes, making as one the subtle parts of the organs of actions, the senses and the four internal organs, and merging all elemental things into the five elements, which are their cause, he makes the earth to merge into water, water into fire, fire into air, air into space, space into ego-sense, ego-sense into mahat (the great one), mahat into the unmanifested, and the unmanifested into the Cosmic Person (Purusha) in regular succession. Virat (gross body), Hiranyagarbha (subtle body) and Isvara (casual body), with their vehicle (Maya) being dissolved, are merged into the Supreme Self (Brahman). The gross body made from the fivefold division of the great elements and shaped by desire-ridden actions (karma), with the extinction of the karmas, with the ripening of good karma, and the undoing of the fivefold division of the elements, attains its casual form and becomes absorbed into immutable inner Self (Kutasta Pratyagatma). The waking state (visva), the dream state (taijasa) and the sleep state (prajna) with their vehicle (ignorance) being dissolved are merged into the immutable self. The egg of macrocosm (the manifest universe) being burnt in the fire of knowledge is absorbed along with its causes into the Su-*

preme Self. Therefore, a Brahmana, having restrained (or stabilized) himself should always strive to achieve the oneness of Tat and Tvam. Then, the Self manifests like the sun freed from the clouds. Meditate upon the Self, seated in the middle, like a lamp placed inside a jar, of the size of the thumb inside the body, having the form of a flame without smoke.

Notes: If manifestation is an outgoing process, involving the division and diversification of elements into various parts of the manifested universe and gross bodies, dissolution is its exact opposite and a reversal process, involving the withdrawal, unification, annihilation and cessation of all phenomena. The Self that goes out into the elemental objective worlds and becomes engaged with binding actions, modifications and the experience of duality and distinction, using Maya (delusion) and Avidya (ignorance) as its tools returns into itself, as if tired of watching the drama and the mayhem of the phenomenal world. It is just like waking up and sleeping. When you wake up, you come from inside to outside. In sleep you go from outside to inside. When you wake up, you are spread out into the world you experience and rarely remain self-aware. In sleep, you are all by yourself, and absorbed in yourself, with no awareness whatsoever of the external world.

4. prakasayantam antahstham dhyayet kutastham avyayam. dhyayan naste munis caiva casupter amritestu yah.

4. One should meditate upon the effulgent, infinite and immutable Self that is inside. The silent ascetic who meditates thus until sleep or death...

Notes: A muni is an ascetic who practice all kinds of silence. He silences his mind and body and remains fixed upon the Self. He has not concern whatsoever, even the concern to stay alive by feeding himself. Munis are rare in the present day world. It is an ideal state difficult to attain.

5. jivanmuktah sa vijneyah sa dhanyah krita-krityavan. jivanmuktapadam tyaktva svadehe kalasatkrite. visatya deha-muktatvam pavano'spandatam iva.

5. He is to be known as a liberated living being (Jivanmukta), blessed, and successful in his effort. When the right time comes to leave his body, he gives up his state of liberated living being and attains freedom for the body, like the wind that comes to stand still.

6.asabdam asparsam arupam avyayam tatha rasam nityam agandhavac ca yat. anady anantam mahatah param dhruvam tad eva sisyaty amalam niramayam.

6. It is that which is without sound, without touch, without form, inexhaustible, and likewise without taste for food, eternal, and without smell also. Without a beginning, without an end, beyond the great (mahat), fixed, without impurities and without sickness is also that.

Chapter 4
The Life of a Jivanmukta

1. atha hainam paingalah prapaccha yajnavalkyam jnaninah kim karma ka ca sthitiriti. sa hovaca yajnavalkyah. amanitvadi sampanno mumuksur eka-vimsati-kulam tarayati. brahma-vinmatrena kulam ekottara-satam tarayati. atmanam rathinam viddhi sariram ratham eva ca. buddhim tu sarathim viddhi manah pragraham eva ca.

1. Then Paingala asked Yajnavalkya, "What is the duty (karma) of a knower? What is their condition?" To him, Yajnavalkya said, "The seeker of liberation, endowed with the wealth of humility and the like, enables twenty one generations of his family to move across (the ocean of births and deaths). By becoming a knower of Brahman alone, one enables a hundred and one generations of his family to cross. Know the Self as the rider of the chariot and the body as the chariot. Know the intelligence as the charioteer and the mind, verily, as the reins."

2. indriyani hayan ahur visayams tesu gocaran. jangamani vimanani hridayani manisinah.

2. "The senses, they say, are the horses, the sense-objects their paths and the hearts of wandering ascetics (Jangamas) are flying machines.

3. atmendriya-mano-yuktam bhoktety ahur maharsayah. tato narayanah saksat hridaye supratisthitah.

4. The Self united with the mind and the senses is the enjoyer, say the great seers. Therefore, he is verily Narayana Himself who is established in the heart.

4. prarabdha-karma-paryantam ahinirmokavad vyavaharati. candravac carate dehi sa muktas caniketanah.

4. Until the ending of the past karma that is destined to bear fruit in his current life (prarabdha karma), he remains (detached) inside (the body) like the snake with slough. Like the moon, wanders around, a liberated person having such a body, without a home.

5. tirthe svapaca-grihe va tanum vihaya yati kaivalyam. pranan avakirya yati kaivalyam.. tam pascad dig-balim kuryad athava khananam caret. pumsah pravrajanam proktam netaraya kadacana.

6. Casting off his body in a sacred place of pilgrimage or in the house of an outcaste, the liberated sage (yati) attains aloneness. Scattering his breaths, he attains aloneness. After that, his body should be offered to the directions as a sacrifice or buried in the earth. Only for a male, the life of a wandering ascetic (pravarajanam) is ordained not for others.

Notes: Dahanam means cremation and khananam means burial. The body of a self-realized person, as per this verse, should be buried or left to elements, but not cremated. This is the tradition. He is also expected to leave his body at a place of pilgrimage or in the house of an outcaste. The latter is suggested because, as a liberated yogi, he has to transcend all caste and class divisions and show no preference whatsoever.

6. nasaucam nagni-karyam ca na pindam nodakakriya. na kuryat parvanadini brahma-bhutaya bhiksave.

6. There is no need to observe purification ceremonies, nor fire sacrifices nor the offerings of balls of rice, nor the offerings of water, nor the fortnightly, monthly or other periodical rituals, is required in case of a begging ascetic who has attained the Self of Brahman.

Notes: These rituals are required in case of those who are not liberated because they need sacrificial food to keep their astral bodies healthy and vigorous in the ancestral world. A liberated person is self-existent and does not depend upon any external support or nourishment. Hence no rituals are required for those who become one with their inmost Self.

7. dagdhasya dahanam nasti pakvasya pacanam yatha. jnanagni-dagdha-dehasya na ca sraddham na ca kriya.

7. What has been cooked require no further cooking. Whas has been burnt (in the fire of austerity) requires no further burning. For a body burnt in the fire of knowledge, there is no need for the sraddha ceremonies and no final sacrifice (antya-kriya).

8. yavaccopadhi-paryantam tavac chusrusayed gurum. guruvad gurubharyayam tat putresu ca vartanam.

8. So long as there is a limitation, deficiency or imperfection, that far one should serve the teacher. His conduct towards the teacher's wife and sons should be the same as his conduct towards the teacher.

9. suddha-manasah suddha-cidrupah sahisnuh so'aham asmi sahisnuh so'aham asmiti prapte jnanena vijnane jneye paramatmani hridi samsthite dehe labdha-santi-padam gate tada prabha-mano-buddhi-sunyam bhavati; amritena triptasya payasa kim prayojanam. evam svatmanam jnatva vedaih prayojanam kim bhavati. jnanamrita-tripta-yogino na kincit

kartavyam asti tad asti cen na satattva-vid-bhavati. durastho'api na durasthah pindavarjitah pindastho'api pratyagatma sarvavyapi bhavati. hridayam nirmalam kritva cintayitvapy anamayam aham eva param sarvam iti pasyetparam sukham.

9. With a pure mind, pure thoughts, forbearance, remembering "I am He," and with the discernment gained through persistence from the state of "I am He, "concentrating his heart upon the Supreme Self, when he establishes firm peace in his body, then his effulgent mind and intellect become empty. What is the use of sweet porridge for one who has enjoyed the nectar or immortality? Even so, to the one who has realized his own Self, of what use the Vedas can be? A yogi who is satisfied with the nectar of knowledge, there is no duty or responsibility whatsoever. If anything is left, he is not a knower of truth. Distant, yet not distant, devoid of a body, yet established in the body, the inner Self becomes all pervading. Making the heart pure, and contemplating upon the well-being (of the world), he obtains the highest bliss thinking thus, "I am the Supreme Self, the All."

10. yatha jale jalam ksiptam ksire ksiram ghrite ghritam. aviseso bhavet tadvaj jivatma paramatmanoh.

10. Just as water mixed in water, milk in milk, and ghee with ghee, become indistinct, so also the individual Self and the Supreme Self.

11. dehe jnanena dipite buddhir akhandakara-rupa yada bhavati tada vidvan brahma-jnanagnina (sarva) karma-bandham nirdahet. tatah pavitram paramesvarakhyam advaita-rupam vimalam-barabham. yathodake toyam anupravistam tathatma-rupo nirupadh-isamsthitah.

11. When the body is lit with the flame of the knowledge and when intelligence becomes indivisible in form, then the knower burns away all the bonds of karma in the fire of Brahman knowledge. Then he becomes pure like the form of the non-dual Supreme Self and bright and peaceful like a cloudless sky. Like water mixed with water, so also the one having the form of the Self becomes (pure) without any limitations or imperfections.

12. akasavat suksmasarira atma na drisyate vayuvad antaratma. sa bahyam abhyantara niscalatma jnanolkaya pasyati cantaratma.

12. *Since the subtle body of the Self has the nature of space, the inner Self, like air, cannot be seen. He, the stable Self, who is both within and without, sees with knowledge and within itself.*

13. yatra yatra mrito jnani yena va kena mrityuna. yatha sarvagatam vyoma tatra tatra layam gatah.

13. *Wherever and in whatever manner a knower may die, he is absorbed (into Brahman) in that very place like the all pervading space (that absorbs everything).*

14. ghatakasam ivatmanam vilayam vetti tattvatah. sa gacchati niralambam jnanalokam samantatah.

14. *Like the space in the (broken) pot, so does the Self (of the knower who died) become dissolved. Then he attains the all pervading world of knowledge, which is without support.*

15. taped varsa-sahasrani eka-pada-sthito narah. etasya dhyana-yogasya kalam narhati sodasim.

15. *A man may practice penance standing on one leg for a thousand years. That does not qualify as much as one sixteenth of the time spent in the practice of the yoga of meditation (dhyana-yoga).*

16. idam jnanam-idam jneyam tat sarvam jnatum icchati. api varsa sahasrayuh sastrantam nadhigacchati.

16. *This is the knowledge, this is the end of knowledge, he who wishes to know all that even after studying for a thousand years will not reach the end of the scriptures.*

17. vijneyo'aksara tanmatro jivitam vapi cancalam. vihaya sastra-jalani yat satyam tad upasatam.

17. *The imperishable alone is to be known, which is very subtle. Life being unstable, giving up the net of scriptures, one should worship that which is true.*

18. ananta-karma saucam ca japo yajnas tathaiva ca. tirtha-yatrabhigamanam yavat tattvam na vindati.

18. *With endless duties, bodily purity, prayers, sacrifices and by going on pilgrimages, with all these the nature of reality is not known.*

19. aham brahmeti niyatam moksa hetur mahatmanam. dve pade bandha-moksaya na mameti mameti ca.

19. For the great souls (mahatmas) who are constantly engaged in, "I am Brahman," is the cause for liberation. Two are the causes for bondage and liberation, mine and not mine."

20. mameti badhyate jantur nirmameti vimucyate. manaso hy unmani bhave dvaitam naivopalabhyate.

21. The thought of mine binds the beings. The thought of not mine liberates. When the mind rises to the state of complete inactivity, then that duality is no more attained.

Notes: Unmani is a state of no-mind. It leads to spiritual madness or intoxication in which the mind ceases all its activity and becomes completely still. It is kind of mindlessness, often experienced by spiritual people, who show signs of madness because their mind ceases to exist practically.

21. yada yaty unmanibhavas tada tat paramam padam. yatra yatra mano yati tatra tatra param padam.

21. When the self-restrained ascetic attains the state of mental inertia then only he reaches that highest state. Wherever the mind of the self-restrained ascetic rests that alone is the highest state.

Notes: Yati means a self-restrained yogi or ascetic. When he becomes still, he enters the supreme state of Brahman. Wherever or in whatever his mind is absorbed, that alone is the abode of Brahman.

22. tatra tatra param brahma sarvatra samavasthitam. hanyan mustibhir akasam ksudhartah khandayet tusam.

22. There (where the mind of Yati rests without a trace) the supreme Brahman is established in everything equally. Just as a hungry person striking the space with his fist or chewing the husks does not appease his hunger...

23. naham brahmeti janati tasya muktirna jayate. ya etad upanisadam nityam adhite so'agniputo bhavati. sa vayuputo bhavati. sa adityaputo bhavati. sa brahmaputo bhavati. sa visnuputo bhavati. sa rudraputo bhavati. sa sarvesu tirthesu snato bhavati. sa sarvesu vedesvadhito bhavati. sa sarva-veda-vrata-caryasu carito bhavati. tenetihasa-purananam rudranam sata-sahasrani japtani phalani bhavanti. pranavanam ayutam japtam bhavati, dasa-purvandasottaranpunati. sa pankti-pavano bhavati. sa mahan bhavati. brahmahatya-surapana-svarnasteya-gurutalpagamana-tat-samyogipatakebhyah puto bhavati. tad visnoh paramam padam sada pasyanti surayah diviva caksuratatam.

23. Who does not know, "I am Brahman," does not attain liberation. Whoever studies this Upanishad everyday becomes as pure as the fire. He becomes as pure as Vayu (air). He becomes as pure as the sun. He becomes as pure as Brahma. He becomes as pure as Vishnu. He becomes as pure as Rudra. He becomes as pure as the one who has bathed in all sacred waters. He becomes like the one who has studied all the Vedas. He becomes like the one who has observed all the rites and rituals prescribed in the Vedas. He attains the fruit of reciting the sacred histories (itihasas), ancient lore (puranas) and the hymns of Rudra a hundred thousand times. He becomes like the one who has uttered the Pranava (Aum) tens and thousands of times. He purifies his family lineage up to ten previous and ten future generations. He purifies those who eat food sitting in the same line as him. He becomes a great person. He is freed from the sins of killing a Brahmana, drinking liquor, stealing gold, sleeping with the wife of the teacher, and association with those who committed these sins. Like an eye spread out in the sky, that is the highest state of Vishnu, which the wise ones always behold.

24. tad vipraso vipanyavo jagrivamsah samindhate visnor yat paramam padam. aum satyam ity upanisat.

24. The Brahmanas, who with their passions subsided, their inner eyes wide open, bring to light the suprme state of Vishnu. Aum, this is the truth of the Upanishad.

Kaivalya Upanishad

Editor's Note

Kaivalya Upanishad belongs to the Atharvaveda. It is considered a minor Upanishad. It provides guidance for those who want to spend their lives in the contemplation of Brahman to achieve Kaivalya or liberation. Like the Svetavatara Upanishad, the Upanishad regards Lord Siva as Supreme Brahman and liberator of souls. The 24th verse mentions Satarudriyam, a devotional prayer from the Yajurveda to Lord Siva containing 100 stanzas, as a purifier and liberator. The seer of the Upanishad is Asvalayana, who is described to have received the knowledge from Lord Brahma himself. The Upanishad is basically for people who follow the path of renunciation (sanyasasrama) to achieve liberation. According to the Upanishad, liberation can be attained only by means of renunciation and by no other means (1.2). The end of that austere effort is "kaivalya," meaning the state of kevalam or aloneness, which is the natural and original state of Brahman, who is One and Only. How to attain this state is also explained in the Upanishad (1.5 and 1.6). Kaivalya Upanishad is meant for the resolute devotees of Lord Siva for whom nothing else is left to achieve except liberation. Its verses are useful for contemplation to stabilize the mind and cultivate detachment, devotion and inner purity.

The following is a revised translation of the Upanishad by Jayaram V.

Invocation

aum bhadram karnebhih srnuyama devah, bhadram pasyemakshabhir yajatrah' sthirair angais tustuvaga sas tanibhih, vyasema deva-hitam yad ayuh, svasti na indro vrddha-sravah, svasti nah pisha visva-vedah, svasti nas tarkshayo arishtanemih, svasti no brhaspatir dadhatu. aum santih santih santih.

Aum! O gods, may we hear with our ears what is auspicious for us. While we perform the sacrifices, may we see what is auspicious. Offering praise with steady limbs and bodies, may we spend our lives for the good of the gods. May Indra, of the ancient glory, be auspicious to us, may the universal god, Pusan, be auspicious to us. May Tarksya of the unhurt wheel bestow blessings upon us. May Brihaspati, the destroyer of evil, be auspiciously inclined towards us.

Translation

The Knowledge of Brahman and Liberation

1. aum athashvalayano bhagavantam paramesthinam upasametyovaca; adhihi bhagavan brahmavidyam varistham sada sadbhih sevyamanam nigudham; yatha 'cirat sarvapapam vyapoyha paratparam purusam yati vidvan.

1. *Aum, then Asvalayana approached the divine Lord and supreme deity (Brahma) and said, "Teach me O divine Lord the knowledge of Brahman, the highest, the hidden, which is always venerated by the wise, and by means of which a wise person, freed from all his sins, reaches the highest."*

2. tasmai sa hovaca pitamahas casraddhabhaktidhyanayogad avaihi; na karmana na prajaya dhanena tyagenaike amritatvam anasuh.

2. *To him the Great Father (Brahma) said, "Know (that supreme knowledge) by faith, devotion, meditation and yoga. Neither by actions, nor by offspring, nor by wealth, but only by means of renunciation can the life eternal be attained.*

Notes: Brahma is the creator god of Trinity manifested by Isvara out of Himself as His reflection in the quality of rajas to undertake the duty of creation and dissemination of spiritual knowledge. He is known as pitamaha, the great grandfather. Although he has an identical name, he is different from Brahman and is an aspect of Him only. This verse explains the means to liberation, namely faith, devotion, meditation and the remaining practices of yoga such as concentration, breath control, observation and rules and restraints and the practice of self-absorption. Liberation is not achieved by performing the duties of a householder, such as producing offspring, earning wealth or performing obligatory duties such as daily sacrifices. It is attained only by giving up worldly life and practicing renunciation. However, the duties of a householder are also important. One has to complete that phase before taking up renunciation.

3. parena nakam nihitam guhayam vibhrajate yad yatayo visanti;

3. Higher than the heaven, hidden in the cave (of the heart), it shines. Those who make strenuous effort enter into it.

4. vedanta vijnana suniscitarthah sannyasayogad yatayah suddha sattvah; te brahmalokesu parantakale paramritah parim ucyanti sarve.

4. The ascetics, who through renunciation and by attaining the highest purity (suddha sattva) strive to affirm the truths of the Vedanta, they living in the world of Brahman until the end of the time, having attained immortality, become liberated

Notes: Vedanta means the knowledge of the Upanishads. The ascetics who renounce worldly life are not merely interested in the intellectual pursuit of the knowledge contained in the Upanishads. They want to ascertain the truths hidden in them from their own experience. Hence they put to practice the essential practices recommended in the scriptures for self-realization.

5. viviktadese ca sukhasanasthah sucih samagriva sirah sarirah; antyasram asthah sakalendriyaninirudhya bhaktya svagurum pranamya

5. Seated comfortably in a secluded place, observing purity, keeping the head, the neck and the body in a straight line, established in the final phase (asrama dharma) of his life, controlling all his senses, offering salutations to his teacher.

Notes: Antyasrama is the final asrama, which is the phase of renunciation (sanyasasrama), which comes in the end after brahmacharya (the phase of a celibate student), griahsthasrama (the phase of a householder), and vanaprastha (the phase of living in the forests). The instruction provided in this verse is especially meant for those who have taken up renunciation to attain kaivalya or aloneness.

6. hritpundarikam virajam visuddham vicintya madhye visadam visokam; acintyam avyaktam anantarupam sivam prasantam amritam brahmayonim

6. Focusing upon the center of the lotus of the heart, which is without passion and pure, and meditating in the center upon that which is pure without sorrow, unthinkable, unmanifested, infinite in form, auspicious, peaceful, eternal and the cause of Brahma.

7. tam adimadhyantavihinam ekam vibhum cidanandam arupam adbhutam; umasahayam paramesvaram prabhum trilocanam nilakantham prasantam; dhyatva munir gacchati bhutayonim samastasaksim tamasah parastat.

7. Without a beginning, middle or an end, who is one, all pervading, of blissful consciousness, without form, wonderful, seated with the goddess Uma, the Supreme Lord, the ruler, bearing three eyes, with a blue neck, ever peaceful by meditating upon Him the sages attain the source of all creation, the witness of all and that which is beyond all darkness.

Notes: As in Svetasvatara Upanishad, here also we see a clear reference to Lord Siva as the very Brahman.

8. sa brahma sa sivah sendrahso aksarah paramah svarat; sa eva visnuh sa pranahsa kalo 'gnih sa candramah

8. He is Brahma, He is Siva, He is Indra. He is the imperishable, Supreme Self-illumined Lord. He alone is Vishnu. He is the life giving breath. He is Time, he is fire, and also the moon.

Notes: This verse extols Lord Siva as the Supreme Lord of the universe. All other gods, including Vishnu, are described as His aspects only.

9. sa eva sarvam yad bhutamyac ca bhavyam sanatanam; jnatva tam mrityum atyetinanyah pantha vimuktaye

9. He alone is all this, all that was and all that will be and eternal. Knowing him one surpasses death. There is no path other than this to liberation.

10. sarvabhutastham atmanam sarvabhutani catmani; sampasyan brahma paramam yati nanyena hetuna

10. By seeing the Self in all beings, and all beings in the Self, one attains the supreme Brahman, not by any other means.

11. atmanam aranim krtva pranavam cottararanim; jnananirmathanabhyasat pasam dahati panditah

11. With oneself as the lower portion of the fire stick and the syllable AUM as the upper part of it, by the practice of kindling the flame of intelligence, the wise burns away all his bonds.

Notes: The reference to pasa, meaning bonds or attachments, suggests that the Upanishad is markedly a Saiva Upanishad.

12. sa eva mayaparimohitatma sariram asthaya karoti sarvam; stryannapanadivicitrabhogaih sa eva jagrat paritriptim eti.

12. That alone becomes the deluded self and, remaining seated in the body, indulges in actions. In the wakeful state he gets gratification through such enjoyments as women, food and drink.

13. svapne sa jivah sukhaduhkhabhokta svamayaya kalpita jivaloke; susupti kale sakale viline tamo 'bhibhutah sukharupam eti.

13. In the dream state, the being experiences happiness or sorrow in a make-believe world created by his own delusion. In deep sleep, when all is absorbed, overwhelmed by darkness, he experiences sukham (happiness).

Notes: When the being (jiva) is in deep sleep, all his troubles are temporarily suspended because under the influence of tamas he simply becomes ignorant of everything. This ignorance, though for a brief period of time, gives him a little break from the harsher realities of the wakeful state. Therefore, the pleasure or happiness (sukham) mentioned here is not a positive state of mental happiness, but a negative state of temporary relief from the modifications of the mind.

14. punas ca janmantara karmayogatsa eva jivah svapiti prabuddhah; puratraye kridati yas ca jivastatas tu jatam sakalam vicitram; adharam anandam akhandabodham yasmin layam yati puratrayam ca.

14. Again the being on account of his deeds in previous lives wakes up and sleeps. He takes delight in the three cities. From him springs all diversity. He is the support, bliss, indivisible consciousness and in him alone dissolve the three states.

Notes: The three cities are the gross, the subtle and the casual bodies of a jiva. The three states are the wakeful, dreaming and deep-sleep states in which the Self participates. They arise and dissolve in him only.

15. etasmaj jayate pranomanah sarvendriyani ca; kham vayur jyotir apas caprithvi visvasya dharini

15. From Him are born the vital breath, mind, all the sense organs, the sky, air, fire, water and the earth, which supports all.

16. yat param brahma sarvatma visvasya yatanam mahat; suksmat suksmataram nityam tat tvam eva tvam eva tat

16. That which is the supreme Brahman, the self of all, who supports the entire universe, subtler than the subtle, eternal, that alone you are, you are that alone.

17, jagrat svapna susupty adi prapancam yat prakasate; tad brahmaham iti jnatva sarva bandhaih pramucyate

17. *That by which the waking, dream and deep sleep worlds are illumined that Brahman I am. Knowing thus one is freed from all fetters.*

18. trisu dhamasu yad bhogyam bhokta bhogas ca yad bhavet; tebhyo vilaksanah saksicinmatro 'ham sadasivah.

18. *I am the witness, pure consciousness and Sadasiva (the ever auspicious) and different from whatever that exists in the three worlds as the enjoyer, the enjoyment or the object of enjoyment.*

19. mayy eva sakalam jatammayi sarvam pratisthitam; mayi sarvam layam yat itad brahmad vayam asmy aham

19. *All this is born from me alone. All this is established in me only. And all this does merge into me alone. I am that Brahman without a plural.*

20. anor aniyan aham eva tad vanmahan aham visvam aham vicitram; puratano 'ham puruso 'ham isohiryanmayo 'ham sivarupam asmi

20. *I am smaller than an atom. So also I am greater than the universe. I am the diversified creation. I am the Ancient. I am the Purusha. I am the Lord of the golden hue. I am Siva in manifestation.*

21. apanipado 'ham acintyasaktih pasyamy acaksuh sa srinomy akarnah; aham vijanami viviktarupam na casti vetta mama cit sada "ham

21. *I am without hands and feet, but with unthinkable prowess. I see without eyes and hear without ears. I am endowed with knowledge. I have a form that is perfect and alone, I am unknown to any and always pure consciousness.*

22. vedair anekair aham eva vedyah vedantakrd vedavid eva caham; na punyapape mama nasti nasah na janma dehendriya buddhir asti.

22. *From the many Vedas I am the one to be known. I am the author of the Upanishads and the knower of the Vedas. Merit or demerit do not attach to me. I am indestructible, and I am not subject to birth, body, sense or intellect.*

23. na bhumir apo na ca vahnir asti na canilo me'sti na cambaram ca asti; evam viditva paramatma rupam guhasayam niskalam advitiyam; samastasaksim sad asad vihinam prayati suddham paramatmarupam.

23. Neither earth nor water nor fire nor air nor ether I have. Knowing the true nature of the Supreme Self, the one who dwells in the cave of the heart, without impurities, without duality, the universal witness, free from (the distinction of) being and non being, one attains the pure form of the Supreme Self.

Notes: The divine consciousness is above and beyond the physical properties of life which is characterized by the presence of the five elements. Hence the expression that these elements are not present in Him.

24. yah satarudriyam adhite so 'gniputo bhavati; sa vayuputo bhavati, sa atmaputo bhavati, sa surapanat puto bhavati, sa brahmahatyat puto bhavati sa suvarnasteyat puto bhavati; sa krtyakrtyat puto bhavati tasmad avimuktam asritobhavaty, aty asrami sarvada sakrd va japet.

24. He who studies Satarudriya becomes purified as fire, becomes pure as air, become purified from (the sin of) harming oneself, becomes purified from (the sin of) drinking wine, becomes purified from killing a Brahmana, becomes purified from stealing gold, and becomes purified from all deeds and misdeeds. Therefore he should take refuge in the Avimukta. He who is in the final ashrama dharma (the phase of renunciation) of his life should always chant this text at least once.

Notes: Satarudriyam is a prayer of 100 stanzas from the Taittiriya Samhita of Yajurveda as an invocation to Rudra or Siva. It is considered sacred by the devotees of Lord Siva. Avimukta is the bound soul, or the embodied Self. One should take refuge in that means, one should fix one's mind upon the inner Self. The nature of Avimukta is explained in the Jabala Upanishad. The final ashrama dharma is the sanyasashram or the phase of renunciation. As we have seen elsewhere, Kaivalya Upanishad is obviously meant for the aged who have renounced the worldly life and awaiting their final journey.

25. anena jnanam apnoti samsararnavanasanam; tasmad evam viditvainam kaivalyam padam asnute.

25. He gains the knowledge by which comes the destruction of the ocean of births and deaths. By knowing it, he attains the state of kaivalyam (aloneness).

Notes: In the previous verse, we have read that the Supreme Self has vivikta rupam, meaning a form that is perfect, detached and solitary. It denotes a state of uniqueness and also aloneness. A liberated self, which unites with the Supreme Self attains that state of aloneness, in which there is no duality and no experience of objectivity and otherness.

Vajrasucika Upanishad

Editor's Note

Vajrasuci means a point that is hard like a diamond or forceful like a thunderbolt. The point may be a reference to its ability to pierce through a traditional argument that Brahmanas are a superior caste or through the ignorance and delusion of an aspirant who want to attain liberation. Vajrasuchika (Vajrasucika) Upanishad belongs to the Samaveda. This is firmly opposed to the orthodox opinion that Brahmanahood (brahmanatvam) comes by birth, and argues forcefully that a person does not become a Brahmana because of the nature of embodiment, because of the body, birth, knowledge, actions, or religious duty, but only by knowing Brahman, who is free from faults, eternal, truth, consciousness and bliss. In this regard, the Upanishad very much reads like a manifesto of the Virasaiva sect of Saivism founded by Basavanana in 12th century BCE.

The authorship of the text was previously ascribed to Asvaghosha and Dharmakirit. Both were Buddhist scholars who hailed from Brahmana families prior to their conversion to Buddhism. A Buddhist text named Vajrasuci was translated in the 10th century BCE by Fahien. While the overall theme regarding the caste and the nature of enlightenment agrees with the basic tenets of Buddhism, the Upanishad has many theistic elements and references to Brahman and Atman, which suggest that it is a Hindu text. Its authorship is ascribed to Shankaracharya himself. It is even possible that the text represented a line of ascetic thought that was much older and has its roots in Saivism.

The Upanishad declares that a person qualifies for liberation because of his character and inclination, not because he hails from a family of Brahmanas, or belongs to the caste of Brahmanas, or because he has the knowledge of the scriptures and can perform religious rites and ceremonies. The Upanishad also states that a Brahmana is a person who has the living presence of Brahman in himself, who has overcome human imperfections and weaknesses and removed from his being the impurities of his consciousness. It is not the mere elevation and transformation of the subtle body that leads him to the exalted status. It is not his intellectual capability, his mental agility or physical beauty of color and form that gives him the identity, but his realization of the highest truth.

Whatever may be its origin, Vajrasuchika Upanishad is a reminder to those who take pride in their caste and family status that a person's spiritual purity does not come by birth or caste or by any other externalities but by union with the inner Self or realization of oneness with Brahman. It cautions those who take pride in their social or religious identity and exhorts the students of the Vedas that their prime duty lies in perfecting themselves morally and spiritually in order to realize Brahman and become qualified to be true Brahmanas. It gives hope to those who come from other castes and those who join Hinduism from other religions and nationalities that they can work for their liberation irrespective of their social or caste background. And if we examine this text in the context of the extreme caste prejudices that prevailed in ancient India we can say that Vajrasuchika Upanishad stands apart as standard text (pramana) on social values and caste equality.

The following is a new translation of the Upanishad by Jayaram V.

Translation

The Knowledge of Vajrasuci

1. vajrasucim pravaksayami jnanam ajnanabhedanam; dusanam jnanahinanam bhusanam jnanacaksusam.

1. *I am now going to teach you the knowledge of Vajrasuci which dispels ignorance, condemns the ignorant and elevates those who possess the eye of wisdom.*

Notes: The ignorant here are those who believe in the traditional notions of the caste system.

2. brahmaksatriyavaisyasudra iti catvaro varnas tesam varnanam brahmana eva pradhana iti vedavacananurupam smrtibhir apy uktam. tatra codyam asti ko va brahmano nama. kim jivah kim dehah kim jatih kim jnanam kim karma kim dharmika iti.

2. *The Brahmana, the Kshatriya, the Vaisya and the Sudra: these are the four castes. The Vedas proclaim that the Brahmana, verily, is the most important among the castes and the law books also affirm it. There is, however, an interesting enquiry about this. Who, indeed, is this one named Brahmana? Is he (the embodied Self known as) a Jiva? Is he the physical body? Is he by birth based class (jati)? Is he by knowledge? Is he by actions? Is he by his religious duty?*

Notes: Varna actually means color. It also means a social division or caste based upon color. Presently there are many castes in Hinduism, based upon traditional occupations and other criteria rather than color. The Vedas constitute the sruti literature or the heard ones. The Smritis are law books. They are called Smritis because they are memorial texts based upon learned knowledge.

3. tatra prathamo jivo brahmana iti cet tan na. atitanagatanekadehanam jivasyaikarupatvad ekasyapi karmavasad anekadehasambhavat sarvasariranam jivasvaikarupatvac ca. tasman na jivo brahmana iti.

3. *Of this the first that the embodied Self is the Brahmana. It is not. In the many past and future bodies, the nature (rupa) of the living Self (jiva) is one and the same. The one (jiva), indeed, because of actions, is born in many bodies, and in all bodies the nature of the jiva is the same only. Therefore, the jiva is not the Brahmana.*

Notes: Rupam means appearance, form or natural state. The argument presented here is that an embodied Self (jiva), even when it is caught in the cycle of births and deaths, remains immutable. The same Self assumes many bodies in the course of its existence upon earth and in each life it assumes a new body, which is not necessarily that of a Brahmana. It can be even an animal body. Therefore, the embodied Self cannot be considered a Brahmana.

4. tarhi deho brahmana iti cet tan na acandaladi paryantanam manusyanam pancabhautikatvena dehasyaikarupatvaj jaramaranadharmadharmadisamyadarsanad brahmanah svetavarnah ksatriyo raktavarno vaisyah pitavarnah sudrah krsnavarna iti niyamabhavat. pitradi sarira dahane putradinam brahma hatyadi dosasambhavac ca tasman na deho brahmana iti.

4. *Then, (as to the argument) that the body is the Brahmana. It is not. Because, down to the outcastes (candalas) in all humans are the same five elements (present). Because of the bodies having the same nature, whereby old age, death, virtue, vice are seen in them. Because, there is no such rule that Brahmanas are of white complexion, Kshatriyas are of red complexion, Vaisyas are of yellow complexion and Sudras are of dark complexion. Because with the cremation of fathers and the like, the sons and the like will become tainted with the impurities of killing a Brahmana and the like. Therefore, the body is not the Brahmana.*

Notes: Very convincing arguments have been put forward here, using the most popular beliefs to refute the notion that the body of a Brahmana is superior to the bodies of other classes of humans. And each of these arguments is true and irrefutable. However, the verse ignores the fact that the bodies of human beings may differ with regard to extent of the sins and impurities that may be present in them on account of their past actions.

5. tarhi jatir brahmana iti cet tan na. tatra jaty antara jantusu aneka jati sambhava maharsayo bahavah santi. rsyasrngo mrgah. kausikah kusat. jambuko jambukat. valmiko valmikat. vyasah kaivartakanyayam. sasaprsthat gautamah. vasisthahurvasyam. agastyah kalase jata iti srutatvat. etesam jatya vinapy agre jnanapratipaditarsayo bahavah santi. tasman na jatih brahmana iti.

5. *Then, that birth based class (jati) is the Brahmana. It is not. There are many divisions based on birth among the animals and great seers were born from them. Rishyasringa was born of a deer, Kaushika from the grass, Jambuka from a Jackal, Valkimi from an ant hill, Vyasa from a fisher girl, Gautama from the back of a hare, Vashista from Urvasi (a celestial nymph), and Agastya from an earthen vessel. Of these, who were from outside (the Brahmana caste), many stood foremost among the sages of wisdom. Therefore a class by birth is not the Brahmana.*

Notes: Sages cannot be born physically from the animals. The connection with a particular object or animal is symbolic. It is possible that these sages came from lower castes or from families that had some occupational or symbolic connection with the animals to which their birth was ascribed.

6. tarhi jnano brahmana iti cet tan na. ksatriyadayo'pi paramarthadarsino 'bhiksa bahavah santi. tasman na jnanam brahmana iti.

6. Then, that by knowledge is the Brahmana. It is not. Many Kshatriyas and others, indeed, saw the highest reality and attained wisdom. Therefore by knowledge is not the Brahmana.

7. tarhi karma brahmana iti cet tan na. sarvesam praninam prarabdhasancitagami karmasadharmya darsanat karmabhipreritah santah janah kriyah kurvantiti. tasman na karma brahmana iti.

7. Then, that action is the Brahmana. It is not. In all beings prarabdha, sancita and agami karma are seen as common. Impelled by karma only good natured people perform their actions. Therefore, action is not the Brahmana.

Notes: Sanchita karma is the residual karma that has accumulated in the past on account of the actions performed in the previous lives. It is the total baggage with leftover karma with which one is born each time. Prarabdha karma is that portion of sancita karma that will be exhausted in the present life. Agami karma is the unexhausted karma of the current life which will be added eventually to the sancita karma.

8. tarhi dharmiko brahmana iti cet tan na. ksatriyadayo hiranyadataro bahavah santi. tasman na dharmiko brahmana iti.

8. Then, that religiosity is the Brahmana. It is not. There have been many Kshatriyas and others who have given away gold. Therefore, religiosity is not the Brahmana.

9. tarhi ko va brahmano nama. yah kascid atmanam advitiyam jatiguna kriyahinam sadurmi-sadbhavetyadi-sarva-dosa-rahitam satya-jnananandananta-svarupam svayam nirvikal-pam asesakal-padharam asesa-bhutantaryamitvena vartama-namantar bahis cakasavad anusyutam akhand-ananda-svabhavam apremeyam anubhavaikavedyam aparoksataya bhasamanam karatalamalakavat saksad aparoksikrtya krtart-hataya kamaragadi-dosa-rahitah-samadamadi-guna sampanno bhava-matsarya-trsnasa-mohadi-rahito dambh-ahankaradibhir asamsprstaceta vartate. evam ukta-laksano yah sa eva brah-mana iti sruti-smrti-puranetihasanam abhiprayah. anyatha hi brahmanatva-siddhir nasty eva. sac-cid-anandam-atmanam advitiyam

brahma bhavayet, sac-cid-anandam-atmanam advitiyam brahma bhavayed ity upanisat.

9. *Then, who, verily is the Brahmana by name? Whoever, after perceiving the Self, like the Amalaka fruit in the palm of his hand, which is without a second, without the distinction of caste, trait and action, which is free from the faults, such as the six stains and six states of existence, having the nature of truth, wisdom, bliss and infinity, by itself without any modifications, but the support for endless modifications, who acts as the indweller of all beings, who pervades the interior and exterior of all like the space, indivisible, of the nature of bliss, immeasurable, within the reach of experience, who can be known only indirectly through reasoning, becomes free from the impurities of desires. passions, becomes endowed with the qualities of sameness, patience and the like, becomes free from emotions, envy, greed, infatuation and the like, and with his mind untainted by vanity, pride and the like, he lives. He who has these declared qualities, he alone is a Brahmana. This is the opinion of the srutis (revelations), smritis (memorial works), puranas (ancient lore) and itihasa (historical works). Otherwise, indeed, Brahmanahood is not attainable at all. Meditate upon the state of Brahman, who is without a second, as truth, consciousness and bliss within oneself. Meditate upon the state of Brahman, who is without a second, as truth, consciousness and bliss within oneself.*

Notes: The six stains are old age, death, sorrow, delusion, hunger and thirst. These are common to all living beings and responsible for their suffering. The six states of being are birth, existence, growth, change, waning and perishing. A person becomes a true brahmana by knowledge of Self alone, but not by birth. This is the final conclusions of the Upanishad. the same truth has been declared in many other scriptures, including the Rigveda (9.112.3), Atharvaveda (4.4.1.5), Mahabharata (Aranya-parva 312.106) and Bhagavata Purana.

Jabala Upanishad

Editor's Note

Jabala Upanishad belongs to the Atharva Veda. This Upanishad should not be confused with the Brihad Jabala Upanishad or Jabali Upanishad. It contains six verses in all in which sage Yajnavalkya features prominently in conversation with Brihaspati, Atri and others. The Upanishad reveals, the importance of the body and the bound soul, the significance of Satarudriyam, and the rules regarding renunciation (sannyasa-jnaana-gocharam) so that one may become a paramahansa, a freed soul. It is predominantly a Saiva Upanishad, which reflects the prevailing beliefs and practices of Saivism including its explicit disapproval of caste distinctions.

The following is a translation of the Jabala Upanishad by Jayaram V.

Invocation

aum purnam adah purnam idam purnat purnam udacyate; purnasya purnam adaya purnam eva vasisyate. Om santih santih santih

Aum! That is full. This also is full. From that full arises this full. Taking the full from the full, the full remains full. Aum, peace, peace, peace.

Chapter 1
Avimutka - The Bound Self

1. aum brihaspatir uvaca yajnavalkyam yadanu kuruksetram devanam devayajanam sarvesam bhutanam brahmasadanam. avimuktan vai kuruksetran devanam devayajanam sarvesam bhutanam brahmasadanam. tasmad yatra kvacana gaccati tad eva manyeta tad avimuktam eva. idam vai kuruksetram devanam devayajanam sarvesam bhutanam brahmasadanam. atra hi jantoh pranesutkramamanesu rudrah tarakam brahma vyacaste yenasavamriti bhutva moksi bhavati tasmad avimuktam eva niseveta avimuktan na vimunced evam evaitad yajnavalkyah.

1. Aum, Brihaspati said to Yajnavalkya, "That which is Kurukshetra is the place of sacrifice for the gods and the Abode of Brahman for all the creatures. Avimukta, the bound one, indeed, is this Kurukshetra, the place of sacrifice for the gods and the Abode of Brahman for all the creatures. Therefore wherever one goes, one should think of it as such: this, verily, is avimukta, the bound one. This is Kurukshetra only, which is the place of sacrifice for the gods and the Abode of Brahman for all creatures. It is there when the breaths of the living beings go upward, Rudra teaches them the secret (taraka) mantra. By it they become immortal and liberated. Therefore, serve avimukta well, do not abandon avimukta. It, verily is so, Yajnavalkya."

Notes: This verse is often interpreted by some with cryptic symbolism, where as the meaning is plain and simple. Kurukshetra is the field, the battleground of life. It is a replica of the entire creation. In other words, it is the body, in which is housed the bound self (avimukta). It is where the gods (bodily organs) perform their actions (devayajanam). It is also the abode of Brahman for all the creatures, because Brahman resides in the bodies of all beings as their very Self. When beings die, then Rudra teaches the secret mantra to the deserving souls, whereby they ascend upward to the immortal world. Avimukta means not liberated, the bound one. Avimukta is the bound soul, Jiva, who is subject to the impurities of egoism (anava), attachment (pasa) and delusion (moha). It is another name for the embodied self or the elemental Self (bhutatama) which is bound to Nature and to the cycle of births and deaths. Although it is bound and impure, this verse says that one should not abandon the bound self. One should serve it well and nourish it well, for it is a sacred place where gods work and Brahman lives. Therefore, for the sake of gods and oneself, one should treat oneself well, considering that the body is a sacrificial altar and an abode of God.

Chapter 2

The location of the Self

1. atha hainamatrih papracca yajnavalkyan ya eso ananto avyaktaatma tan katham aham vijaniyam iti, sa hovaca yajnavalkyah so avimukta upasyo ya esoananto avyakta atma so avimukte pratisthita iti, so avimuktah kasmin pratisthita iti. varanayam nasyam ca madhye pratisthita iti, ka vai varana ka ca nasiti, sarvan indriyakritan dosanvarayat iti tena varana bhavati, sarvan indriyakritan papann asayat iti tena nasi bhavatiti, kataman casya sthanam bhavatiti, bhruvor ghranasya ca yah sandhih sa esa dyaur lokasya parasya ca sandhir bhavatiti, etad vai sandhin sandhyam brahmavida upasata iti so avimukta upasya iti, so avimuktan jnanam acasteyo vai tad evam vedeti.

2. *Thereafter Atri asked Yajnavalkya, "How may I know that Self which is inexpressible and infinite?"*

Yajnavalkya said, "Worship the avimukta, the bound one, for that which is the infinite and the inexpressible Self is established in the avimukta only."

"In what then the avimukta is established?"

"It is established between that which is varana and which is nasi."

"What is varana and what is nasi?"

"That which removes all the impurities arising from actions of the sense organs is varana. That which removes all the sins committed by the sense organs is nasi."

"What is their resting place?"

"The meeting place between the eye brows and the nose. It is the meeting place between the world of gods and the immortal heaven. The knowers of Brahman call it twilight (sandhya). That avimukta should

meditate upon. He who knows this thus, gains the knowledge that leads to liberation."

Notes: Varanasi is the bridge that liberates the avimukta, the bound soul. It is physically located in the place between the eye-brows and the nose. By concentrating upon it, one can remove all the impurities and sins in the body. The place is compared to the twilight zone upon which the pious brahmanas meditate during their daily sacrifices both in the morning and the evening.

Chapter 3
The Importance of Satarudriyam

3. atha hainam brahmacarina ucuh kim japy enamritatvam bruhiti, sa hovaca yajnavalkyah, satarudriyenety etany eva ha va amritasya namani, etairha va amrito bhavatiti evam evaitad yajnavalkyah.

3. Then, the celibate student of the Vedas asked (Yajnavalkya), "By reciting which (mantra) one may attain immortality?"

Yajnavalkay (replied in answer), "By satarudriyam, the names of the immortal, one becomes immortal."

Notes: Satarudriya, meaning hundred forms of Rudra, is an invocation found in the Yajurveda addressed to the universal form of Rudra, or Lord Siva, extolling him with his various benign and fierce forms, names, powers and manifestations. The hymn also brings out the deeper connection between the all devouring Agni and Rudra, the lord of destruction. References to it are found abundantly in the Puranas of Lord Siva. Its chanting is considered highly purifying.

Chapter 4
The Practice of Renuciartion

1. atha hainan janako vaideho yajnavalkyam upasam etyovaca bhagavan sannyasam bruhiti, sa hovaca yajnavalkyah, brahmacaryam parisamapya grihi bhaveth, grihi bhutva vani bhaveth, vani bhutva pravrajeth, yadi vetaratha brahmacaryad eva pravrajet grihad va vanad va, atha punaravrati va vrati va snatako va asnatako votsannagniko va yad ahar eva virajet tad ahar eva pravrajeth, taddhaike prajapatyam evestim kurvanti, tadu tatha na kuryadagneyimeva kuryath, agnir ha vai pranah pranam eva tatha karoti, traidhataviyam eva kuryath, etayaiva trayo dhatavo yad uta sattvam rajas tama iti, ayam te yonir ritvijo yato jatah pranad arocathah, tam pranam janann agna arohatha no vardhaya rayimh, ity anena mantren agnim ajighreth, esa ha va agner yonir yah pranah pranan gacca

svahety evam evaitad aha, gramad agnim ahritya purvad agnim aghrapayeth, yady agnim na vindet apsu juhuyat, apo vai sarva devatah sarvabhyo devatabhyo juhomi svaheti hutvodhritya prasniyat sajyan havir anamayam moksam antrah trayyaivan vadet, etad brahma etad upasitavyam, evam evaitad bhagavann iti vai yajnavalkyah.

1. *Then Janaka of Videha approached Yajnavalkya and said, "Godman, please speak to me about renunciation."*

To him, said Yajnavalkya, "After completing education practicing celibacy, one should become a householder. After completing the life of a householder one should become a forest-dweller. After completing the life of a forest-dweller, one should renounce. Alternatively, one may renounce even while pursuing the study of the Vedas as a celibate student, or living as a householder or as a forest-dweller. Whether he has observed or not observed the vows (of a householder), whether he is a student or not, whether he has not maintained the sacrificial fire or discontinued them, whatever day the distaste (for worldly life) dawns upon him he may renounce. Some suggest the prajapatya sacrifice (for those who want to take up renunciation). That does not have to be performed. One should only perform the fire sacrifice. Fire, verily is breath. Therefore, for keeping (the fire in the) breath one should perform it. Then he should perform the triple-impurities (tridhataviya) sacrifice. These three impurities (which need to be burnt in the sacrifice) are sattva, rajas and tamas. (Having performed the sacrifice) he should then utter the following verse, 'O fire, this breath which is the source of your birth, and from whom having born, you shine. Knowing thus, may you ascend into breath (and merge in it). Then increase my wealth (of breath). This one, the breath, verily, is the source of fire.' Therefore, this is what is asked of fire, 'O Fire, whose source is breath, may you go into you source.' Svaha. (As to the one who has not maintained a domestic fire of his own or discontinued it), having procured the fire from (any house in) the village, he should inhale the fire as said before. If he unable to procure fire, he should pour his offering in the water for water, verily, is all gods. He should then perform the sacrifice reciting, 'I am hereby offering this to all the gods. Svaha.' He should eat the remains of the burnt offering with ghee as it is beneficial. He should then utter Pranava (Aum), the mantra of liberation (whose recitation is equal to the recitation of) the three Vedas. It is Brahman and it should be worshipped."

"Indeed, so be it Godman, Yajnavalkya?" (said Janaka upon hearing it).

Notes: This very long verse states the rules for taking up the life of renunciation. One may renounce life in the normal course after completing the first three stages (ashramas) of human life, namely the life of a student, the householder's life and the life of a forest dweller, or anytime when one is seized with an intense desire to renounce worldly life. The later part of the verse suggest how one should initiate oneself into renunciation by performing certain sacrificial rituals. These are meant to assist the initiate who is expected not to carry fire or lit it once he becomes a recluse. From then on, he has to use his breath as a substitute for fire. He has to use that even to generate heat in his body and keep himself warm during cold winters, since he cannot cover himself with warm clothing. From the time he takes renunciation, he has to live by breath only and sustain himself on limited food, using breath to suppress his hunger and thirst.

Chapter 5
The True Sacred Thread

1. atha hainamatrih papracca yajnavalkyam priccami tva yajnavalkya ayajnopaviti katham brahmana iti, sa hovaca yajnavalkyah, idam evasya tad yajnopavitan ya atmapah prasyacamyayan vidhih parivrajaka namh,viradhvane va anasake va apam pravese va agni pravese va mahaprasthane va, atha parivradvivarnavasa mundo'parigrahah suciradrohi bhaiksano brahmabhuyaya bhavatiti, yad yaturah syan manasa vaca sannyaset, esa pantha brahmana hanuvittasstenaiti sannyasi brahmavidity evam evaisa bhagavan yajnavalkya.

1. Then Atri asked Yajnavalkya, "Please tell me Yajnavalkya, without a sacred thread, how can one be a Brahmana?"

To him, Yajnavalkya said, " This (Self) alone is the sacred thread of him who purifies himself by offering and sipping water. This is the ordained method (vidhi) for those who have renounced worldly life (parivrajakas). (Regarding others who want to renounce but are not yet ready), one may choose death by becoming a warrior, by fasting, by entering into water, by entering into fire or by walking his last walk until the end. Now, the wandering ascetic, who wears colored robes, whose head is shaven, who practices non-covetousness (aparigraha), who is pure, who does not think of harming others, who lives on alms, he attains the state of Brahman. If he is sick, he may renounce the world by thought and speech. This path is prescribed for those who want to know Brahman. He who renounces thus, becomes the knower of Brahman."

"Indeed, so be it Godman, Yajnavalkya?" (said Janaka upon hearing it).

Chapter 6
Description of Great Souls - Paramahansas

1. tatra paramahansanam asanvartak aruni svetaketu durvasa ribhu nidagha jada-bharata dattatreya raivataka prabhritayo, avyaktalingah avyakta carah anunmatta unmatta vadacarantas tridandam kamandalum sikyam patram jala pavitram sikham yajnopavitam ca ity etat sarvam bhuh svahety apsu parityajy atmanam anvicceth, yatha jata rupadharo nirgrantho nisparigrahastat tad brahmamarge samyak sampannah suddhamanasah prana samdharanartham yathoktakale vimukto bhaiksam acarann udara patrena labha labhayoh samo bhutva sunyagara deva grihatrinakuta valmika vriksam ulakulalasalag nihotra grihanadipulina girikuhara kandara kotara nirjhara sthandilesu tesvaniketavasya prayatno nirmamah sukladhyanaparayano, adhyatma nistho,asubha karma, nirmulanaparah sannyasena dehatyagan karoti sa paramahanso nama paramahanso nameti.

1. There are Samvartaka, Aruni, Svetaketu, Durvasa, Ribhu, Nidagha, Jada-Bharata, Dattatreya, Raivataka,and others who are known by the name Paramahansas. They bear no distinguishing marks, act in mysterious ways, free from intoxication but behave as if they are intoxicated. Throwing into water the three pronged staff (tridandam), the water jug (kamandalam), tuft of hair on the back of the head, the sacred thread, and saying bhuh svaha, they (who want to become Paramahansas) should search for the Self. Resorting to nakedness they had at birth, without any attachments, without holding on to anything, they should follow the path of Brahman. With a pure mind that is endowed with stable intelligence, for the sake of sustaining their breath, with the alms they collect at the appointed times, they should fill the vessel of their stomachs, remaining equal to whether they received the alms or not. They must live in an empty house, a temple, a shelter made of grass or straw, an anthill, the base of a tree, a potter's house, a house where sacred fire is lit, the sandy bank of a river, a hill, a cave, a hollow of a tree, a water fall or a mountain torrent in a deserted place. Without effort, free from egoism, with the mind firmly established in the Self, intent upon ending the consequences of impure actions, they finally give up their bodies on the path of renunciation. That one goes by the name paramahansa, yes, he goes by the name paramahansa.

Bibliography

Aiyar, Narayanasvami K. Thirty minor Upaniṣads: revised edition includes Sanskrit texts, English translation. Delhi, India: Parimal Publications, 1997.

Ananthacharya, Chakravarti. Philosophy of Upanishads. Bangalore, India: Ultra Publications, 1999.

Archak, K.B. Upaniṣad and Śaivism. New Delhi, india: Sundeep Prakashan, 2002.

Aurobindo, Sri. The Upanishads, with Sanskrit text, English translation and commentary. Twin Lakes, WI: Lotus Light Publications, 1996.

Barnett, L. D. Brahma-knowledge, an outline of the philosophy of the Vedānta as set forth by the Upanishads and by Sankara.London, J. Murray, 1911.

Basham, A.L. The Origins and Development of Classical Hinduism. New York: Oxford University Press, 1991.

Bhattacharya, A.N. One hundred and twelve Upaniṣads and their philosophy: a critical exposition of Upaniṣadic philosophy with original text in Devanāgarī. Delhi, India: Parimal Publications, 1987.

Brown, George William. The human body in the Upanishads. Jubbulpore, India, The Christian Mission Press, 1921.

Chakravarti, Sures Chandra. The philosophy of the Upanishads. Delhi, India: Nag Publishers, 1979.

Deodikar, Sanjay Govind. Upanisads and early Buddhism. Delhi, India : Eastern Book Linkers, 1992.

Desai, S.G. A critical study of the later Upanishads. Mumbai, India : Bharatiya Vidya Bhavan, 1996.

Deussen, Paul, and Rev. Geden, A. S. The philosophy of the Upanishads. Edinburgh, Clark, 1908.

Deussen, Paul, and Bedekar, V.M., and Palsule, G.B. Sixty Upaniṣads of the Veda. Delhi, India : Motilal Banarsidass, 1980.

Devi, Chitrita. Upanishads for all. New Delhi, India: S. Chand [1973 i.e. 1972].

Diwakar, R.R., and Radhakrishnan, S., Intro. The Upanisads in story and dialogue. Mumbai, India: Hindi Kitabs, 1950.

Easwaran, Eknath. Essence of the Upanishads: A Key to Indian Spirituality. Canada: Nilgiri Press & Blue Mountain Center of Meditation, 2009.

_____. The Upanishads: The Classics of Indian Spirituality. Canada: The Blue Mountain Center of Meditation, 1987, 2007.

_____., Nagler, Michael N., fwd. The Upanishads. Tomales, CA : Nilgiri Press, 2007.

Egnes, Thomas, and Reddy, Kumuda. Eternal Stories from the Upanishads. New Delhi, India: Smriti Books, 2002.

Elenjimittam, Anthony. The Upanishads: Isa, Katha, Mundaka, Mandukya, with an introduction and commentary. Mumbai, India: Aquinas Publications, 1977.

Frawley, David. The creative vision of the early Upanisads. Denver, Colo.: D. Frawley, 1982.

Gambhirananda, Swami. Eight Upanishads: With the Commentary of Sankaracaya, Vol 1 and 2. Kolkata, India: Advaita Ashrama, 2003 and 2004.

Ghose, Aurobindo Sri. The Upanishads. Pondicherry, India: Aurobindo Ashram Trust, 1996.

Giri, Swami Satyeswarananda. The Upanishads. San Diego : Sanskrit Classics, 2006.

Gren-Eklund, Gunilla. A study of nominal sentences in the oldest Upanisads.Uppsala : Univ.; Stockholm : Almqvist & Wiksell international (distr.), 1978.

Grover, Usha. Symbolism in the Āranyakas and their impact on the Upaniṣads: a remarkable cultural upheaval which ever inspires the future thought. New Delhi : Guruvar Publications, 1987.

Hock, Henrich Hans. An early Upaniṣadic reader : with notes, glossary, and an appendix of related Vedic texts. Delhi, India : Motilal Banarsidass Publishers, 2007.

Hume, Robert Ernest. The thirteen principal Upanishads [microform]: translated from the Sanskrit with an outline of the philosophy of the Upanishads and an annotated bibliography. London ; New York : Oxford University Press, 1931.

Johnston, Charles. The great Upanishads. New York: Quarterly Book Department [c1927].

Kadankavil, Kurian T. The quest of the real: a study of the philosophical methodology of Mundakopanishad. Bangalore, India: Dharmaram Publications, 1975.

Keith, Arthur Berriedale. The religion and philosophy of the Veda and Upanishads. Cambridge, Mass. : Harvard University Press, 1925.

Keith, Arthur Berriedale. The religion and philosophy of the Veda and Upanishads. Cambridge, Mass., Harvard university press; London, H. Milford, Oxford university press, 1925.

Krishnamurti, V.G. From J. Krishnamurti to the Upanishads : world order for the 21st century : an Indian vision. Kolkata, India : Writers Workshop, 1990.

Kriyananda, Swami Saraswati. Nine principal Upanishads, with text, translitteration [sic], translation, and notes. Monghyr, India : Bihar School of Yoga, 1975.

Kulkarni, T.R. Upanishads and yoga; an empirical approach to the understanding. Mumbai, India: Bharatiya Vidya Bhavan, 1972.

Madhavananda, Swami. Minor Upanishads. With original text, introd., English rendering, and comments. Kolkata, India: Advaita Ashrama, 1968.

Majumdār, Sridhar. The Vedanta philosophy : in English with original sutras and explanatory quotations from Upanishads, Bhagavad Gītā etc. and their English translations. Varanasi, India: Chowkhamba Sanskrit Series Office, 2000.

Manohar, Mrinalini Vivek. The earlier and later Upaniṣads : a comparative study. Delhi, India: Bharatiya Kala Prakashan, 2011.

Mascaro, Juan. The Upanishads. New York: Penguin Putnam Inc., 1965.

Mead, G.R.S., and Chaṭṭopādhyāya, Jagadīsha Chandra (Roy Choudhuri). The Upanishads / translated into English, with a preamble and arguments. Adyar, Madras, India : Theosophical Publishing House, 1930.

Milburn, R. Gordon. The religious mysticism of the Upanishads. London, Theosophical publishing house, 1924.

Mukherji Anil Kumar, Das, Saroj Kumar, fwd. Upanishad in the eyes of Rabindra Nath Tagore: an anthology of the poet Tagore's writings, interpretative of and related to Upanishadic verse. Kolkata, India: Dasgupta, 1975.

Mukhopadhyaya, Govindagopal. Studies in the Upaniṣads. Kathmandu, Nepal: Distributed by Pilgrims Book House, 1999.

Muller, Max F. Sacred Books of the East, Vol. 1. Oxford: Clarenden Press, 1900.

_____. The Upanishads. New York : Christian Literature Co., 1897.

Muni, Angirasa. The Upanisads / introduction and translation. Fort Wayne, IN: Sacred Books, 1999.

Narla, V.R. An essay on the Upanishads: a critical study. Hyderabad, India: Narla Institute of New Thought, c1989.

Nikam, N. A. Ten principal Upanishads: some fundamental ideas: a dialectical and analytical study. Mumbai, India: Somaiya Publications, 1974.

Nikhilananda, Swami. Upanishads, Vol.1-4. New York: Ramakrishna Vivekanada Center, 1986, 1990, 1990, 1994.

Olivelle, Patrick. The early Upaniṣads: annotated text and translation. New Delhi, India: Munshiram Manoharlal Publishers, 1998.

Olivelle, Patrick. The early Upanisads: annotated text and translation. New York: Oxford University Press, 1998.

Olivelle, Patrick. Upanishads: A new Translation. Oxford, New York: Oxford University Press, 1996.

Pandit, M.P. Upanishads: Gateways of Knowledge. Wilmot, WI: Lotus Light Publications, 1988.

Paramananda, Swami. The Upanishads: Translated and commentated. Volume 1. Boston, MA: The Vedanta Center, 1919.

Parrinder, Geoffrey . The wisdom of the forest: selections from the Hindu Upanishads. New York: New Directions Pub. Corp., 1976.

_____. The wisdom of the forest: sages of the Indian Upanishads / translated [from the Sanskrit]. London : Sheldon Press, 1975.

_____. Upanishads, Gita and Bible: a comparative study of Hindu and Christian scriptures. London: Sheldon Press, 1975.

Pathak, Meena P. (Meena Pinakin). study of Taittirīya Upanisad. Delhi: Bharatiya Kala Prakashan, 1999.

Prabhavananda, Swami. The Upanishads: Breath of the Eternal. New York: Penguin Putnam Inc., 2002.

Raja, C. Kunhan, ed., and Pandits of Adayar Library. Daśopanishads, with the commentary of Sri Upanishad-brahmayogin. Chennai, India: Adyar Library (Theosophical Society) 1935-36.

Puligandla, R. "That thou art" : the wisdom of the Upanishads. Fremont, Calif. : Asian Humanities Press, c2002.

Puligandla. R. Reality and mysticism: perspectives in the Upanisads. the University of Michigan, MI: D K Printworld (P) Limited, 1997.

Pundalik, Pandit Madhav. Mystic approach to the Veda and the Upanishads. Chennai, India: Sri Aurobindo Library [1952].

Purohit, Swami. The ten principal Upanishads put into English. New York: Macmillan, 1975, c1937.

Radhakrishnan, S. Indian philosophy. London, Allen & Unwin; New York, Humanities Press [1966].

_____. The philosophy of the Upanisads, with a foreword by Rabindranath Tagore and an Introduction by Edmond Holmes. London, G. Allen & Unwin ltd.; New York, The Macmillan Company [1935].

_____. The Principal Upanishads: Edited With Introduction, Text, Translation and Notes. New Delhi, India: HarperCollins Publishers, India, 1994

Raghavachar, S.S. Sri Ramanuja on the Upanishads. Chennai, India: Prof. M. Rangacharya Memorial Trust; [can be had of M. C. Krishnan, 1972].

Rajagopalachari, C. Upanishads for the lay reader. New Delhi, India: Hindustan Times [1956].

Rajagopalachari, Chakravarti. Upanishads. Mumbai, India: Bharatiya Vidya Bhavan, 1991.

Rama, Swami. Wisdom of the ancient sages: Mundaka Upanishad. Honesdale, Pa.: Himalayan International Institute of Yoga Science and Philosophy of the U.S.A., c1990.

Ranade, R.D. A constructive survey of Upanishadic philosophy; being an introduction to the thought of the Upanishads. Mumbai, India: Bharatiya Vidya Bhavan, 1968.

Reddy, Madhusudan. Yoga of the rishis: the Upanishadic approach to death and immortality. Hyderabad, India: Institute of Human Study ; Delhi: Distributed by Indian Books Centre, 1985.

Rehman, Saif-ur. Indian philosophy: some common concepts in the Vedas, Upanishads & early Buddhism. [Lahore]: [publisher not identified], [2012?].

Rodrigues, Antonio F.X. In search of meaning: a phenomenological reading of the Upanishads. Bangalore, India: Redemptorist Publications India, [198-?].

Roebuck, Valerie. The Upanishads. London, New York: Penguin Books, 2003.

Roer, E., ed. The twelve principal Upaniṣads: text in Devanāgari and translation with notes in English from the commentaries of Śaṅkarācārya, and the gloss of Ānandagiri. Delhi, India: Nag Publishers, 1978-1979.

Sarasvati, Svami Satya Prakash. Parables and dialogues from the Upaniṣads. Delhi, India: S. Chand, 1975.

Saraswati, Swami Sivananda. The essence of principal Upanishads. Rishikesh, India: Yoga-Vedanta Forest Academy, Divine Life Society, 1961.

Scharfstein, Ben-Ami A comparative history of world philosophy: from the Upanishads to Kant. Albany: State University of New York Press, c1998.

Sen, Pritam. God's love in Upanishad philosophies. Mumbai, India: Bharatiya Vidya Bhavan, 1995.

Seru, S.L. The thirteen principal Upanisads: an introduction on Vedanta-sara text with English translation and notes. Delhi, India: Nag Publishers, 1997.

Sharma, Shubhra. Life in the Upanishads. New Delhi, India: Ahinav Publications, 1985.

Shearer, Alistair & Russell, Peter; photos. by Lannoy, Richard. The Upanishads. New York: Harper & Row, c1978.

Shearer, Alistair and Russell, Peter. The Upanishads. Bell Tower, New York: Sacred Teachings, 2003.

Singh, Maan. The Upaniṣadic etymologies. Delhi: Nirmal Publication, 1994.

Singh, Satya Prakash. Upanisadic symbolism. New Delhi, India: Meharchand Lachhmandas, 1981.

Sircar, Mahendranath. Hindu mysticism according to the Upaniṣads. New Delhi: Oriental Books Reprint Corp. : distributed by Munshiram Manoharlal Publishers, 1974.

Sreeram, Lala. The metaphysics of the Upanishads, or Vichar Sagar/ translated with copious notes. New Delhi : Asian Publication Services, 1979.

Sri Upanishad-brahma-yogin. The Yoga Upanishads, with the commentary of. [Madras] Pub. for the Adyar library (Theosophical society) 1920.

Srinivasachari, P.N. The wisdom of the Upanisads. Madras: Sri Krishna Library, 1947.

Subrahmanian, V.K. The Upanishads and the Bible. New Delhi: Abhinav Publications, 2002.

Swāmi, Shree Purohit, and Yeats, W. B. The ten principal Upanishads; put into English. London: Faber, 1970.

Tathagatananda, Swami. Journey of the Upanishads to the West. New York, NY : Vedanta Society, 2002.

Thachil, Jose. The Upaniṣads, a socio-religious appraisal. New Delhi, India : Intercultural Publications, 1993.

Vasus, Srisa Chandra. The Upaniṣads with the commentary of Madhvachárya: part I, Īśa, Kaṭha, Praśna, Muṇḍaka and Mâṅḍuka. Allahabad, India: Panini Office, 1909.

V, Jayaram. Brahman. New Albany, OH: Pure Life Vision LLC, 2010.

Vidyaranva, Srisa Chandra. Studies in the first six Upanisads and the Isa and Kena Upanisads, with the commentary of Sankara. Allahabad, India: Panini Office, 1919 [i.e. 1918].

Witz, Klaus G.The supreme wisdom of the Upaniṣads: an introduction. Delhi, India: Motilal Banarsidass Publishers, 1998.

Symbolism Of The Cover Design

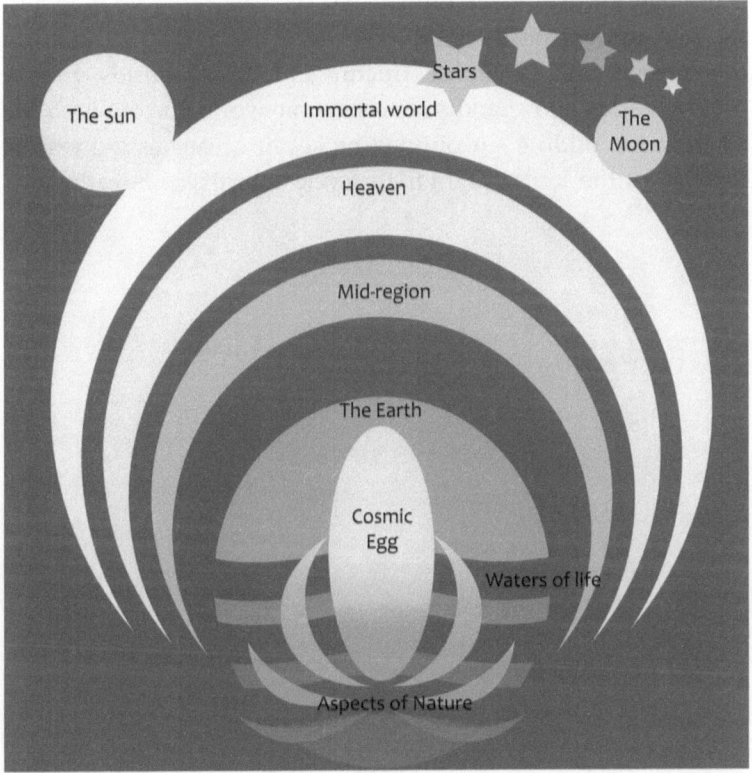

Editor: The cover illustration of this book, designed by Jayaram V, is based upon the structure of the universe as described in the Vedic scriptures. The Vedas envisage a four-tier universe consisting of the earth (bhu), the mid-region (bhuva), the sky-region (svah) and the infinite world of Brahman (maha). The heaven is adorned with two deities, the sun and the moon and the constellation of stars. The sun represents immortality, light, knowledge, constancy, heat (tapas), food, and breath. The moon represents change, impermanence, dreams and rebirth. Life manifests upon earth in the form of a cosmic egg with Manifested Brahman as the source of all diversity. Energy and consciousnesses fuse together to manifest beings of intelligence. Creation is cyclical and Brahman as Isvara or Hiranyagarbha is responsible for the creation, preservation and dissolution of the worlds. In the end everything returns to its primal state of latency, except the highest heaven, or the world of Brahman. In addition to the four, the

Upanishads also refer to another world, the world beneath the earth inhabited by insects, worms and demons to which the souls that indulge in mortal sins go. This early Vedic model of the four upper worlds or regions was subsequently replaced in the Puranas with a complex structure of fourteen worlds with six divine worlds above and seven demonic worlds below with the earth in the middle surrounded by seven oceans as the resting ground for the souls caught in the cycle of births and deaths.

Pure Life Vision Books
Chandogya Upanishad

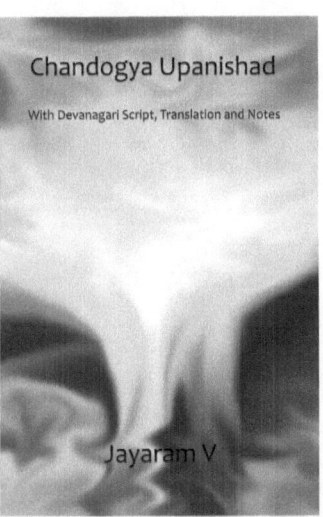

Historically, the Chandogya Upanishad is one of the most ancient Upanishads, which played a significant role in the emergence of the Vedanta Philosophy and internalization of the Vedic ritual. It is also the largest among the Principal Upanishads with 629 verses, eight chapters and 154 sections. This is a complete translation of the Upanishad by Jayaram V.

- New translation
- Original Sanskrit verses in transliterated Devanagari
- With Explanatory notes and Bibliography
- ISBN: 978-1-935760-08-5
- Book type: Perfect Bound (paperback)
- Cover Gloss. Dimensions: 6x9. Pages: 215

Discounts up to 50% are available on bulk orders. **Order your copy from** http://www.PureLifeVision.com.

Pure Life Vision Books
Brihadaranyaka Upanishad

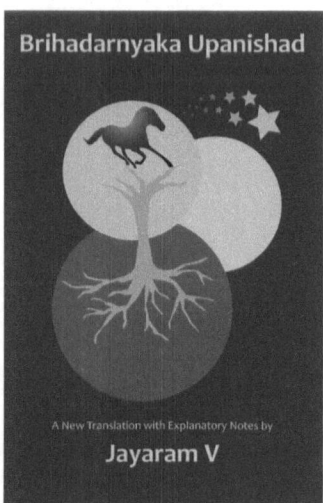

The first major translation of the Brihadaranyaka Upanishad in the 21st century. This Upanishad presents many secret doctrines of Hinduism and the significance of certain important Vedic sacrifices. This translation by Jayaram V is useful for both scholars and serious practitioners of Hinduism.

- New translation,
- Original Sanskrit verses in transliterated Devanagari
- With Explanatory notes and Bibliography
- ISBN: 978-1-935760-07-8
- Book type: Perfect Bound (paperback)
- Cover Gloss. Dimensions: 6x9
- No of pages 204

Discounts up to 50% are available on bulk orders. **Order your copy from http://www.PureLifeVision.com**

Pure Life Vision Books

The Bhagavadgita Complete Translation

- Most comprehensive work on the Bhagavadgita in recent times
- Complete text with word to word translation
- Detailed commentary without sectarian bias
- Original and inspiring
- Authoritative and scholarly
- No of pages 874
- Dimensions: 6.14 x 9.21
- ISBN: 978-1-935760-04-7

Discounts up to 50% are available on bulk purchases. **Order your copy from** http://www.PureLifeVision.com

Pure Life Vision Books
The Bhagavadgita
A Simple Translation

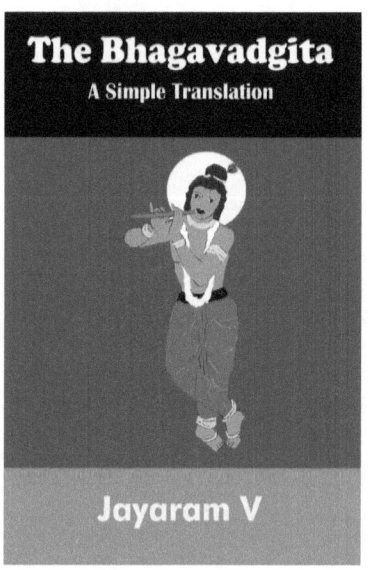

- Abridged version
- Complete text with word for word translation
- Ideal for recitation and reference
- Perfect Bound (paperback), Cover Matte
- Page count: 304
- Dimensions: 6.14 x 9.21
- ISBN: 978-1-935760-17-7

Discounts up to 50% are available on bulk orders. For bulk orders, please contact the publishers at the following link http://www.PureLifeVision.com

Pure Life Vision Books

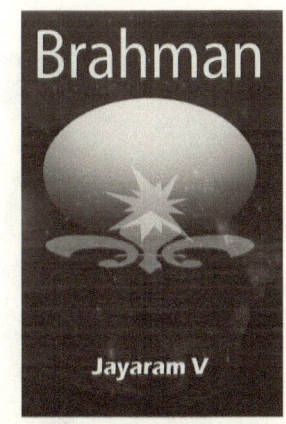

Discounts up to 50% are available on bulk orders. **Order your copies from** http://www.PureLifeVision.com.

Pure Life Vision Books
Think Success – Combined Volume

- Combined volume
- Contains 44 mind-expanding articles
- Comprehensive information on self-help
- Motivational, inspiring and uplifting
- Improves your self-awareness and confidence
- Prepares you for success and achievement
- Guides you to excellence
- No of pages 492
- Dimensions: 6 x 9
- ISBN: 978-1-935760-03-0
- Book type: Bound Blue Cloth w/Jacket on Creme

Discounts up to 50% are available on bulk orders. **Order your copy from** http://www.PureLifeVision.com.

Pure Life Vision Books
Essays on the Bhagavadgita

In this collection of essays, you will find a critical analysis of the philosophy, principles and practice of the Bhagavadgita and their relevance to human life. You will understand the true meaning of yoga in the context of the teachings of Lord Krishna and the importance of various yogas. This book will increase your understanding of the Bhagavadgita immensely and help you in the practice of its teachings.

- 35 Informative articles
- With Bibliography
- ISBN: 978-1-935760-09-2
- Book type: Perfect Bound (paperback)
- Cover Matte. Dimensions: 6x9

Discounts up to 50% are available on bulk orders. **Order your copy from http://www.PureLifeVision.com**

Pure Life Vision Books
Introduction to Hinduism

Hinduism is the oldest living religion of the world. It is also the most complex in terms of its philosophy and practices and difficult to understand. This book gives you a thorough and scholarly understanding of the basic and essential aspects of the eternal tradition, useful to both lay practitioners and students alike.

- Covers significant aspects of Hinduism
- Written in easy to understand language
- With Bibliography
- ISBN: 978-1-935760-11-5
- Book type: Perfect Bound (paperback)
- Cover Matte. Dimensions: 6x9

Discounts up to 50% are available on bulk orders. **Order your copy from** http://www.PureLifeVision.com

www.ingramcontent.com/pod-product-compliance
Lightning Source LLC
Chambersburg PA
CBHW030304080526
44584CB00012B/441